CW00500741

INTERNET DIRECTORY UK in easy steps

Geoff Preston

COMPUTER STEP

In easy steps is an imprint of Computer Step
Southfield Road . Southam
Warwickshire CV33 OFB . England

Tel: 01926 817999 Fax: 01926 817005
http://www.computerstep.com

Notice of Liability

Every effort has been made to ensure that this book contains accurate and current information. However, Computer Step and the author shall not be liable for any loss or damage suffered by readers as a result of any information contained herein.

Trademarks

All trademarks are acknowledged as belonging to their respective companies.

Printed and bound in the United Kingdom

ISBN 1-84078-010-X

Contents

Chapter One

Introduction

Not for nothing has the Internet been labelled the most hyped phenomenon of the decade. But is the Internet a really useful tool or is it just a passing fad?

Covers

What is the Internet?

The name 'Internet' is a very appropriate title. An **inter**national **net**work of computers, representing a huge fount of knowledge which anyone with a computer connected to a telephone line can access. Internet statistics are mind-boggling. One estimate suggests that the amount of material on the 'Net' doubles every couple of months. Another claim is that every few seconds another individual from somewhere in the world becomes an Internet subscriber.

This indeed is the super-highway of information. But just as anyone can search the Internet for the information they require, so too can anyone contribute to the global fount of knowledge. Free speech now takes on a whole new meaning. Anyone can put anything on the Internet which can then be accessed worldwide. Pornography, anarchistic philosophies, riot incitement, explosives manufacture, you name it, it's sure to be there. Even sites which do not contain material of this type vary in quality enormously.

What this book sets out to do is sort the wheat from the chaff. I've sorted out a variety of Internet sites which I've placed into categories. There should be something here for everyone – leisure (including computer games), personal finance, business, travel, education and news, to name but a few.

REMEMBER

If you want to see the web at its best, open a commercial site which has had fistfuls of money thrown at it.

Many of the sites featured are commercial ones and for this I make no apology. Companies have quickly recognised that the Internet is a very cheap way of getting their message to all corners of the globe. Many have enormous advertising budgets and therefore can afford to pay the very top web page designers to create web sites. The result is some of the best sites available. In particular, motor car manufacturers seem to spare no expense in creating their sites. Hi-tech companies like manufacturers of consumer electronics also inject a great deal of money into their sites.

Other sites featured have more modest budgets but nevertheless serve the global community and are of no lesser importance.

This is not an exhaustive study of the top sites on the Internet but a very small collection of sites which should be more than just of passing interest to UK users. Inevitably, more will have been left out than included.

What do you need to get started?

Four things really, the first being a computer, although not necessarily a computer as you may imagine it. To connect to the Internet, most people will use a personal desktop computer comprising a screen (to enable the user to see what's happening), a keyboard (to enable the user to enter text), a pointing device (mouse or rollerball to select items) and the clever bit that does all the working out.

HANDY TIP

Buy the fastest modem you can.

Modem

The other component required is a method of connecting all this to a phone line, and this is called a modem.

There are two types of modem available: internal and external. An internal modem plugs into the computer, the external variety is, well, external. The advantage of an internal modem is that it takes its power from the computer and therefore does not require an additional power supply. It also doesn't need a cable to be plugged into the back of the computer and hence it doesn't use one of the precious sockets which seem to be required for half-a-dozen other peripherals. But it does occupy one of the sockets inside the computer which are potentially more valuable. An external modem uses desk space which is probably also at a premium, and because it requires a power supply and a cable to connect to the computer, its very presence adds to the two platefuls of spaghetti you've already got behind your desk.

What is important is that you buy the fastest modem you can afford. Top of the range is 56k followed by 33.3k and then 28.8k.

Set Top Box

If all you want to do is surf the net, then you can do away with much of this hardware and opt instead for one of the new generation set-top boxes which are becoming increasingly popular. A typical set-top box plugs into your television set (and hence disposes of the monitor) and also does away with all the bits you don't need for surfing. Many are supplied with infra-red QWERTY keyboards with built-in pointing device. Set-top boxes are about one third of the price of a mid-range computer.

A Phone Line

However you connect to the web, you have the on-going cost of phone calls.

The second item required is a phone line. Now it might be that you already have a telephone and as long as the installation terminates with a socket somewhere near where you intend surfing, you can use that. But remember, whilst you're surfing, the line is engaged and so there will be no outgoing or incoming calls. For this reason many people opt for a second phone line which isn't as extravagant as would first appear. Most phone companies are offering very good deals on second lines, often with free installation. But if you really want to set the web alight, go for an ISDN line. This will give the fastest access times, but comes at a price.

ISP

A good ISP will provide a service which accesses the Internet with a local phone call.

The third element needed to get you on-line is an account with an Internet Service Provider or ISP. There are many to choose from but they all offer much the same service. Typically, unlimited access time, five email addresses and 5Mbytes of your own web space will cost about £15 per month. Some are cheaper and have limited access after which you pay extra whilst some don't have all the email addresses but offer more web space. The trick is to compare very carefully and don't sign up for too long in case you change your mind and decide a different service provider would be more appropriate.

Whichever ISP you choose, ensure that all access is by a local call and check whether they offer on-line support, and if there is a charge for that.

Browser

Finally, you'll need a browser. This is a computer program that enables you to view pages of information from the Internet. If the service you're considering doesn't provide a browser, don't worry. If you've got Windows 95 or Windows 98, it is supplied with Internet Explorer. The only other serious contender on the PC front is Netscape Navigator.

Once you have the hardware, the phone line, the browser and the ISP sorted out, you're ready to surf.

HANDY TIP

For more detailed information on getting connected to the Internet, see 'Internet UK' by Chris Russell, also in the 'in easy steps' series.

There are several browsers for all platforms, but the most popular are arch-rivals Netscape Navigator (by Netscape Communications Inc) and Internet Explorer (by Microsoft).

Searching

Web Searches

The web is too large to be able to plough through without some guidance. The best way to find the information you need, if you don't have a specific address, is to use one of the search engines.

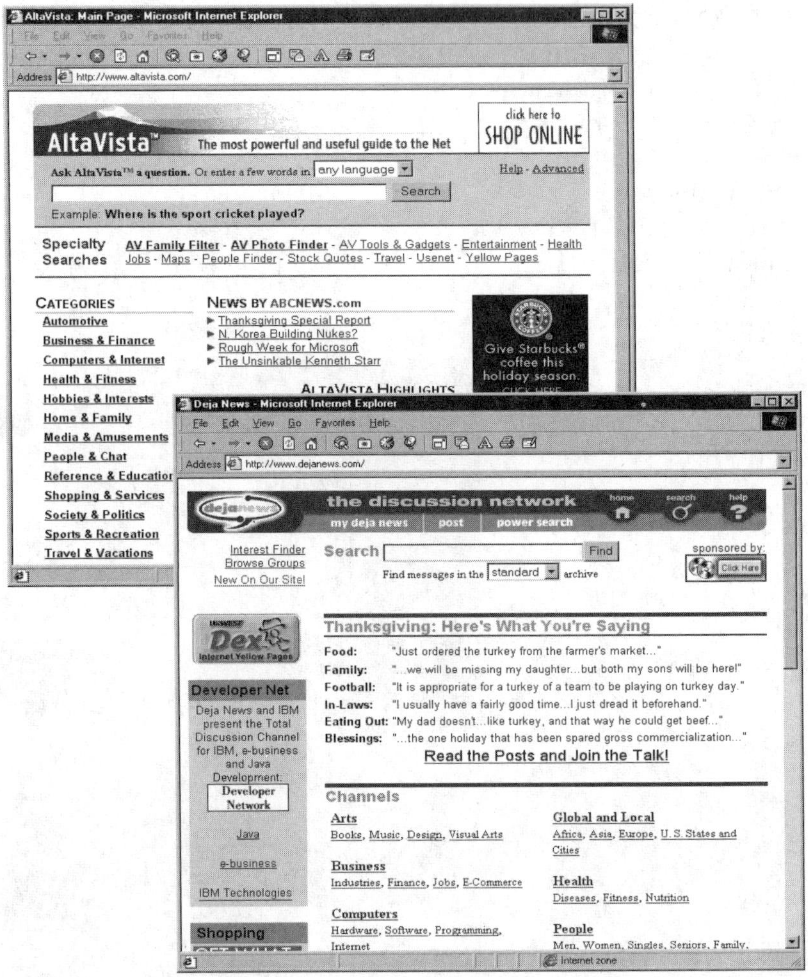

BEWARE

Entering a single word can generate thousands of sites.

There are several search engines to choose from and you will soon discover the one that best suits your needs although they are all used in much the same way. At its simplest, type in a word, click on the Search button and you will be presented with a list of sites containing that word.

Email Searches

This is the Internet equivalent of directory enquiries. There are now an estimated 20,000,000 email addresses and the number is growing by the minute.

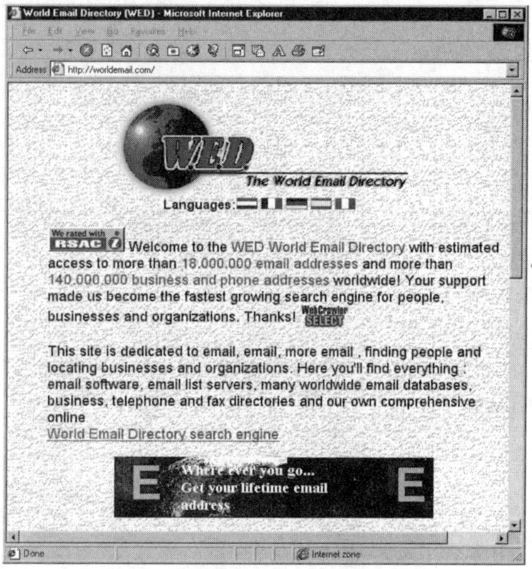
World Email Directory (WED) - Microsoft Internet Explorer
Address http://worldemail.com/
WED
The World Email Directory
Languages:
We rated with RSAC
Welcome to the WED World Email Directory with estimated access to more than 18,000,000 email addresses and more than 140,000,000 business and phone addresses worldwide! Your support made us become the fastest growing search engine for people, businesses and organizations. Thanks!
WebCrawler SELECT
This site is dedicated to email, email, more email , finding people and locating businesses and organizations. Here you'll find everything : email software, email list servers, many worldwide email databases, business, telephone and fax directories and our own comprehensive online
World Email Directory search engine
Where ever you go... Get your lifetime email address
Done
Internet zone

HANDY TIP

Log into one of these engines and add your own email address.

To locate a person, go to either *http://www.whowhere.com* or *http://worldemail.com* to access one of the search engines that specialise in searching email addresses.

REMEMBER

These are the major search engines.

Alta Vista – *http://www.altavista.com*

DejaNews – *http://www.dejanews.com*

Excite – *http://www.excite.com*

Four 11 – *http://www.four11.com*

Hard Seek – *http://www.hardseek.com/default.cfm*

InfoSeek – *http://www2.infoseek.com*

Lycos – *http://lycos.com*

Reference – *http://www.reference.com*

WebCrawler – *http://webcrawler.com*

Yahoo – *http://www.yahoo.com*

WebRings

A clever way of accessing several web sites on the same subject is to go to a webring. A webring is a group of web sites linked to each other in a circle. On each webring web site are links to take you either forward or back around the webring. If you keep going in one direction you'll eventually get back to where you started.

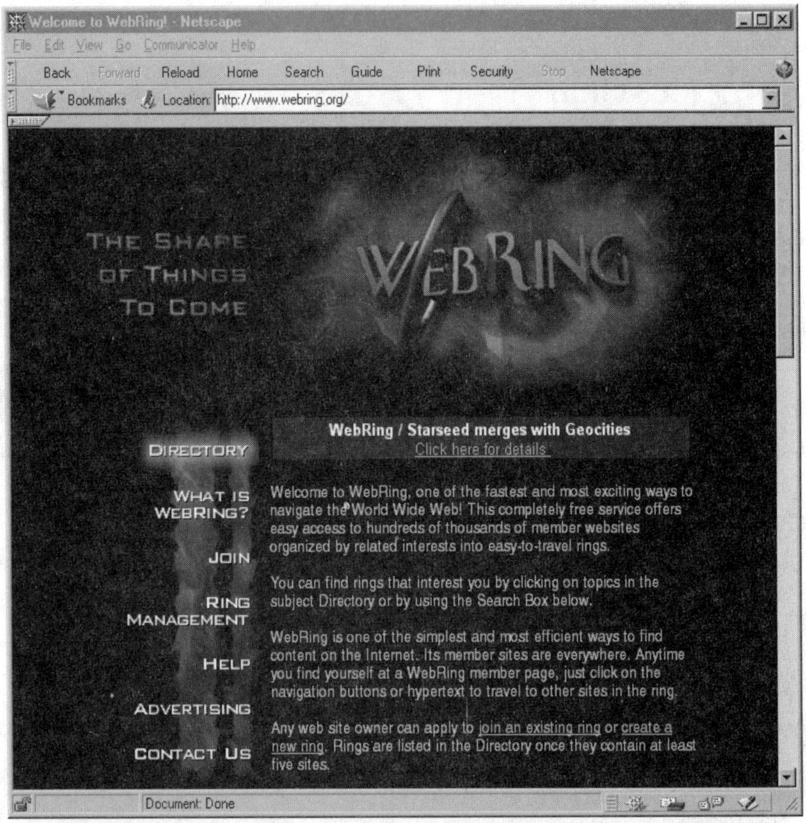

Welcome to WebRing! - Netscape
File Edit View Go Communicator Help
Back Forward Reload Home Search Guide Print Security Stop Netscape
Bookmarks Location: http://www.webring.org/
THE SHAPE OF THINGS TO COME
WEBRING
WebRing / Starseed merges with Geocities
Click here for details
DIRECTORY
WHAT IS WEBRING?
JOIN
RING MANAGEMENT
HELP
ADVERTISING
CONTACT US
Welcome to WebRing, one of the fastest and most exciting ways to navigate the World Wide Web! This completely free service offers easy access to hundreds of thousands of member websites organized by related interests into easy-to-travel rings.
You can find rings that interest you by clicking on topics in the subject Directory or by using the Search Box below.
WebRing is one of the simplest and most efficient ways to find content on the Internet. Its member sites are everywhere. Anytime you find yourself at a WebRing member page, just click on the navigation buttons or hypertext to travel to other sites in the ring.
Any web site owner can apply to join an existing ring or create a new ring. Rings are listed in the Directory once they contain at least five sites.
Document: Done

HANDY TIP

Use your browser's 'Favorites' feature to store useful pages from the webring.

From time to time sites are added to webrings with the result that some rings have become very large.

Anyone can add their own web site to a webring and details of how to do this may be found on the WebRing Homepage.

There are hundreds of webrings on a huge variety of topics ranging from the obscure to the widely popular which can be accessed from *http://www.webring.org.*

Chapter Two

Finance on the Web

Money, it is said, makes the world go round. The Internet is a great place to carry out your financial dealings as well as for looking up information about financial deals and getting advice on your finances, both immediate and long term. Make sure that the site from which you pull down information is regularly updated.

Covers

Internet Banking

Several Banks and Building Societies offer their customers banking via the Internet. The advantage is that you can make transactions, order statements and carry out a variety of other banking tasks from the comfort of your armchair and at any time of the day or night, 365 days a year. The only thing you can't do is actually withdraw cash.

First Direct is a branch of the Midland Bank/HSBC which began offering a very successful 24 hour telephone banking service where customers simply dial a local telephone number and get balances, move money, arrange loans and generally do most things they would do in a traditional bank.

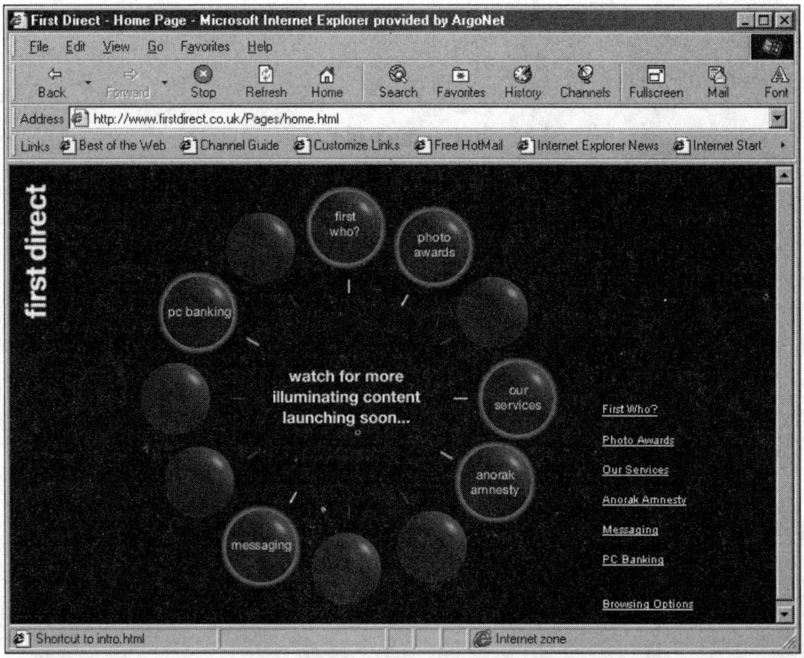

First Direct recently introduced Internet banking to run alongside the telephone service and this too is becoming very popular. Once enrolled, you will be provided with a CD ROM containing all the software required which is installed on your PC. Once installed and registered, you'll have access to your bank account.

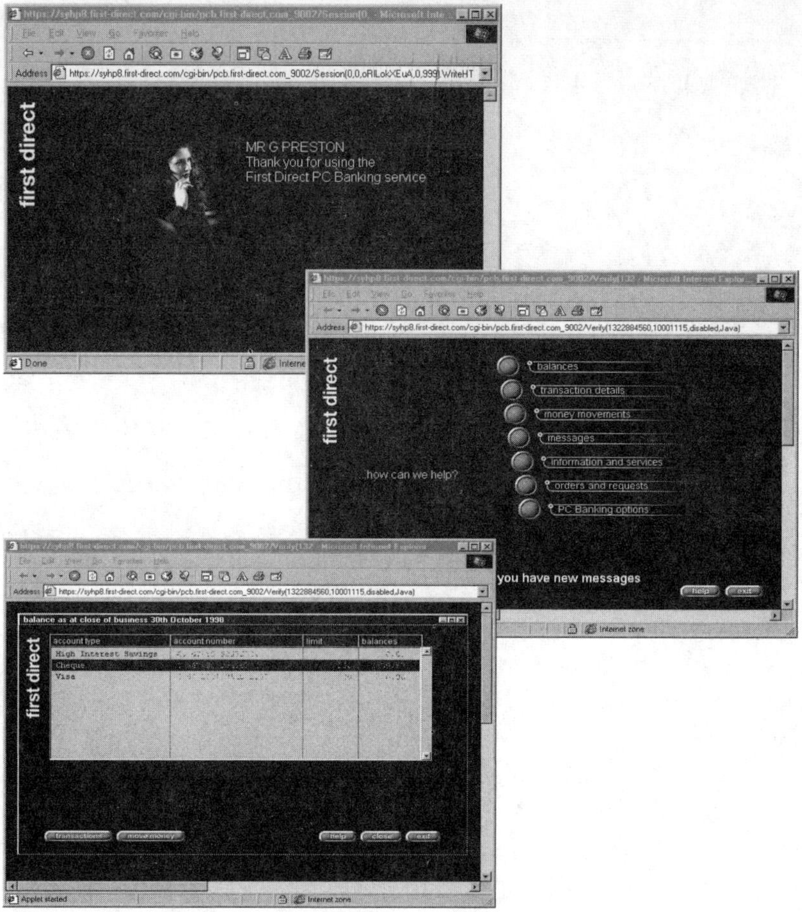

REMEMBER

Keep your password safe – it's the key to open your bank account.

The First Direct web site can be viewed at *http://www.firstdirect.co.uk.*

There is a link from their homepage which will provide you with information about opening a First Direct bank account.

Internet banking has had some bad press, unfairly in my opinion. Stories abound about hackers intercepting individuals' bank accounts and moving money, but these stories are largely bogus. Internet banking sites like First Direct are as safe as any traditional banking method – and some would argue that they can in fact be safer.

Clearing Banks

Most major banks have web sites and it's worth checking them out from time to time to see who has the best deals for loans and deposits. As one would expect from large multi-national companies, the sites are very well organised and contain lots of useful information, although one shouldn't forget these sites are also adverts.

The sites for the four UK clearing banks are :

Barclays – *http://www.barclays.com*

Lloyds – *http://www.lloydsbank.co.uk*

Midland – *http://www.midlandbank.co.uk*

National Westminster – *http://www.natwest.co.uk*

Credit Cards

The UK's two major credit cards have web sites in which they provide a great deal of information about their cards and other services they provide, such as insurance.

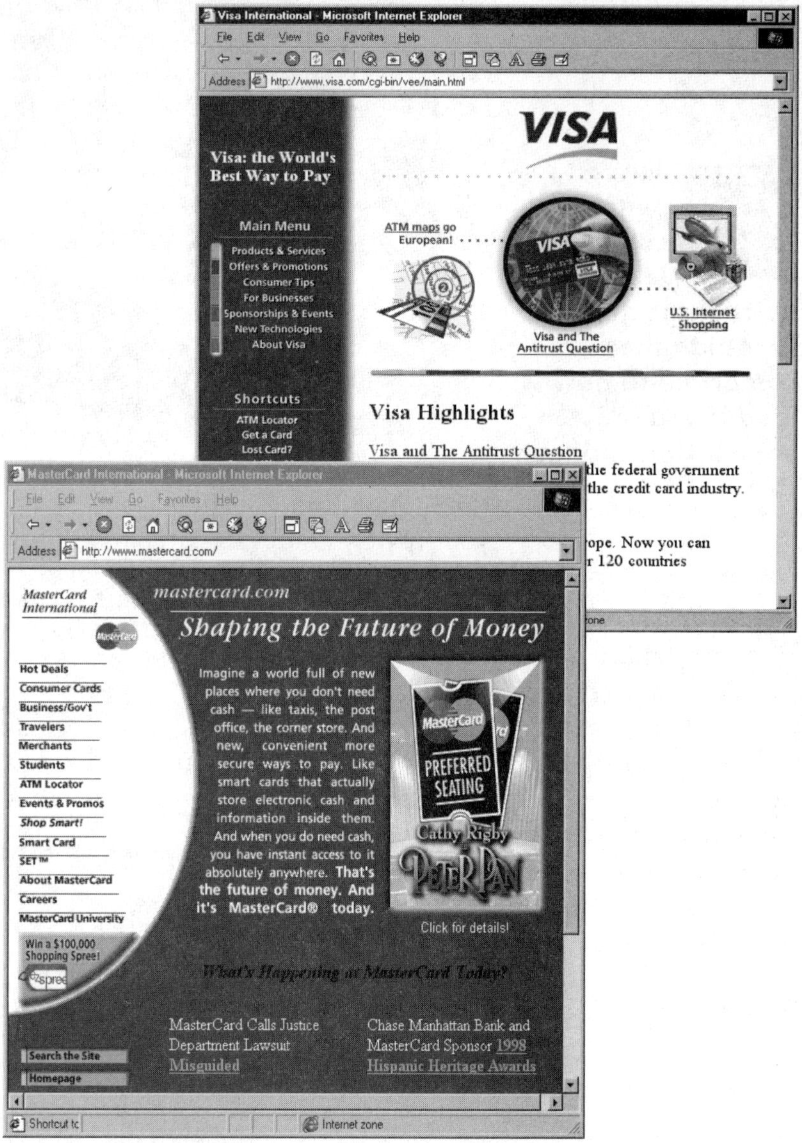

Visa is at *http://www.visa.com* and MasterCard is at *http://www.mastercard.com.*

EGG

Most pages contain at least one quite large graphic. It could take sometime to download if you only have a slow modem.

This is another of the growing number of sites requiring the installation of 'Shockwave' (a plug-in control enabling you to view elaborate sites with multimedia effects).

You'll need to register on this site by entering your name. You will be given a password which you'll need to keep for future reference.

Have a pencil and paper handy to copy down the password, which is case sensitive.

The site offers help and advice on all personal financial matters including insurance, loans and mortgages. There is an email service offering more personal advice.

EGG is at *http://www.egg.com.*

Interactive Finance Services

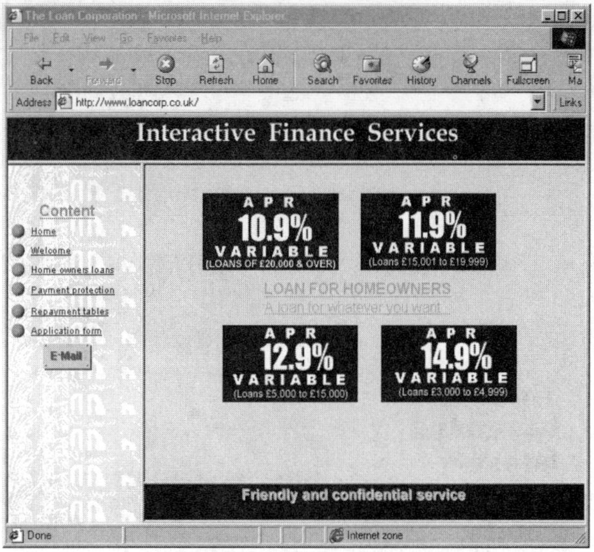

This site offers loans to homeowners at very competitive rates. You apply for a loan over the Internet by completing an on-line form giving the usual information about salary and expenditure. The reply comes back very quickly.

Your home could be at risk if you do not keep up payments on a mortgage or other loan secured on it.

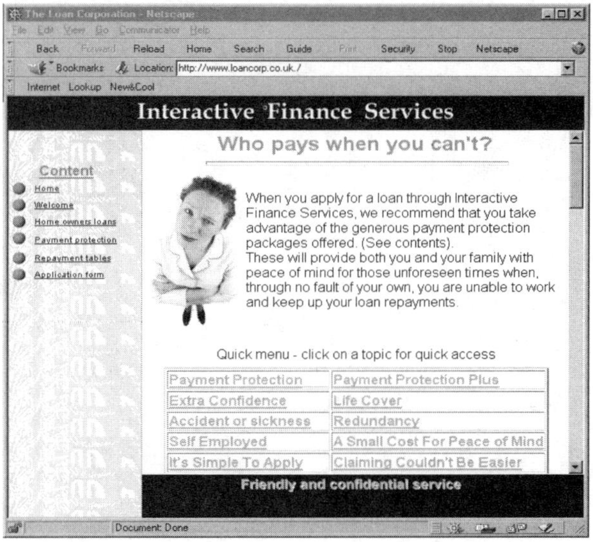

Interactive Finance Services may be found at *http://www.loancorp.co.uk.*

Interactive Investor

For those who enjoy dabbling with shares, this site is invaluable. Amongst other features, it lists the FTSI prices which can be displayed either in alphabetical order or by the amount they rose or fell. Additional information is available about Personal Equity Plans or PEPs, as well as other long term financial investments.

HANDY TIP

This site has all the latest prices and is very accurate.

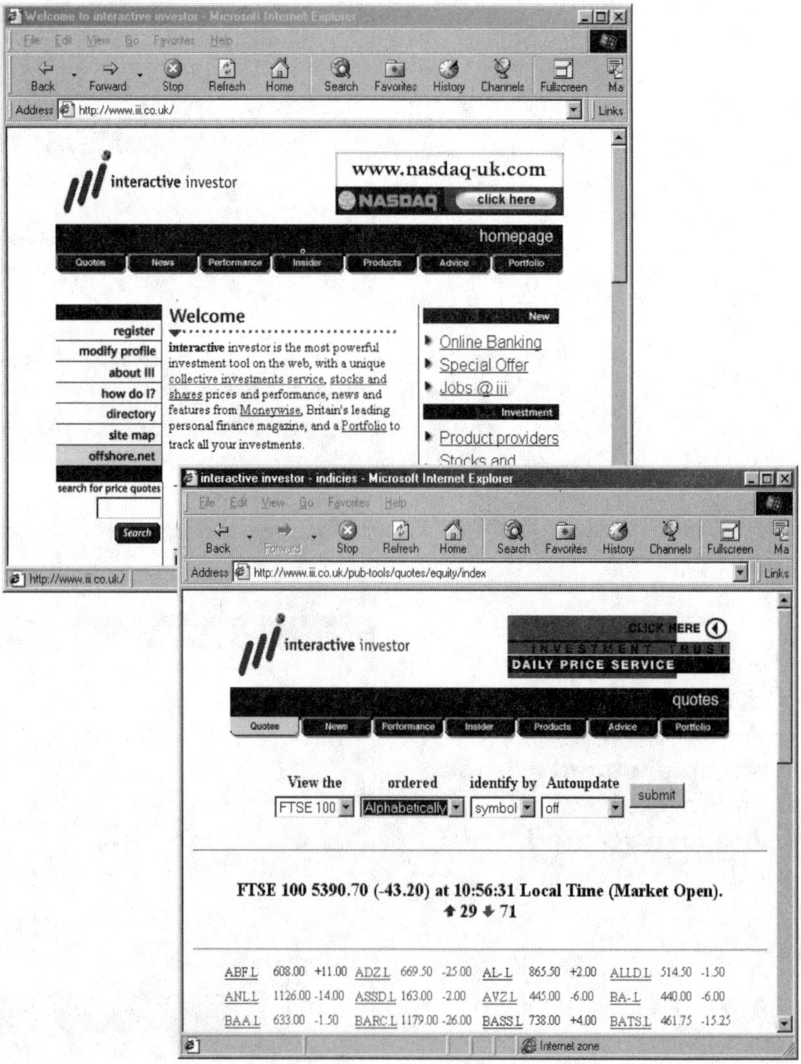

The Interactive Investor may be found by going to *http://www.iii.co.uk*.

Universal Currency Converter

This is a clever and very useful site. Simply, it will convert an input sum of money from almost any currency into another. Begin by entering the amount of money to be converted. Next, choose the currency you want to convert from, and the one to convert to. Finally, click on the Convert button at the bottom of the page. The current exchange rates will be applied to the sum of money entered, and the result will be output on the next page.

If you have a portable computer, this is a handy site to access whilst on holiday.

Although accurate, there is a disclaimer stating that accuracy is not guaranteed.

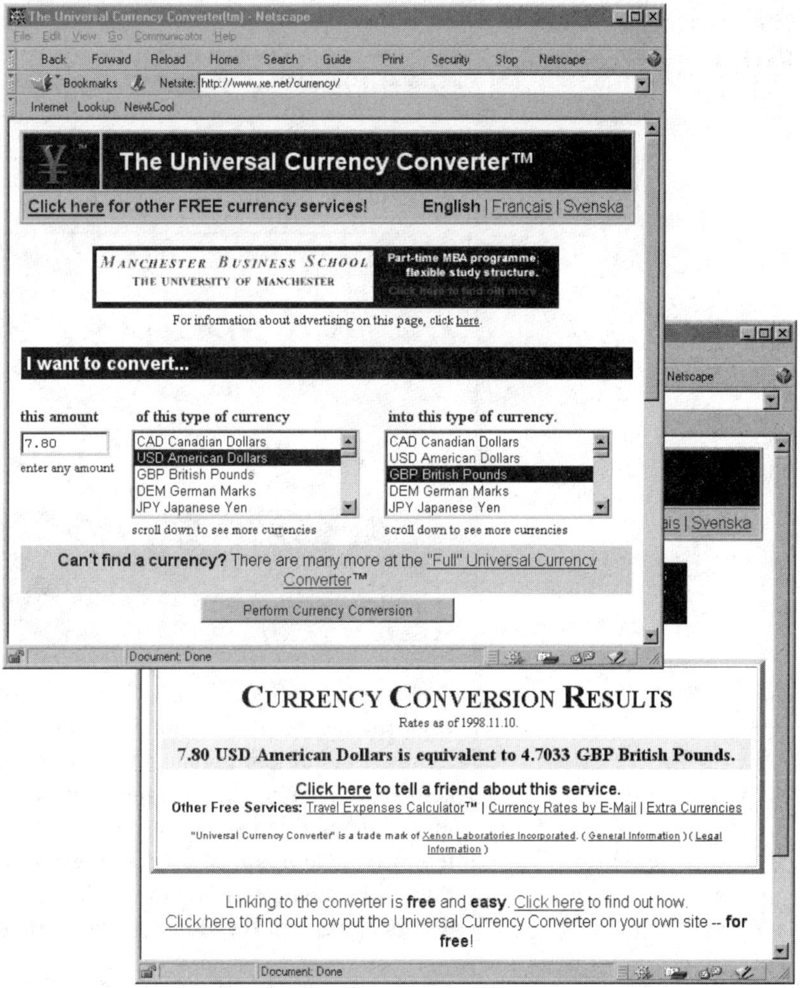

The Universal Currency Converter is at *http://www.xe.net/currency*.

MoneyWeb

The MoneyWeb site contains lots of good basic information on all financial matters including pensions, mortgages, life insurance and investments.

BEWARE

This site is for information only and does not constitute advice within the terms of the FSA 1986.

This site contains several calculators to enable you to work out a variety of benefits.

MONEYWEB - Solid information for the layman, speculations and ...
File Edit View Go Favorites Help
Address http://www.moneyweb.co.uk/
MoneyWeb
Visit our sponsor.
Why give your money to the
Welcome to MONEYWEB, " probably the most comprehensive UK Personal Finance site" - the Financial Times. Lots of good basic information on all matters concerning pensions, mortgages, investments. life insurance etc. Also valuable information for industry professionals, looking at Compliance on the Internet and other issues, plus the opportunuity to join FinServUK, mailing list based discussion group for industry professionals.
Internet zone

Moneyweb is at *http://www.moneyweb.co.uk.*

Money World

The list of companies advertising on this site is very impressive indeed. Bradford and Bingley, Scottish Widows, Legal and General and Eagle Star to name but a few.

The MoneyWorld site contains an amazing amount of material including a financial jargon buster. Just about every banking and finance term is explained in clear, easy-to-understand language.

You can also use this site to find out the current performance (for saving and borrowing) of all sorts of financial services.

One of the most useful areas of this site is the section offering help for homebuyers.

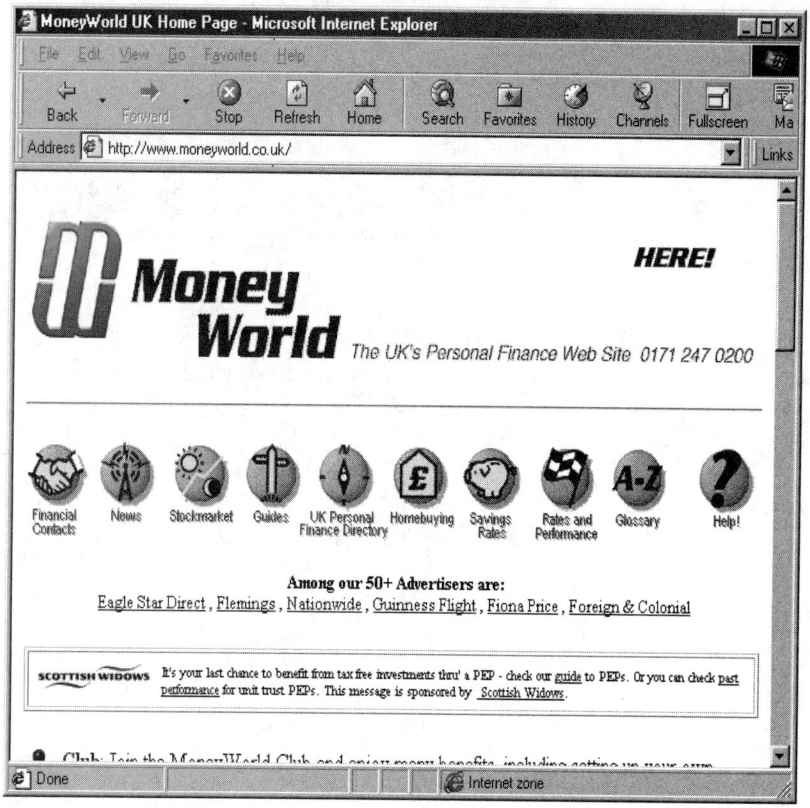

Money World is at *http://www.moneyworld.co.uk.*

Nationwide

The Nationwide site is packed with current information about their services.

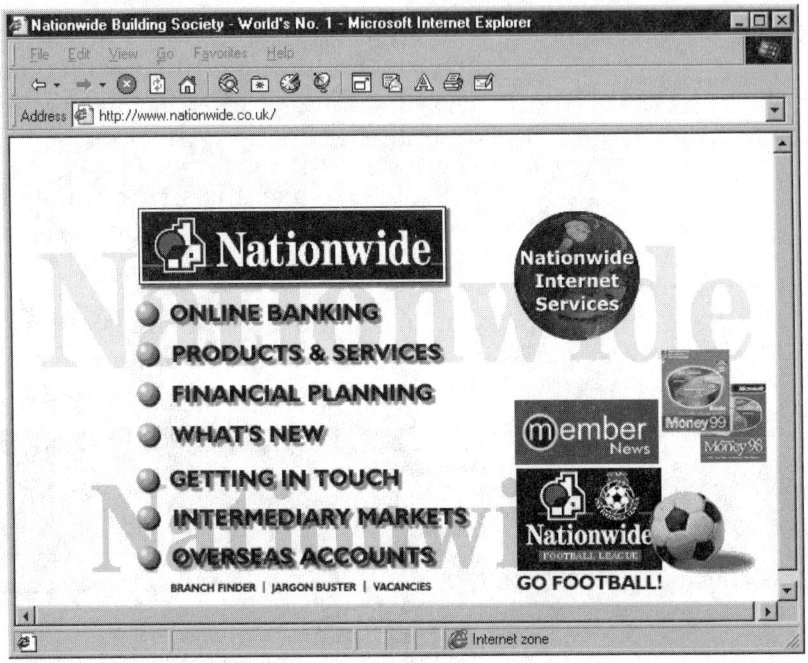

On-line banking is their latest offering and there is a link on the site to enable you to apply for this service. As outlined previously, this facility is particularly useful for regularly keeping track of your bank accounts.

Nationwide are also an internet service provider and providing you have a Nationwide bank account you can also enjoy the ISP services offered.

The Nationwide web site includes a useful section on financial planning which is well worth reading.

As the sponsors of the Football League, there is also a section on the League with information about most of the clubs in the top divisions. You can also view the Football League table.

Nationwide is at *http://www.nationwide.co.uk.*

Electronic Share Information

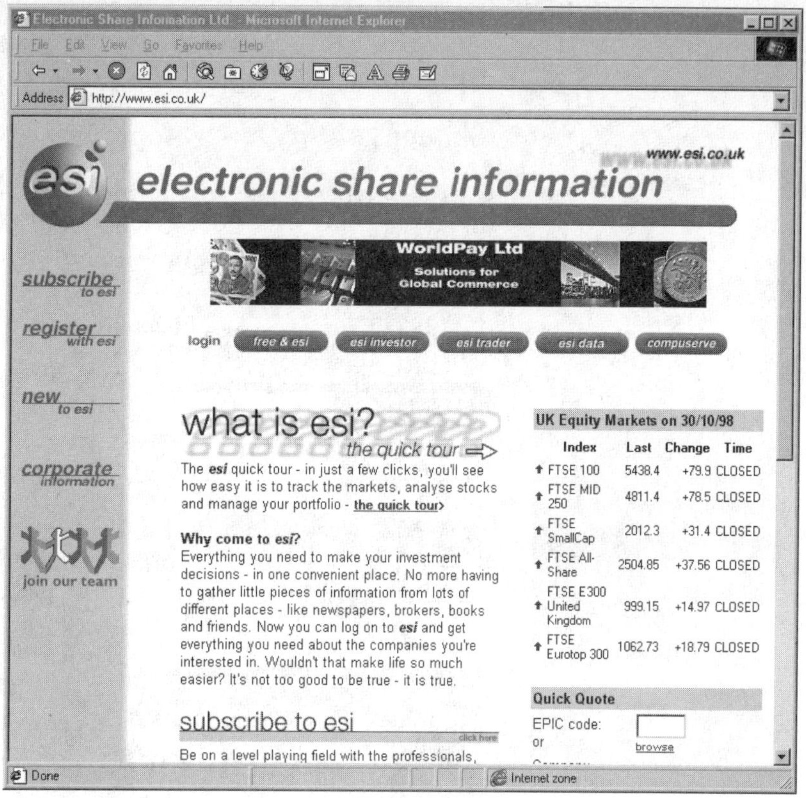

Information you provide may be passed on to other reputable companies who offer goods and services which may be of interest to you. This can be suppressed if required.

An alternative site for getting the latest prices on your shares is the Electronic Share Information site at *http://www.esi.co.uk*.

The Electronic Share Information web site contains everything you need to make investment decisions. The advantage of a well maintained site such as this is that the prices are always up to date.

To get the most from this site you should register. The on-line form requires that you provide some security information which you'll need to quote when you re-enter the site.

Once registered, you'll have access to a full range of financial services to enable you to be on a level playing field with the professionals.

Other Financial Sites

Halifax – *http:/www.halifax.co.uk*

Alliance & Leicester – *http://www.alliance-leicester.com*

Skipton – *http://www.skipton.co.uk*

Xest – *http://www.xest.com*

Chapter Three

Internet Shopping

Like Internet banking, shopping on the Internet has a mixed press. Some see it as a dream come true, others as little more than a gimmick which wastes more time than it saves.

Covers

Tesco Shopping

Whatever is available at a Tesco store can also be purchased via the Internet and will be delivered for a fee of £5.

The advantage of this method is that you don't have to be physically present in the shop to do your shopping. Payment is by credit card, over a secure connection which means there is no chance of your card number falling into the wrong hands.

HANDY TIP **Create a file of items you use every week and begin your shopping list with these.**

All the benefits (such as discounts that you would get by attending the shop in person) are passed on to you as an Internet shopper.

BEWARE **You won't be able to see the items, only their description.**

The problem with this system is that it has become so popular, you'll need to book the delivery several days in advance. Therefore you'll need to plan next week's meals quite early on during the previous week to ensure you get a delivery time to suit you.

To find out more about Tesco's Home Shopping, begin by going to *http://www.tesco.co.uk* and clicking on the Internet Superstore link.

In addition to Internet shopping, Tesco have their own web site which is packed with useful information, including recipes and a comprehensive wine guide.

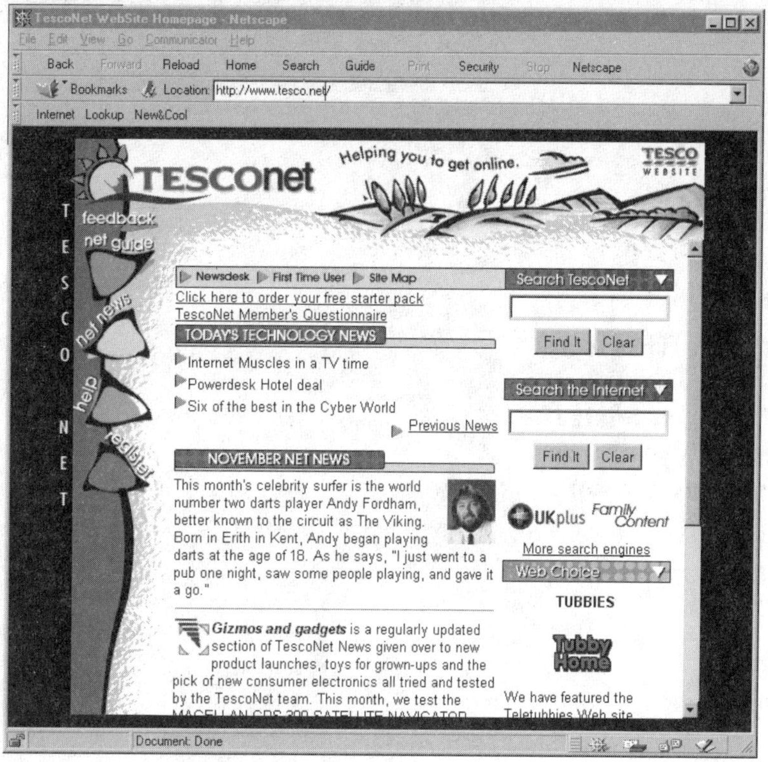

HANDY TIP

If you're prone to 'impulse' buying, this is a great way to cut down your food bill.

There is a list of new items to look out for and a useful search facility which will help you locate the items you want to know about.

Tesco are also heavily involved in education and this too is reflected in their web site.

The site features a news section which reports on all manner of topics including technology. Look out for the reviews of toys for grown-ups and reviews of technological products – at the time of writing, this was a satellite navigation system! It's all a long way from the original Tesco concept: "Pile it high and sell it cheap."

IKEA

For those whose fashion consciousness extends to the home, IKEA is the place to go. There are numerous shops both in the UK and overseas.

IKEA Worldwide - Netscape
File Edit View Go Communicator Help
Back Forward Reload Home Search Guide Print Security Stop Netscape
Bookmarks Location: http://www.ikea.com/content/
Internet Lookup New&Cool
IKEA
IKEA around the World: Select a Country
better living
Visit homes around the world and discover what smart solutions people used to help create better everyday living situations.
living with kids
Discover all of the fun stuff, as well as practical kids furnishings, that IKEA has for the most important people in the world!
product guide
You'll find some of our most popular products along with assembly tips, interactive guides and inspirational ideas.
about IKEA
What's in a name? Find out about IKEA, our unique design approach and how we keep prices so low and
what's new
Create a custom IVAR storage system with the IVAR design tool to make the most out of your space. Then print a list of components to take to your local IKEA store.
November 18th marks the grand opening of IKEA Chicago, one of the biggest IKEA stores in the world.
Introducing VARDE, a flexible, practical and whole new way to think about the kitchen.
Document: Done
Netscape
/locator/locator.asp&formid=30
Internet Lookup New&Cool
IKEA
home
search
International
better living
living with kids
product guide
about IKEA
IKEA near you
Store Locator
Store Experience
what's new
store locator
To find the store nearest you use the pull-down menu below.
United Kingdom
United Kingdom
Birmingham
Leeds
London (Brent park)
London (Croydon)
London (Thurrock)
If you haven't been to an IKEA store before, get ready for a truly unique shopping experience
Document: Done

HANDY TIP

This is a useful site to visit if you're re-designing a room.

This site has several useful sections, including living with children which gives some useful tips for furnishing children's rooms. IKEA can be found at *http://www.ikea. com.*

The Body Shop

This is not so much a shopping site as a web site about the shop. The name Body Shop has become synonymous with fair trade, natural products and non-animal testing.

For lovers of Body Shop products, this site provides a wealth of information about them, about the company itself and its trade links.

HANDY TIP

This is an excellent site to use in schools.

The Body Shop - Skin & Hair Care - Microsoft Internet Explorer
Address http://www.bodyshop.co.uk/
Home
Worldwide:
Select...
Go
monday nov 09
Welcome to The Body Shop Website
MAKE YOUR MARK
1998 marks the 50th anniversary of the Universal Declaration of Human Rights. To celebrate, The Body Shop and Amnesty International have joined forces to launch the world's largest consumer- based human rights campaign - 'Make Your Mark for Human Rights'. Find out more in our updated Action Section.
On 10 December 1998, the campaign culminates in a major international concert in Paris. Visit out News Section to find out more.
We've recently launched some
Home
Action
Company & Values
Questions & Answers
Community Trade
News
Full Voice
Products
Done
Internet zone
The Body Shop - Microsoft In
Address http://www.bodyshop.c
Community Trade
Programme
Go
"We absolutely believe in the power of community economic initiatives to effect change in our lives. Our trade with these communities is our way of participating in and encouraging these initiatives. It is not just about creating another product or market for The Body Shop. It is about exchange and value, trade and respect, friendship and trust."
Home
Action
Company & Values
Questions & Answers
Community Trade
News
Full Voice
Products
Internet zone

The Body Shop site is at *http://www.bodyshop.co.uk.*

Racing Green

Racing Green is part of the Arcadia Group which includes Burton and Dorothy Perkins. Their web site shows all of their products available through mail order and also includes on-line ordering.

BEWARE **Ensure you order the correct size and colour for each item you order.**

HANDY TIP **Have your credit card handy.**

Once an order is started, each page gives you an opportunity to add to your virtual shopping basket. The bill is totalled for you and secure credit card payment is available.

The Racing Green web site is at *www.racinggreen.co.uk.*

Next

Staying with fashion, the Next web site offers the user an on-line catalogue showing many of the Next products. Originally fashion clothes for those who no longer qualify for a Club 18–30 holiday, Next now sell accessories and a range of stylish household products and children's clothes.

HANDY TIP

Keep a look out for on-line ordering.

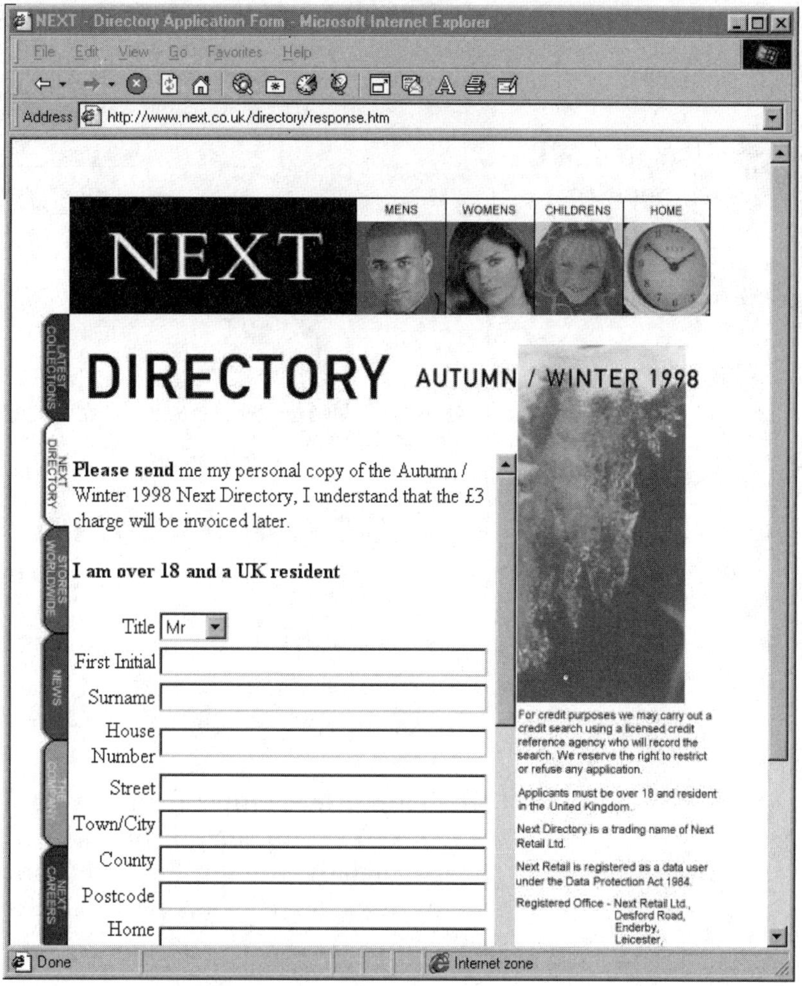
NEXT - Directory Application Form - Microsoft Internet Explorer
File Edit View Go Favorites Help
Address http://www.next.co.uk/directory/response.htm
MENS
WOMENS
CHILDRENS
HOME
NEXT
LATEST COLLECTIONS
NEXT DIRECTORY
STORES WORLDWIDE
NEWS
THE COMPANY
NEXT CAREERS
DIRECTORY AUTUMN / WINTER 1998
Please send me my personal copy of the Autumn / Winter 1998 Next Directory, I understand that the £3 charge will be invoiced later.
I am over 18 and a UK resident
Title Mr
First Initial
Surname
House Number
Street
Town/City
County
Postcode
Home
For credit purposes we may carry out a credit search using a licensed credit reference agency who will record the search. We reserve the right to restrict or refuse any application.
Applicants must be over 18 and resident in the United Kingdom.
Next Directory is a trading name of Next Retail Ltd.
Next Retail is registered as a data user under the Data Protection Act 1984.
Registered Office - Next Retail Ltd., Desford Road, Enderby, Leicester,
Done
Internet zone

Although on-line shopping is not yet available, you can order a catalogue by completing the on-line form. You'll be invoiced for £3.

The Next web site is at *http://www.next.co.uk*.

Fashion clothes shopping

For some people, shopping for clothes is like an extended holiday and the ultimate retail therapy. Personally, I can't think of anything worse than queuing up at changing rooms, being badgered by commission-hungry sales assistants and then having to haul several heavy bags home on an over-crowded train. If you feel the same, Kingshill have the answer.

REMEMBER

You don't need to leave your armchair to shop here.

Kingshill offer clothes from several top fashion names which you can browse through from the comfort of your own armchair. It's not dissimilar to strolling through a shop. Just click on a fashion name and look through the collection.

You don't have to be a member to view the site, but you do need to register to make a purchase.

Go to *http://www.kingshill.co.uk* to get to Kingshill's front page. You can order a catalogue for £3 and once registered you can shop without leaving your home.

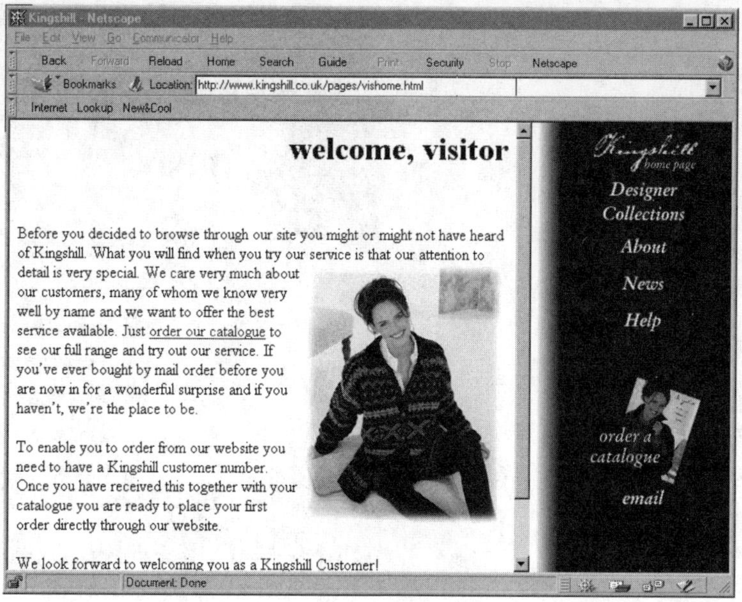
Kingshill - Netscape
File Edit View Go Communicator Help
Back Forward Reload Home Search Guide Print Security Stop Netscape
Bookmarks Location: http://www.kingshill.co.uk/pages/vishome.html
Internet Lookup New&Cool
welcome, visitor
Before you decided to browse through our site you might or might not have heard of Kingshill. What you will find when you try our service is that our attention to detail is very special. We care very much about our customers, many of whom we know very well by name and we want to offer the best service available. Just order our catalogue to see our full range and try out our service. If you've ever bought by mail order before you are now in for a wonderful surprise and if you haven't, we're the place to be.
To enable you to order from our website you need to have a Kingshill customer number. Once you have received this together with your catalogue you are ready to place your first order directly through our website.
We look forward to welcoming you as a Kingshill Customer!
Kingshill
home page
Designer Collections
About
News
Help
order a catalogue
email
Document: Done

REMEMBER **There are several brand names in this store.**

Once registered, you can wander through several top design names and place items in your virtual shopping basket. If you haven't registered, go to the sight and browse through the stock.

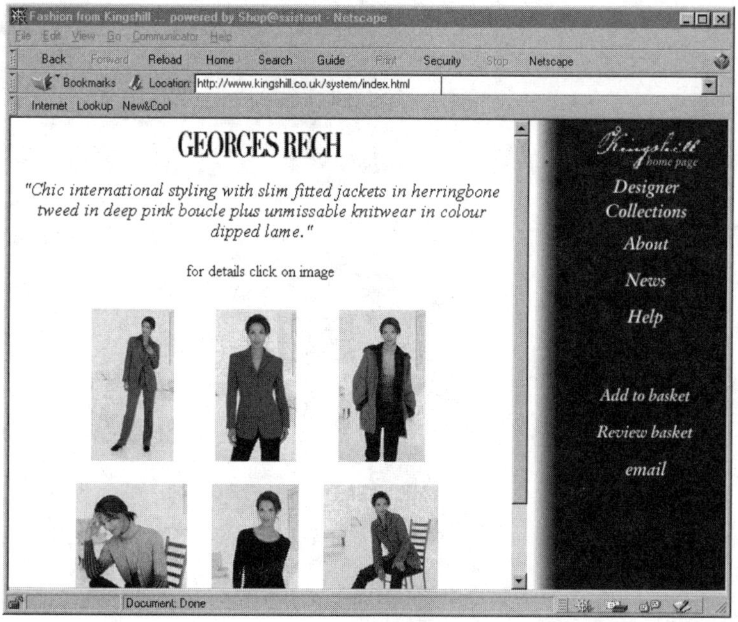
Fashion from Kingshill ... powered by Shop@ssistant - Netscape
File Edit View Go Communicator Help
Back Forward Reload Home Search Guide Print Security Stop Netscape
Bookmarks Location: http://www.kingshill.co.uk/system/index.html
Internet Lookup New&Cool
GEORGES RECH
"Chic international styling with slim fitted jackets in herringbone tweed in deep pink boucle plus unmissable knitwear in colour dipped lame."
for details click on image
Kingshill
home page
Designer Collections
About
News
Help
Add to basket
Review basket
email
Document: Done

Sainsbury

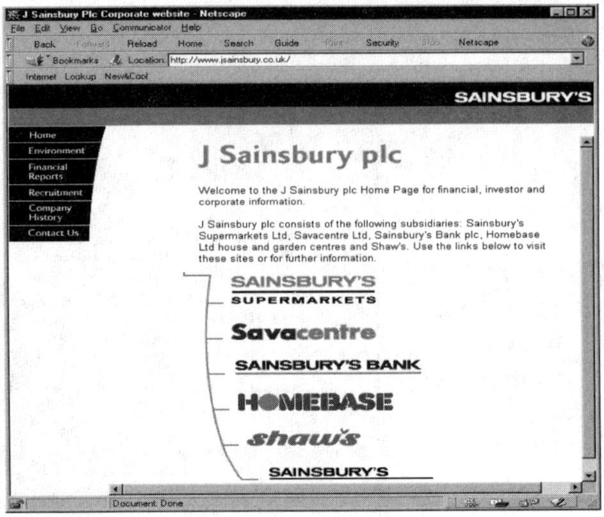
J Sainsbury Plc Corporate website - Netscape
http://www.jsainsbury.co.uk/
SAINSBURY'S
Home
Environment
Financial Reports
Recruitment
Company History
Contact Us
J Sainsbury plc
Welcome to the J Sainsbury plc Home Page for financial, investor and corporate information.
J Sainsbury plc consists of the following subsidiaries: Sainsbury's Supermarkets Ltd, Savacentre Ltd, Sainsbury's Bank plc, Homebase Ltd house and garden centres and Shaw's. Use the links below to visit these sites or for further information.
SAINSBURY'S SUPERMARKETS
Savacentre
SAINSBURY'S BANK
HOMEBASE
shaw's
SAINSBURY'S
Document: Done

HANDY TIP **The Sainsbury site also contains links for other shops in the chain.**

The Sainsbury web site offers customers the chance to order on-line but also gives other value-added features such as recipes and information about the Sainsbury reward card scheme.

When the site is entered, click on the '10,000 good reasons to click here' slogan to register for on-line purchasing.

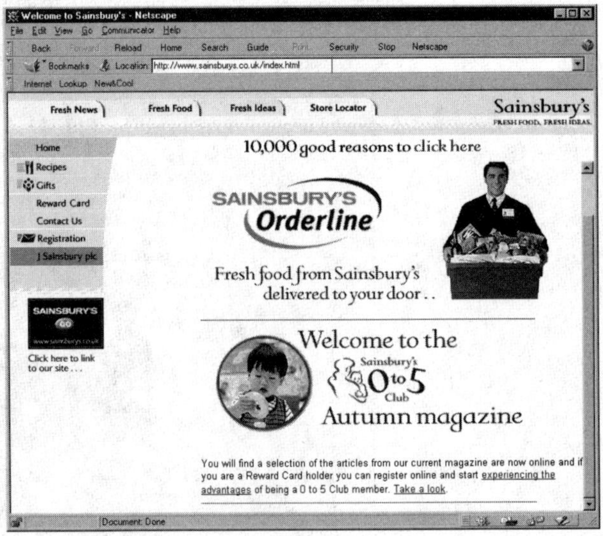
Welcome to Sainsbury's - Netscape
http://www.sainsburys.co.uk/index.html
Fresh News
Fresh Food
Fresh Ideas
Store Locator
Sainsbury's
Home
Recipes
Gifts
Reward Card
Contact Us
Registration
J Sainsbury plc
10,000 good reasons to click here
SAINSBURY'S Orderline
Fresh food from Sainsbury's delivered to your door . .
Click here to link to our site . . .
Welcome to the
Sainsbury's 0 to 5 Club
Autumn magazine
You will find a selection of the articles from our current magazine are now online and if you are a Reward Card holder you can register online and start experiencing the advantages of being a 0 to 5 Club member. Take a look.
Document: Done

Sainsbury's are at *http://www.jsainsbury.co.uk.*

Homebase

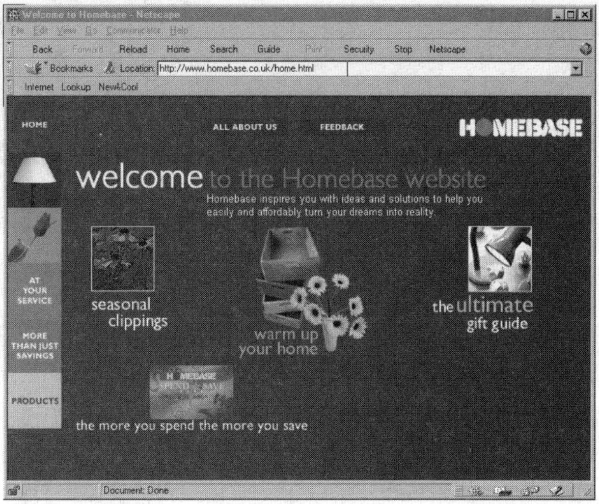

Homebase is Sainsbury's 'do-it-yourself' shop. Although you can't actually shop at this site, you can wander around and get some ideas for improvements for both house and garden. There are details about the Homebase 'Spend and Save Card' as well as seasonal tips to brighten up your home and garden.

HANDY TIP **If you're stuck for decorating ideas, look no further.**

The section on choosing gifts is a particularly interesting and useful one aimed at people who, like me, never quite know what to buy for a birthday present.

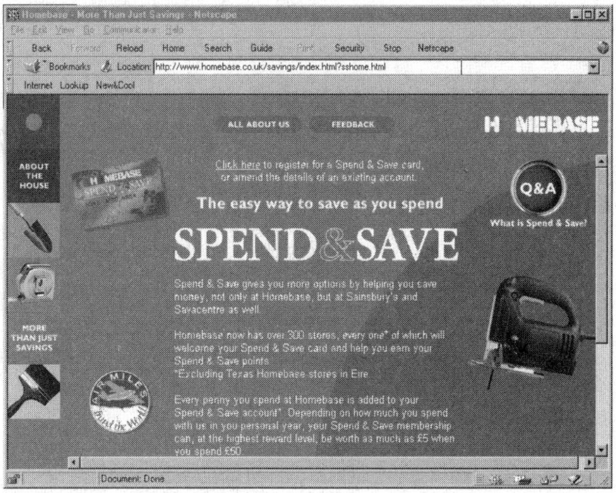

Visit Homebase at *http://www.homebase.co.uk.*

ASDA

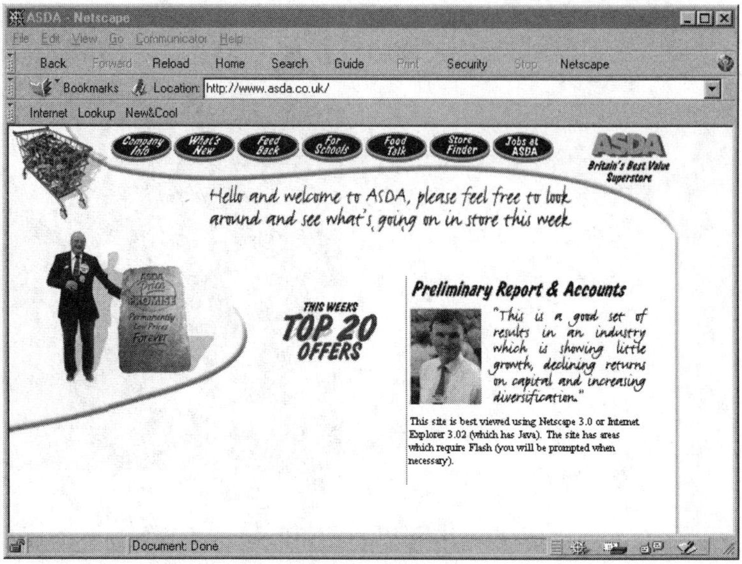

HANDY TIP Check out this site every week to take advantage of the best offers.

ASDA are currently advertising quality and value and this is reflected in their web site. The highlight of this site is the week's top 20 offers.

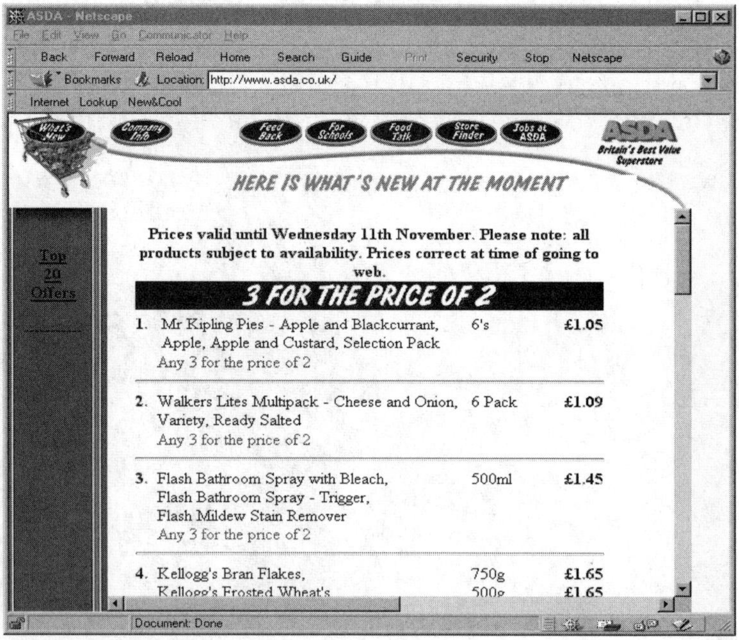

HANDY TIP There are ASDA jobs advertised on this site.

ASDA is at *http://www.asda.co.uk*.

Traidcraft

Traidcraft is an organisation which trades with workers in developing countries and imports their products for sale in this country.

What makes Traidcraft stand out is that it deals fairly with the workers and pays them a sensible wage for the work they have done.

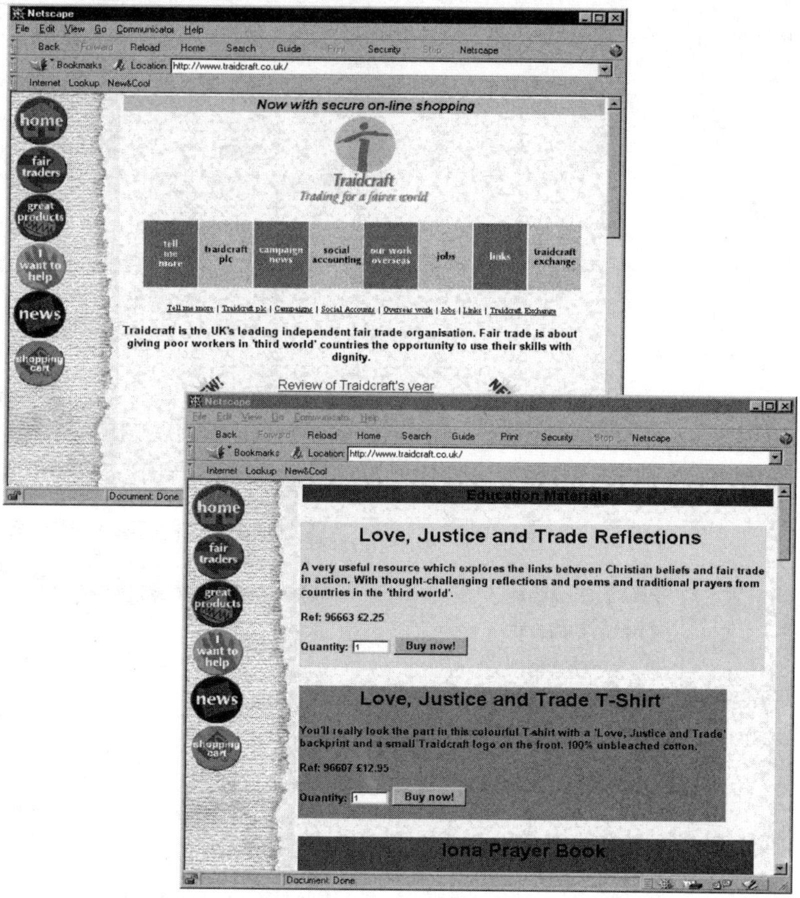
Netscape
http://www.traidcraft.co.uk/
Now with secure on-line shopping
Traidcraft
Trading for a fairer world
Traidcraft is the UK's leading independent fair trade organisation. Fair trade is about giving poor workers in 'third world' countries the opportunity to use their skills with dignity.
Review of Traidcraft's year
Love, Justice and Trade Reflections
A very useful resource which explores the links between Christian beliefs and fair trade in action. With thought-challenging reflections and poems and traditional prayers from countries in the 'third world'.
Ref: 96663 £2.25
Buy now!
Love, Justice and Trade T-Shirt
Ref: 96607 £12.95
Buy now!
Iona Prayer Book
Document: Done

REMEMBER **Although some products may be slightly more expensive, they have been traded fairly.**

In short, the people of developing countries are not being exploited to provide goods, so that we in the developed world can buy more of the products at lower prices.

You can now order on-line from Traidcraft, whose web site is at *http://www.traidcraft.co.uk.*

The Shopping Zone

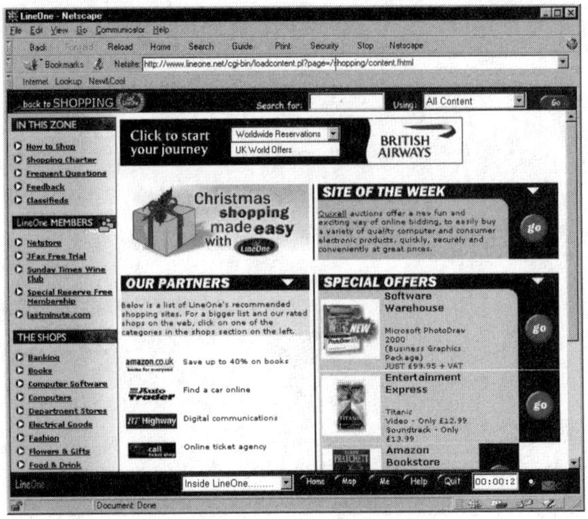

This is probably the definitive site for information about web shopping. The Shopping Zone lists most shops that offer on-line shopping and rates them according to which services they offer.

Details about secure payments are listed and other services are given a star rating.

HANDY TIP

Make sure credit card payment is through a secure connection.

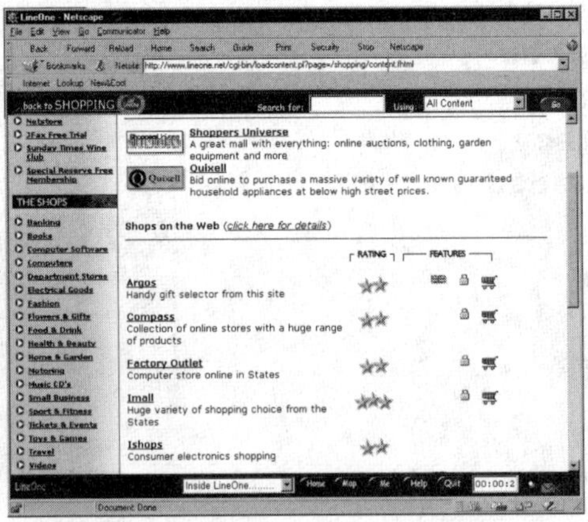

The information about on-line services is thoughtfully divided into categories such as banks, bookshops, computers, department stores, music, fashion and videos.

The Shopping Zone is at *http://shopping.lineone.net.*

Dixons

HANDY TIP **Comparing prices on the web is much easier than trudging around shops.**

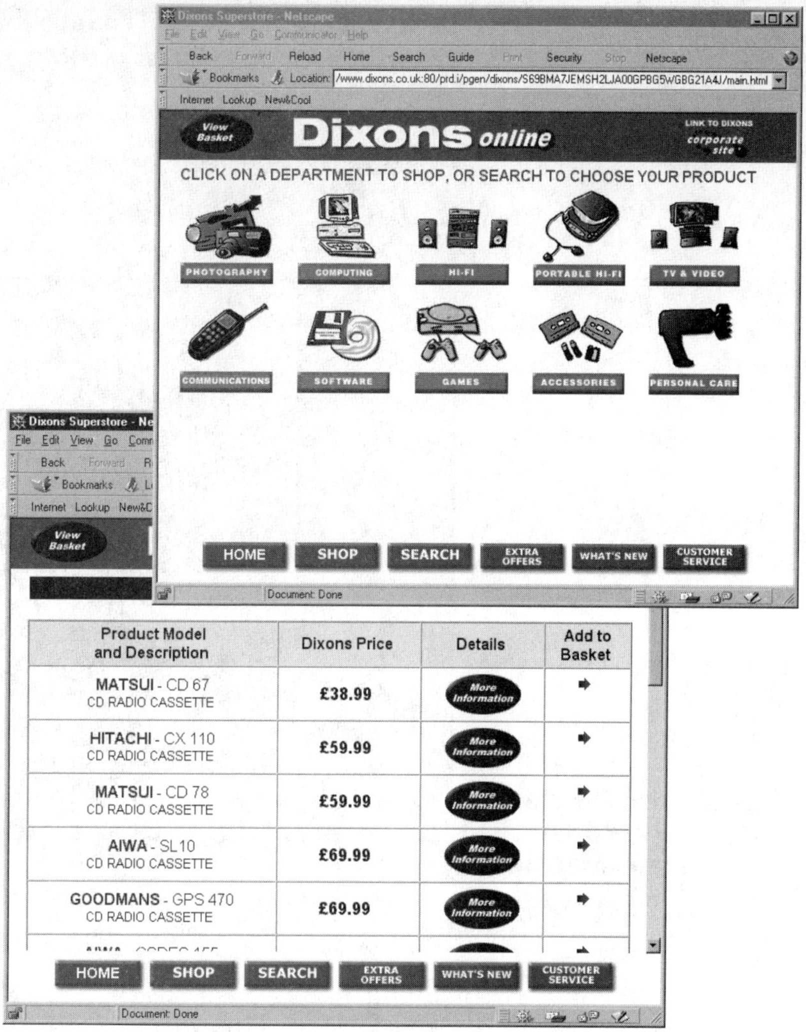

Of all the on-line shopping sites, this seems to be one of the easiest to use. On the first page you're asked to choose the overall category of product you wish to purchase (computer, hifi, portable hifi, communications etc). You then select a specific item within that category.

Further information on each product is available before deciding whether to purchase on-line.

Dixons are at *http://www.dixons.co.uk.*

Electric Postcard

This is just a lovely idea. Technically it's little more than an email with a picture, but it could mean so much more to someone.

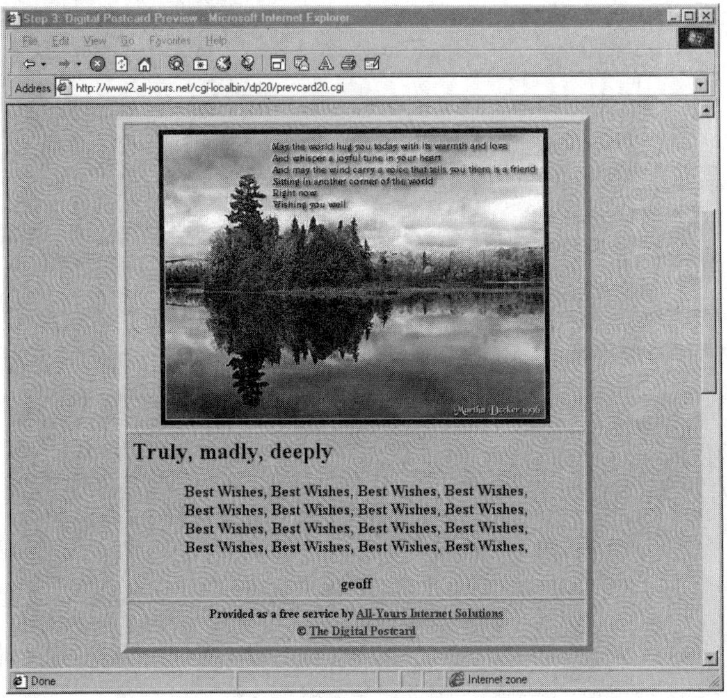
Step 3: Digital Postcard Preview - Microsoft Internet Explorer
File Edit View Go Favorites Help
Address http://www2.all-yours.net/cgi-localbin/dp20/prevcard20.cgi
May the world hug you today with its warmth and love
And whisper a joyful tune in your heart
And may the wind carry a voice that tells you there is a friend
Sitting in another corner of the world
Right now
Wishing you well
Truly, madly, deeply
Best Wishes, Best Wishes, Best Wishes, Best Wishes,
Best Wishes, Best Wishes, Best Wishes, Best Wishes,
Best Wishes, Best Wishes, Best Wishes, Best Wishes,
Best Wishes, Best Wishes, Best Wishes, Best Wishes,
geoff
Provided as a free service by All-Yours Internet Solutions
© The Digital Postcard
Done
Internet zone

HANDY TIP

Send your loved one a romantic message.

There are several similar sites to choose from, but they all work in much the same way.

Begin by choosing a suitable picture for the occasion from those provided. This will be the postcard. Then, enter the email address of the recipient, your email address and the all important message. Some sites allow you to add music or use animated cards. Finally, click the 'deliver' button and your virtual postcard is sent.

The recipient receives an email to log onto the Internet site (usually clicking on the link will do it) and there waiting for them will be the card with the message.

You can send an electric postcard by entering *http://www2.all-yours.net/postcard.*

Chapter Four

Food and Drink

For some, food is so much more than just fuel to keep going. If you want to find out more about the food you eat, or you just want a new recipe to try out on your friends, the Internet is the place to go.

Covers

British Meat

Meat in general, and British meat in particular, has had its fair share of bad publicity. Recent scares about the safety of meat and meat products have made us all question the meat industry.

This site gives us an insight into the British meat industry for both consumers and those in the industry.

HANDY TIP **Check out the meat recipes on this site.**

For many of us, the main route from the title page will be to the excellent recipes using favourite cuts of lamb, beef and pork. I can't claim to have tried them all, but those I have are excellent.

Like many good web sites, the British Meat site has a page of links to other sites. In this case, the links are to other good food sites.

The British Meat web site may be found at *http://www.britishmeat.org.uk*.

Boddington's Beer

HANDY TIP **This site contains a handy screen saver to download.**

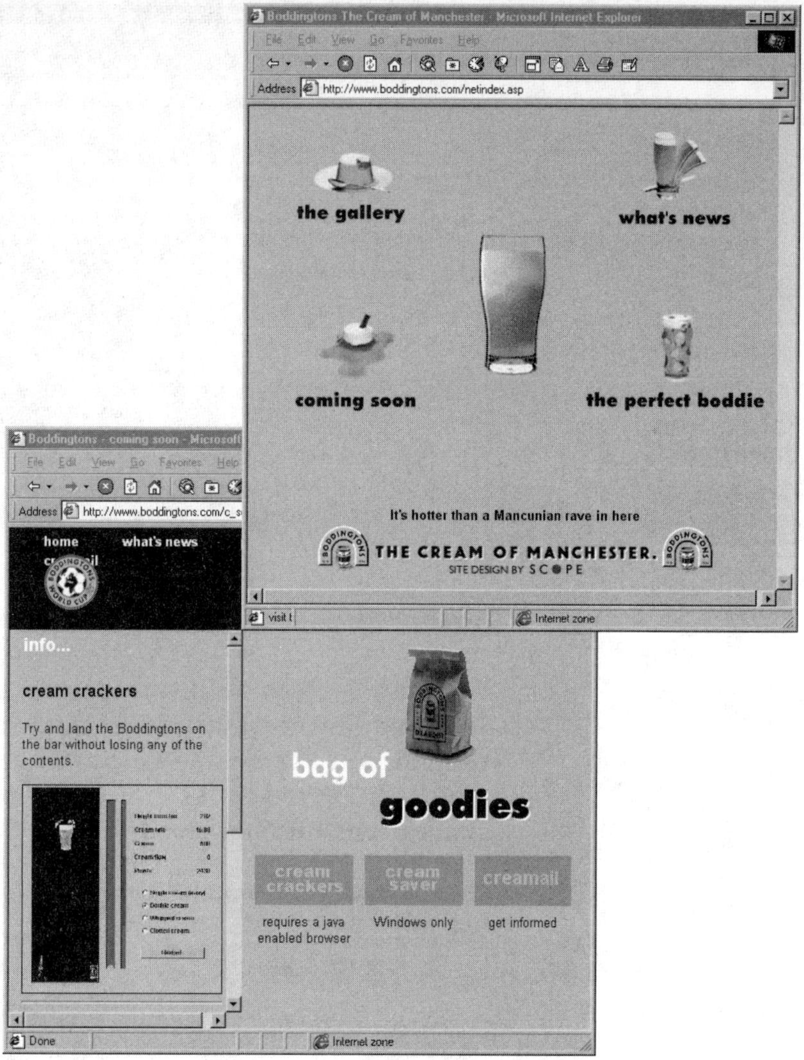

The brewers of the beer dubbed the 'Cream of Manchester' have a particularly light-hearted site providing the user with all manner of snippets about their beer.

One of the highlights is a screensaver which can be downloaded and used on your computer.

The Cream of Web sites may be found at *http://www.boddingtons.com/netindex.asp*.

Cheese . . .

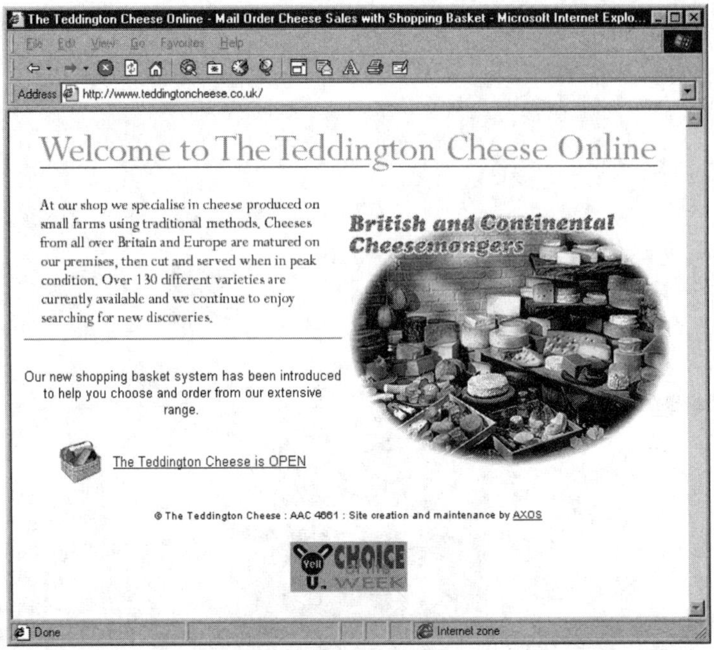

The Teddington Cheese Online - Mail Order Cheese Sales with Shopping Basket - Microsoft Internet Explo...
Address http://www.teddingtoncheese.co.uk/
Welcome to The Teddington Cheese Online
At our shop we specialise in cheese produced on small farms using traditional methods. Cheeses from all over Britain and Europe are matured on our premises, then cut and served when in peak condition. Over 130 different varieties are currently available and we continue to enjoy searching for new discoveries.
British and Continental Cheesemongers
Our new shopping basket system has been introduced to help you choose and order from our extensive range.
The Teddington Cheese is OPEN
© The Teddington Cheese : AAC 4661 : Site creation and maintenance by AXOS
CHOICE
Done
Internet zone

REMEMBER

You can order on-line from this site.

For connoisseurs of fine cheese, this is the place to come. Teddington Cheese have over 130 varieties of fine cheeses from around the world, which can be ordered on-line if required. There are descriptions of cheeses and some suggestions for cheeseboards.

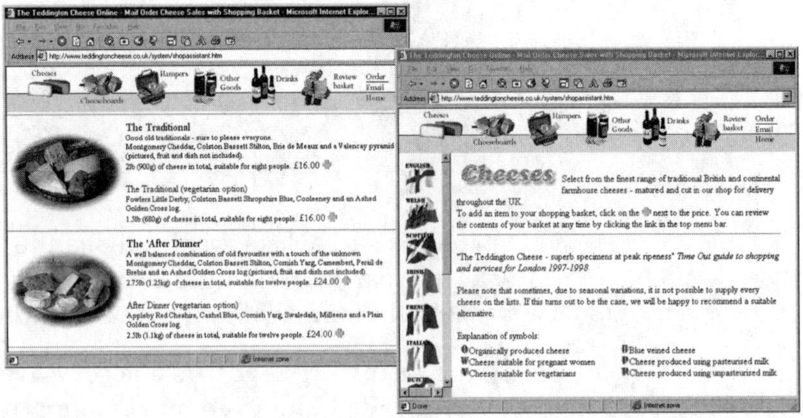

The Traditional
The 'After Dinner'
Cheeses

Teddington Cheese On-line may be found at *http://www.teddingtoncheese.co.uk/*

. . . and Wine

It's not always easy to find a wine you really like. I find that some really cheap wines are very good, some expensive wines, to me, taste like vinegar.

REMEMBER

The best wine to buy is the one you like.

For lovers of fine wine, the Wine Spectator web site is the place to visit.

This site is crammed full of information about fine wines for both the expert and the novice.

The Wine Spectator is at *http://www.winespectator.com.*

Eating at Home

Domino's Pizza

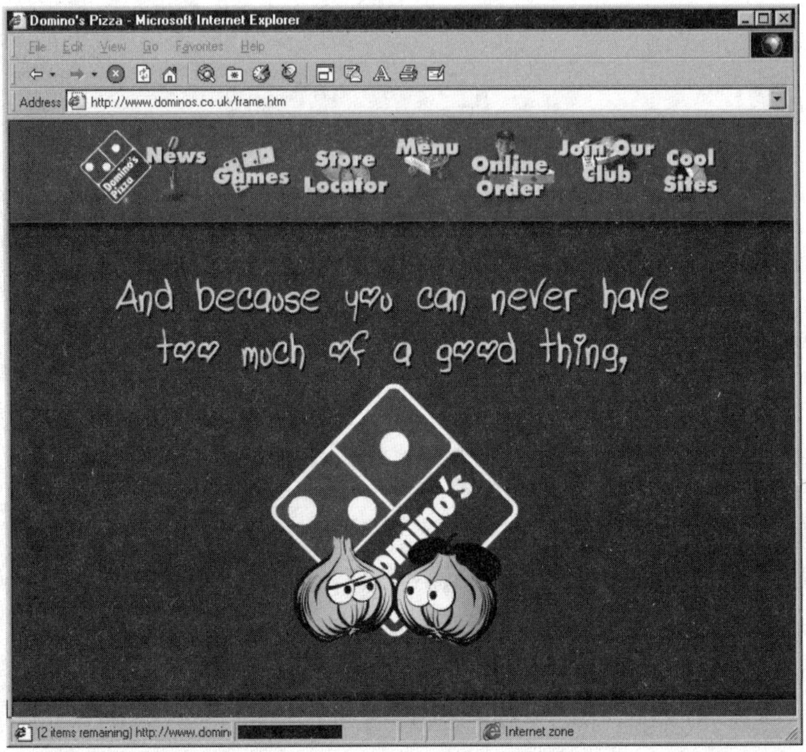

REMEMBER

You can order on-line from this site.

I've found the box often tastes better than the contents of many home-delivered pizzas. Domino's, on the other hand, produces an excellent range of 'custom-made' pizzas which are cooked to perfection and don't taste like oil-soaked cardboard.

The Domino's web site contains news about the chain of outlets as well as giving you information about becoming a franchee – a lucrative occupation, I understand. There are some games to play (most of which have a pizza connection) and there's the chance to join the Domino's Pizza Club.

Their web site at *http://www.dominos.co.uk* has an on-line ordering service. To help you order your pizza, there's a store locator and a menu to enable you to 'design' your own pizza.

Ben and Jerry's Ice Cream

What better after a pizza than some ice cream. The trouble with much of the commercial ice-cream is that it's manufacture doesn't even include milk, let alone cream. Ice cream dates back to Victorian times when it was made from cream and fruit, and then frozen by placing it in a mould which was turned in ice.

Ben and Jerry's ice cream is much the same, except that the freezing process is a little more in keeping with the 20th Century.

In addition to information about the ice cream, including details of their latest flavour, there are games to be played and some fun activities for the kids.

BEWARE

This ice cream is addictive!

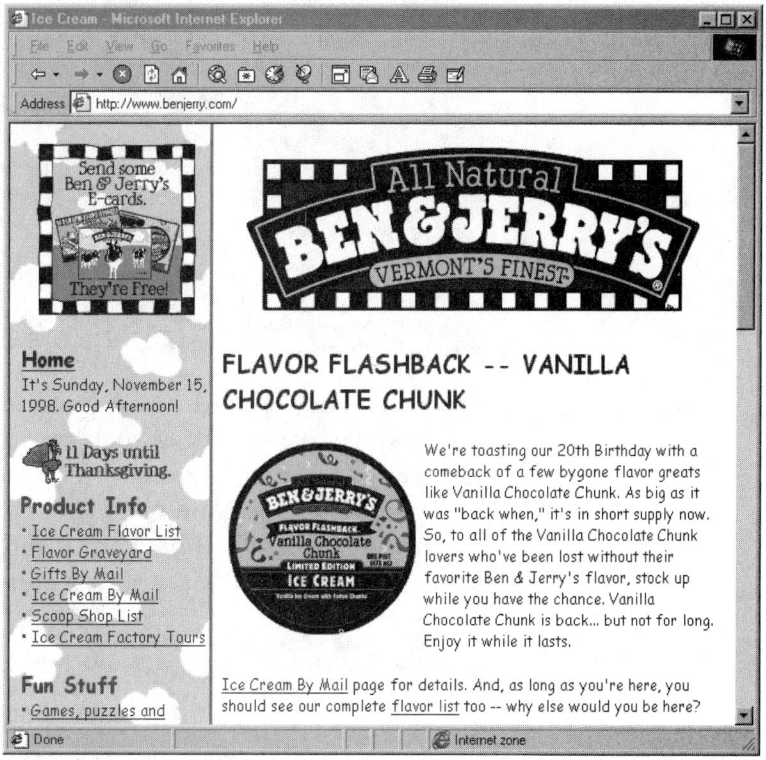
Ice Cream - Microsoft Internet Explorer
File Edit View Go Favorites Help
Address http://www.benjerry.com/
Send some Ben & Jerry's E-cards. They're Free!
All Natural
BEN & JERRY'S
VERMONT'S FINEST
Home
It's Sunday, November 15, 1998. Good Afternoon!
11 Days until Thanksgiving.
Product Info
Ice Cream Flavor List
Flavor Graveyard
Gifts By Mail
Ice Cream By Mail
Scoop Shop List
Ice Cream Factory Tours
Fun Stuff
Games, puzzles and
FLAVOR FLASHBACK -- VANILLA CHOCOLATE CHUNK
We're toasting our 20th Birthday with a comeback of a few bygone flavor greats like Vanilla Chocolate Chunk. As big as it was "back when," it's in short supply now. So, to all of the Vanilla Chocolate Chunk lovers who've been lost without their favorite Ben & Jerry's flavor, stock up while you have the chance. Vanilla Chocolate Chunk is back... but not for long. Enjoy it while it lasts.
BEN & JERRY'S
FLAVOR FLASHBACK
Vanilla Chocolate Chunk
LIMITED EDITION
ICE CREAM
Ice Cream By Mail page for details. And, as long as you're here, you should see our complete flavor list too -- why else would you be here?
Done
Internet zone

Ben and Jerry's ice cream web site may be found at *http://www.benjerry.com.*

Chocolate

Cadbury's Chocolate

Chocoholics will love this.

I immediately put on 2 pounds just smelling it. Chocolate was first used by the Aztecs, although it was very bitter compared to chocolate bought today. The process by which chocolate is made is a long and fascinating one. Not to mention scientific.

Chocoholics may find these sites difficult to avoid.

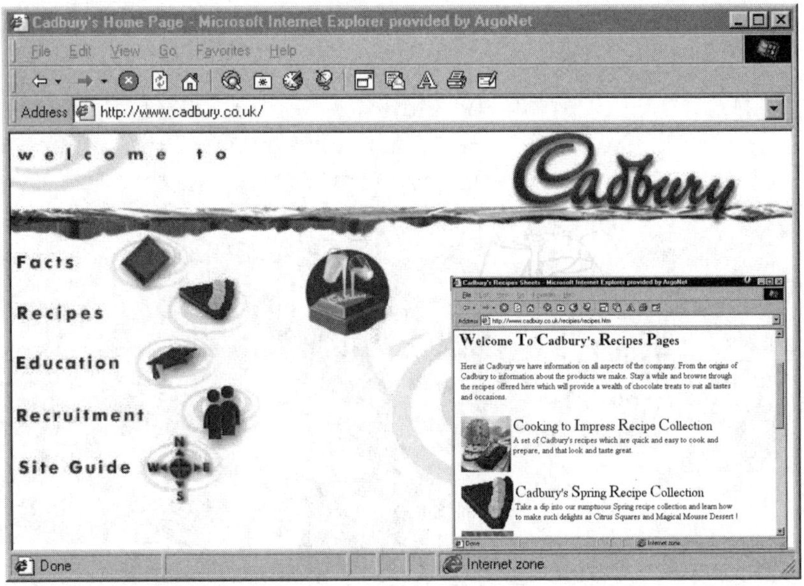

Cadbury is probably the best known chocolate in this country. Their web site is at *http://www.cadbury.co.uk* and is a particularly interesting site. Rather than just outlining their products, this site gives a vast amount of information about the history of chocolate, where it is grown, the modern manufacturing process and its distribution.

There is an education section, which is well worth visiting, and a recruitment section.

Apart from eating chocolate as a confection, chocolate is also a cooking ingredient and Cadbury have included a recipe section which contains some truly mouthwatering recipes.

Godiva's World of Chocolate

Continuing the waist-expanding theme, the World of Chocolate site by Godiva details their range of high-quality chocolates with mouth-watering illustrations. Godiva are at *http://www.godiva.com.*

HANDY TIP

Virtual Chocolates are less fattening than real ones.

You can also use the web to send someone a virtual chocolate. If you're not sure what that is, go to *http://www.virtualchocolate.com.*

Coffee

We seem to take so much for granted. A cup of coffee arrives at our desk and we swill it down without a second thought. Yet the route from the bean to the cup is a long and fascinating one.

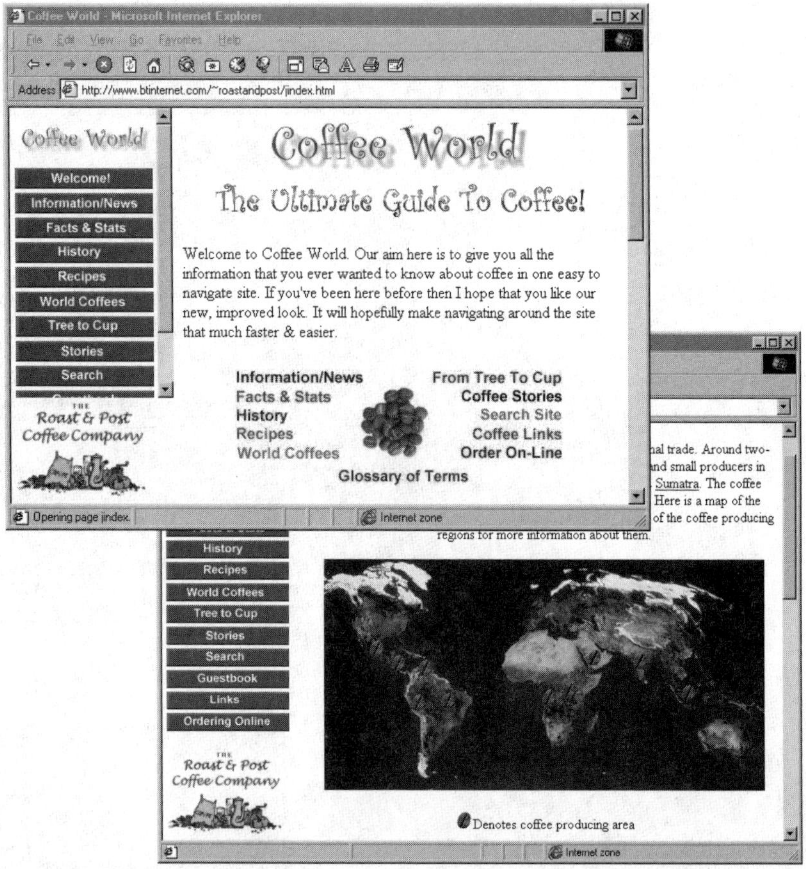

REMEMBER

Like wine, there is a lot of nonsense talked about coffee. This site will help sort out the truth.

The Coffee World web site offers an insight into the production of coffee and includes a huge number of facts about it. The map shows where most of the world's coffee is grown and gives an explanation of the different types and blends available.

The Coffee World web site may be visited at *http://www.btinternet.com/~roastandpost/index.html,* where there is an on-line ordering service.

Jam

I was well into my 20's before I tasted shop-bought jam. My grandfather used to swear that shop-bought raspberry jam contained sawdust to simulate the pips. So, my grandmother used to make it. The recipe was simple: it contained fruit and sugar and nothing else.

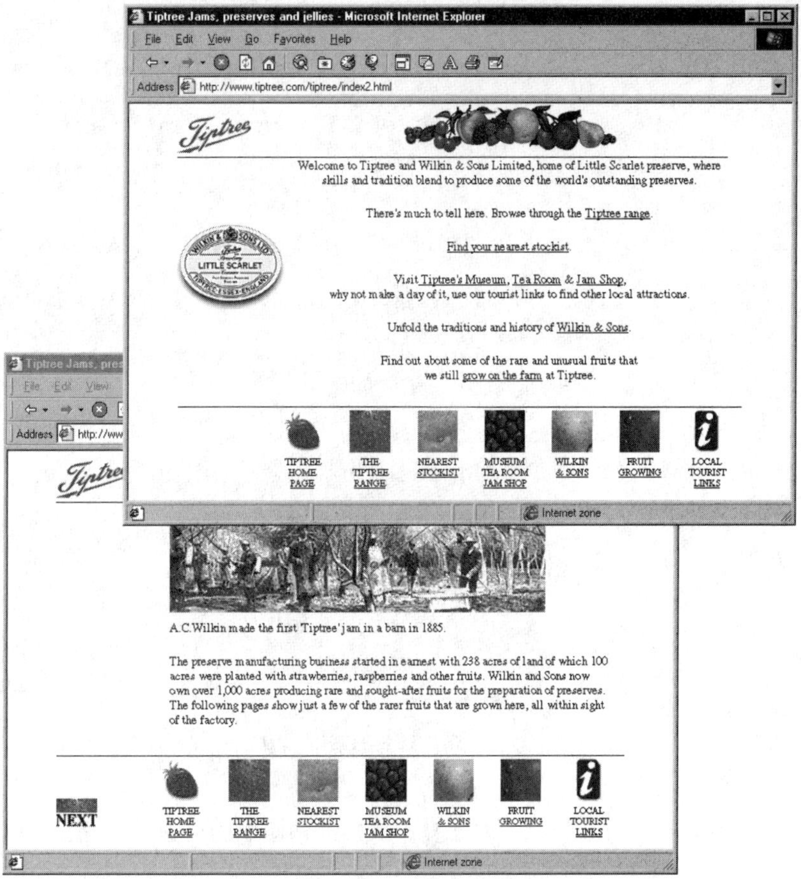
Tiptree Jams, preserves and jellies - Microsoft Internet Explorer
File Edit View Go Favorites Help
Address http://www.tiptree.com/tiptree/index2.html
Tiptree
Welcome to Tiptree and Wilkin & Sons Limited, home of Little Scarlet preserve, where skills and tradition blend to produce some of the world's outstanding preserves.
There's much to tell here. Browse through the Tiptree range.
Find your nearest stockist.
Visit Tiptree's Museum, Tea Room & Jam Shop, why not make a day of it, use our tourist links to find other local attractions.
Unfold the traditions and history of Wilkin & Sons.
Find out about some of the rare and unusual fruits that we still grow on the farm at Tiptree.
TIPTREE HOME PAGE
THE TIPTREE RANGE
NEAREST STOCKIST
MUSEUM TEA ROOM JAM SHOP
WILKIN & SONS
FRUIT GROWING
LOCAL TOURIST LINKS
Internet zone
A.C.Wilkin made the first Tiptree' jam in a barn in 1885.
The preserve manufacturing business started in earnest with 238 acres of land of which 100 acres were planted with strawberries, raspberries and other fruits. Wilkin and Sons now own over 1,000 acres producing rare and sought-after fruits for the preparation of preserves. The following pages show just a few of the rarer fruits that are grown here, all within sight of the factory.
NEXT

BEWARE

Not all jam is made in the same way as grandmothers'.

Whilst not containing impurities such as sawdust, many modern shop bought jams contain a great deal more than fruit and sugar. The Tiptree web site clearly demonstrates how their jam has hardly changed for years. Information includes fruit growing, the company itself and tourist information.

Tiptree jams: *http://www.tiptree.com/tiptree/index2.html.*

Other Sites

Chocnet – *http://orders.mkn.co.uk/choc/.en*

Clipper Teas – *http://www.clipper-teas.co.uk*

Epicurious Food – *http://food.epicurious.com*

Farmshop Directory – *http://www.farmshop.net/directory/start.asp*

French Wine Collection – *http://www.somerfield.co.uk*

FruitNet UK – *http://orders.mkn.co.uk/fruit/.en*

Heinz – *http://www.heinz.co.uk*

Honey Bureau – *http://www.honey-bureau.demon.co.uk*

Kelloggs Cereals – *http://www.kelloggs.com*

Lunch On-line – *http://lunch.online.offworld.co.uk*

Magnum Fine Wines – *http://www.magnum.co.uk*

Moet & Chandon – *http://www.moet.com*

Müller – *http://www.muller.co.uk*

Mushroomers – *http://members.aol.com/basidium/mushpepl.html*

Organics Direct – *http://www.organicsdirect.com*

Smokehouse – *http://www.zetnet.co.uk/smoke/options.htm*

Sugar Information Service – *http://www.sugarinfo.co.uk*

Traditional Sweets – *http://www.sela.co.uk*

Tia Maria *http://www.tiamaria.co.uk*

Tizer – *http://www.tizer.co.uk/index_01.htm*

Van den Bergh Foods – *http://www.vdbfoods.co.uk*

Wine – *http://wine.net/index.html*

Chapter Five

Healthy Living

We eat too much, drink too much, eat the wrong things and we don't take enough exercise. Oh yes, and we spend too much time in front of computers. We are not a healthy race!

The Internet can provide some help, but before ploughing on with a list of sites to increase longevity, a few words of caution. It has long been recognised that giving a layman a medical book with which to carryout self-diagnosis is not always sound. If you really think something is wrong, it's best to seek qualified medical advice.

Covers

Women's Health

Ask a Woman Doctor

HANDY TIP

Go to these sites for help and advice about female health issues.

a forum for Women's Health - Microsoft Internet Explorer
File Edit View Go Favorites Help
Address http://www.womenshealth.org/
Ask a Woman Doctor
Subjects
general/other
social/psych.
reproductive
wellness
Lifecycle
reproductive
midlife
mature
girls
Search the Forum
What's New?
a forum for
Women's Health
welcome
Welcome to a forum for Women's Health - your internet resource for women's health information. The forum hosts a Collection of facts, information, advice, and suggestions to help you deal with your health concerns. All content on these pages is designed, written, and
we're on AOL
HEY! We're on AOL now! Just type in keyword: ELECTRA to view our site. Come see it for live chats and more information. Our chat schedule is posted in the "What's New?" section.
Done
Internet zone

There is no shortage of help specifically aimed at women on the web. The Ask a Woman Doctor web site offers women a range of information provided by doctors.

Ask a Woman Doctor can be found at *http://www.womenshealth.org.*

Women's Nutritional Advisory Service

This service offers Women resident in the UK several services such as telephone advice lines, self-help books and general self-help advice.

Women's Nutritional Advisory Service is at *http://www.wnas.org.uk.*

For an alternative approach to helping with health problems, try *http://www.weleda.co.uk.*

Tampax

REMEMBER

Although this is a commercial site, it does contain some very helpful information.

The Tampax web site exists primarily to promote their products but goes much further by providing forums on a variety on women's issues. The Tampax site is at *http://www.tampax.com.*

National Osteoporosis Society

Osteoporosis is the thinning of the bones which usually begins after the menopause. The National Osteoporosis Society (*http://www.nos.org.uk*) will provide women with help and advice.

The list of headings on the front page shows some of the issues covered by this very valuable and well constructed site.

Seek advice before using medication.

Progesterone Cream

The site claims that in a three year study of post-menopausal osteoporosis patients, women who used Natural Progesterone Cream actually increased bone density by an average of 8% in the first year, by 4% in the second year and 2% in subsequent years, against the USA national average of a 1.5% annual loss. Natural Progesterone Cream is also claimed to provide relief from PMT. The site is at *http://www.progesterone.co.uk*.

British Pregnancy Advisory Service

REMEMBER **This site also provides advice about abortions and vasectomy.**

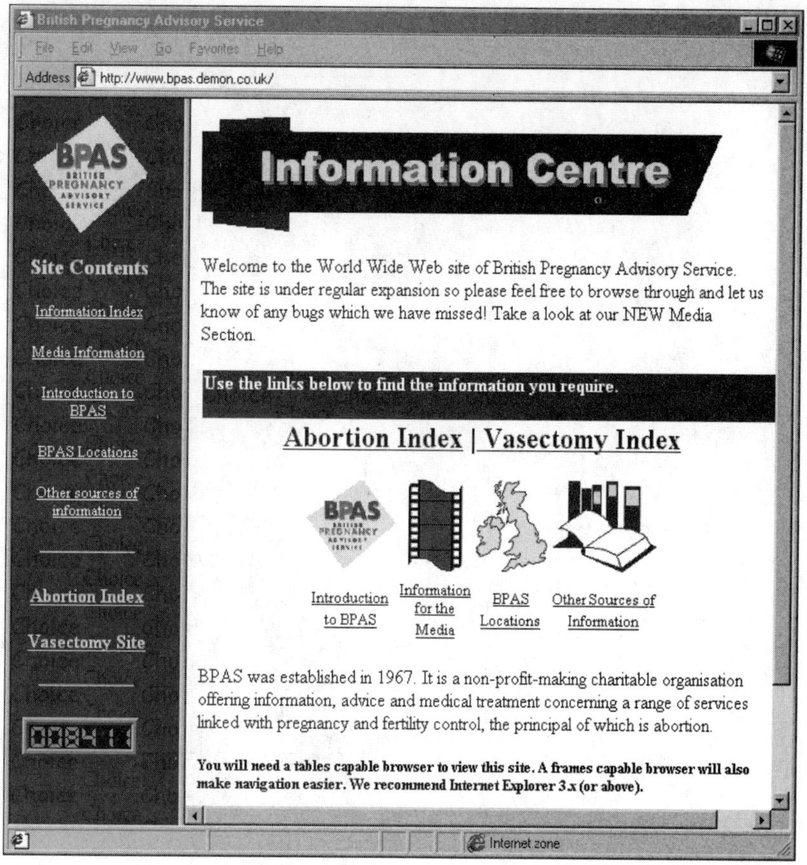
British Pregnancy Advisory Service
File Edit View Go Favorites Help
Address http://www.bpas.demon.co.uk/
BPAS BRITISH PREGNANCY ADVISORY SERVICE
Site Contents
Information Index
Media Information
Introduction to BPAS
BPAS Locations
Other sources of information
Abortion Index
Vasectomy Site
Information Centre
Welcome to the World Wide Web site of British Pregnancy Advisory Service. The site is under regular expansion so please feel free to browse through and let us know of any bugs which we have missed! Take a look at our NEW Media Section.
Use the links below to find the information you require.
Abortion Index | Vasectomy Index
Introduction to BPAS
Information for the Media
BPAS Locations
Other Sources of Information
BPAS was established in 1967. It is a non-profit-making charitable organisation offering information, advice and medical treatment concerning a range of services linked with pregnancy and fertility control, the principal of which is abortion.
You will need a tables capable browser to view this site. A frames capable browser will also make navigation easier. We recommend Internet Explorer 3.x (or above).
Internet zone

The British Pregnancy Advisory Service provides help and advice on all matters relating to pregnancy, including how not to become pregnant and dealing with an unwanted pregnancy. Their site may be found at *http:// www.bpas.demon.co.uk.*

BEWARE **Only enter this site if you really want to know!**

Beauty Check

Inner health is vital, but how one feels about oneself is also important. The feeling about oneself is frequently based on confidence about appearance and this site will give you an independent critical appraisal of how you look. If you feel in need of a beauty check, go to *http:// www.justhow.co.uk.*

Men's Health

Men's Health

HANDY TIP

Go to these sites for help and advice about male health issues.

Like women, men too have their fair share of health problems. Men's Health is a monthly magazine which offers help and advice to men about their health. This web site is at *http://www.menshealth.co.uk.*

Viagra

The male anti-impotence drug, Viagra, must be the best known drug since aspirin. Certainly, I can't remember a drug receiving so much attention even before it was launched. For men suffering with impotence a visit to *http://www.viagra.com* might put them onto the right path.

Healthgate

Healthgate is another site offering advice for male problems. There is an excellent search facility here and it can be found at *http://www.healthgate.co.uk.*

If in doubt, seek medical advice.

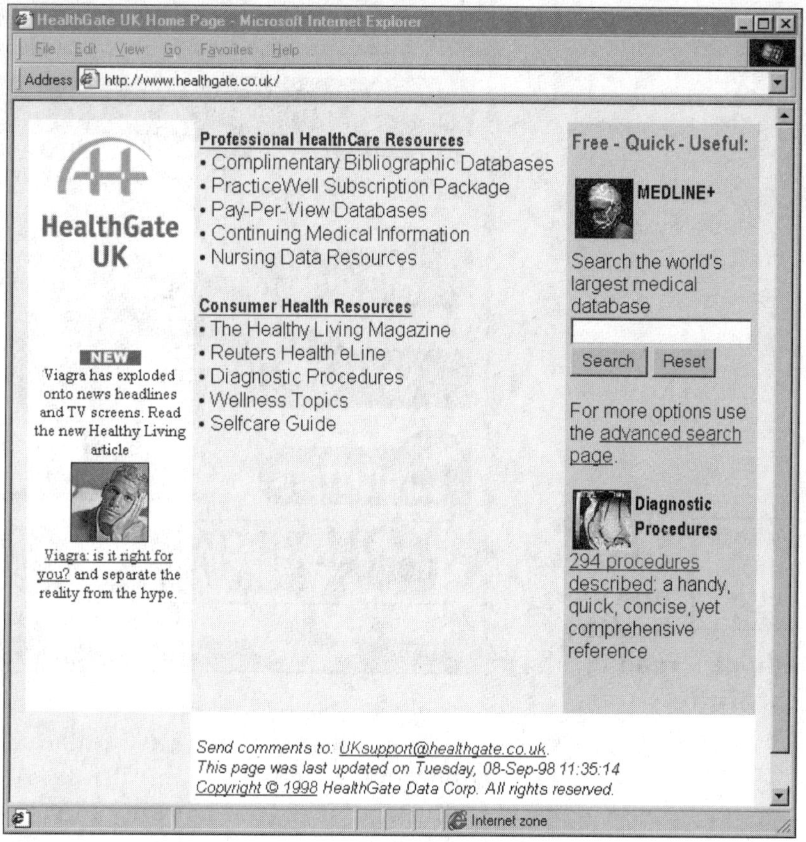

Condoms

Condoms are more than just contraceptives.

Apart from their contraceptive use, a condom will prevent the spread of sexually transmitted diseases. Some men use them as a matter of course, others can't seem to manage them. Whichever category you fit into, *http://www.condom.co.uk* will take you to the site for more information.

Probably the most famous of all brands of condom are Durex and their site is at *http://www.durex.com.*

Men's Fitness

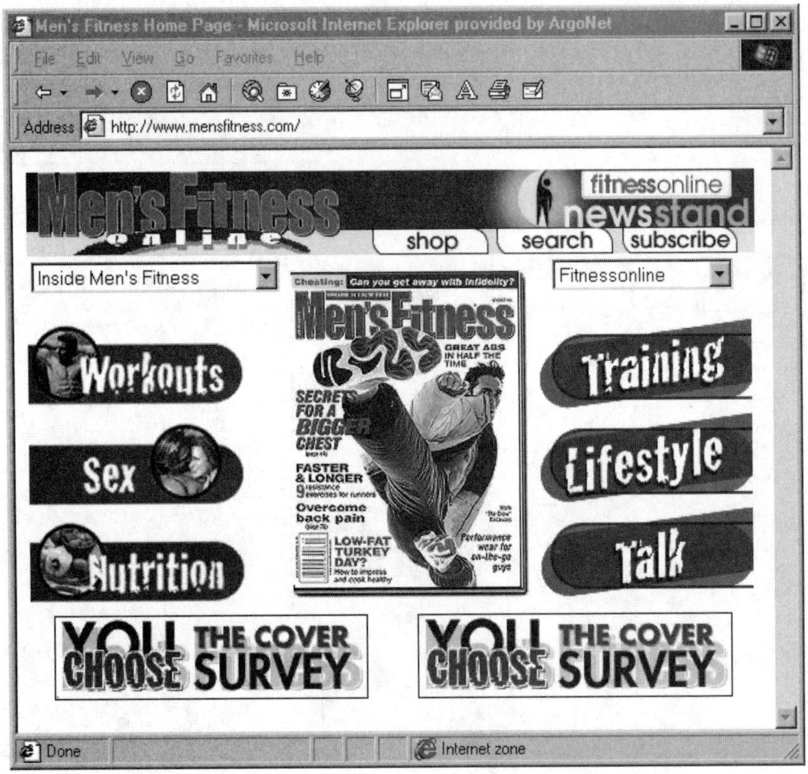

HANDY TIP This site contains lots of healthy advice – read it carefully.

Although fitness is not just a male issue, this site is concerned only with male fitness. As can be seen from the front page, it covers not only muscle building, but nutrition and lifestyle – both of which contribute very significantly to an overall state of health.

The site does not shy away from any issue, and yet it never degenerates into foul or inappropriate language. Everything is covered in a plain and simple style which is easily accessible.

Regular features include workouts, sex, training and nutrition.

Visit this site at *http://www.mensfitness.com.*

Men's Sexual Issues

A recent survey found that men are far less likely to seek medical advice, especially when it's a sexual or a bowel problem. For those who do find it difficult to talk about these matters, this site might help you change your mind.

It deals with sexual issues such as premature ejaculation, and testicular self-examination.

REMEMBER

You must type the address exactly as given.

Slightly 'off-beat' in its approach, it contains some vital hints and advice for keeping the lower regions in order.

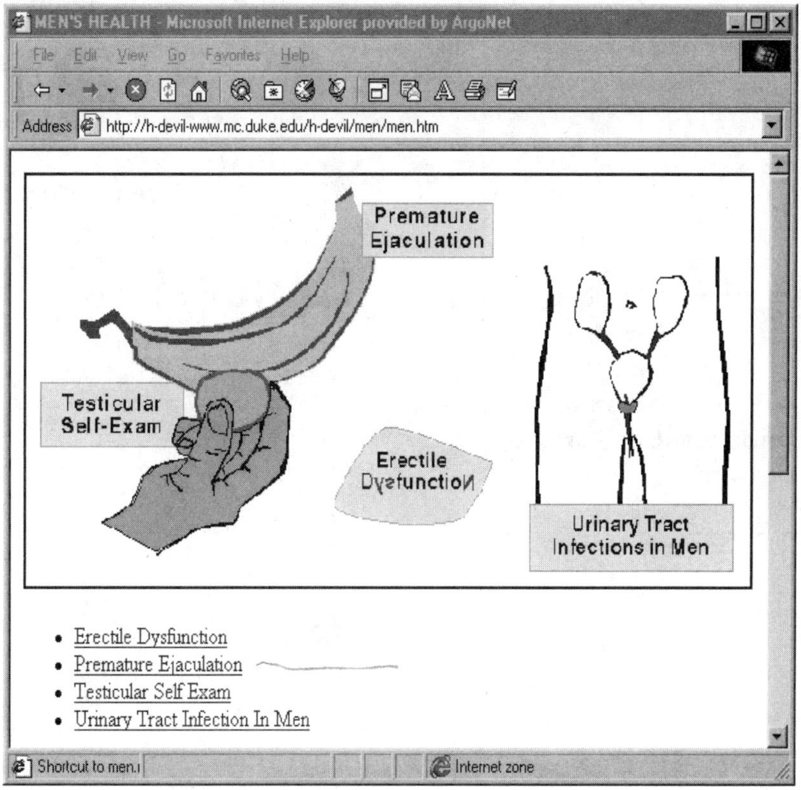

To visit this site, enter *http://h-devil-www.mc.duke.edu/h-devil/men/men.htm.*

Cancer

Young or old, black or white, male or female, cancer knows no boundaries. Having witnessed the effects, not only on the patient, but on the family, I know only too well what it can do.

For the patient, there is medical help, but it's often the families that also need help and support. The Cancer web site is at *http://medweb.bham.ac.uk/cancerhelp/public/orgs/useorgs.html.*

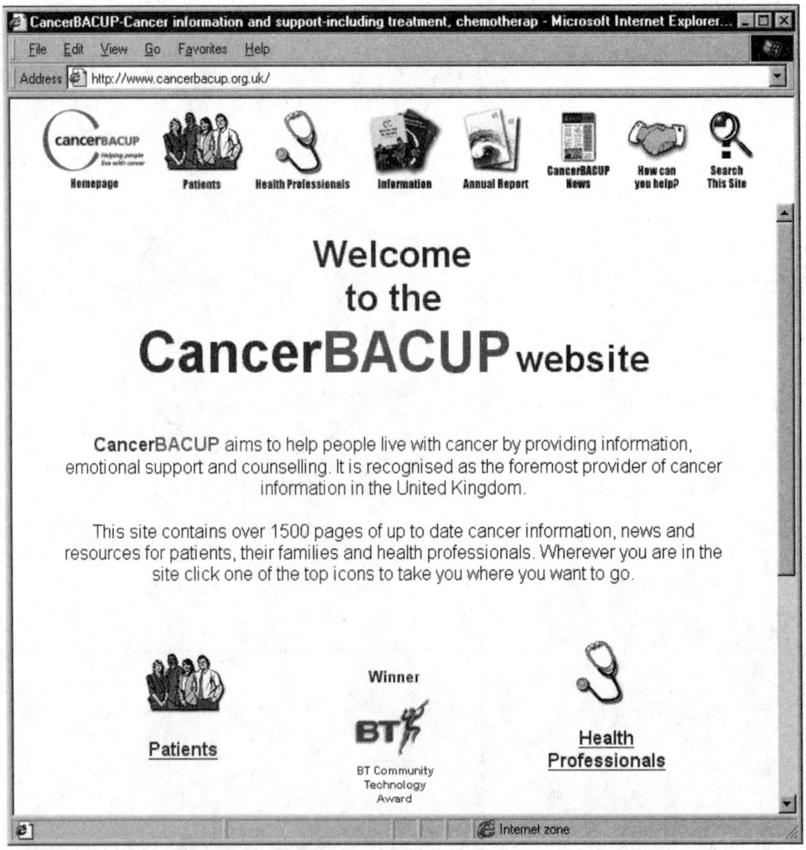

CancerBACUP-Cancer information and support-including treatment, chemotherap - Microsoft Internet Explorer...
File Edit View Go Favorites Help
Address http://www.cancerbacup.org.uk/
cancerBACUP
Homepage
Patients
Health Professionals
Information
Annual Report
CancerBACUP News
How can you help?
Search This Site
Welcome to the CancerBACUP website
CancerBACUP aims to help people live with cancer by providing information, emotional support and counselling. It is recognised as the foremost provider of cancer information in the United Kingdom.
This site contains over 1500 pages of up to date cancer information, news and resources for patients, their families and health professionals. Wherever you are in the site click one of the top icons to take you where you want to go.
Patients
Winner
BT
BT Community Technology Award
Health Professionals
Internet zone

REMEMBER **Support for the family is often as important as for the patient.**

Cancerbacup (note the spelling) will point patients and carers in the right direction. Go to *http://www.cancerbacup.org.uk.*

Breast Cancer

If you're over 50, you'll be invited to get a mammogram; if not, start at *http://www.breastcancerfund.org.*

HANDY TIP **Regular checks will help reduce the possibility of surgery.**

The Breast Cancer Fund - Microsoft Internet Explorer
http://breastcancerfund.org/
MAY THE WINDS BRING SERENITY AND REMEMBRANCE
MAY THE WINDS BRING HEALING
MAY WE BE FREE FROM ILLNESS
THE BREAST CANCER FUND
About TBCF
The Disease
Grants
Newsletter
Art & Healing
Events
Advocacy
Resources
Can I Help?
Events HOT News!
McKinley Climb
Art.Rage.Us
Lilith Concert Tour
This web site designed and maintained by PointLine Interactive Studio.
Internet zone

Cervical Cancer

A regular smear test will help detect this cancer. Find out more by going to *http://www.nccc-online.org.*

REMEMBER **If in doubt, seek medical advice.**

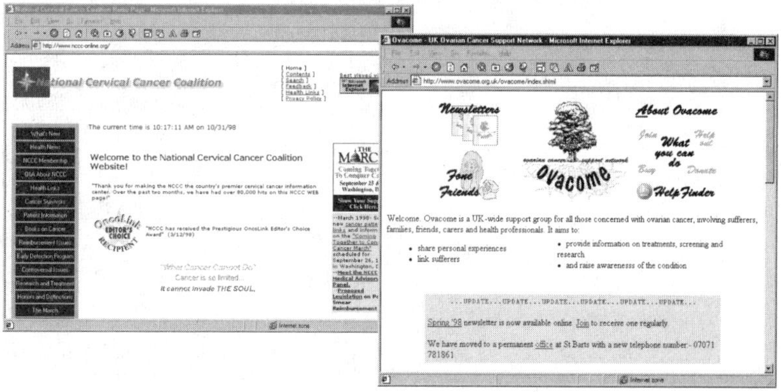
National Cervical Cancer Coalition
Welcome to the National Cervical Cancer Coalition Website!
Ovacome - UK Ovarian Cancer Support Network - Microsoft Internet Explorer
http://www.ovacome.org.uk/ovacome/index.shtml
Newsletters
About Ovacome
What you can do
Fone Friends
Ovacome
HelpFinder
Welcome. Ovacome is a UK-wide support group for all those concerned with ovarian cancer, involving sufferers, families, friends, carers and health professionals. It aims to:
share personal experiences
link sufferers
provide information on treatments, screening and research
and raise awareness of the condition

Ovarian Cancer

Jenny Agutter is the Patron of Ovacome. Their web site is at *http://www.ovacome.org.uk.*

Prostate Cancer

REMEMBER

Early diagnosis is favourable. Regular checks will help.

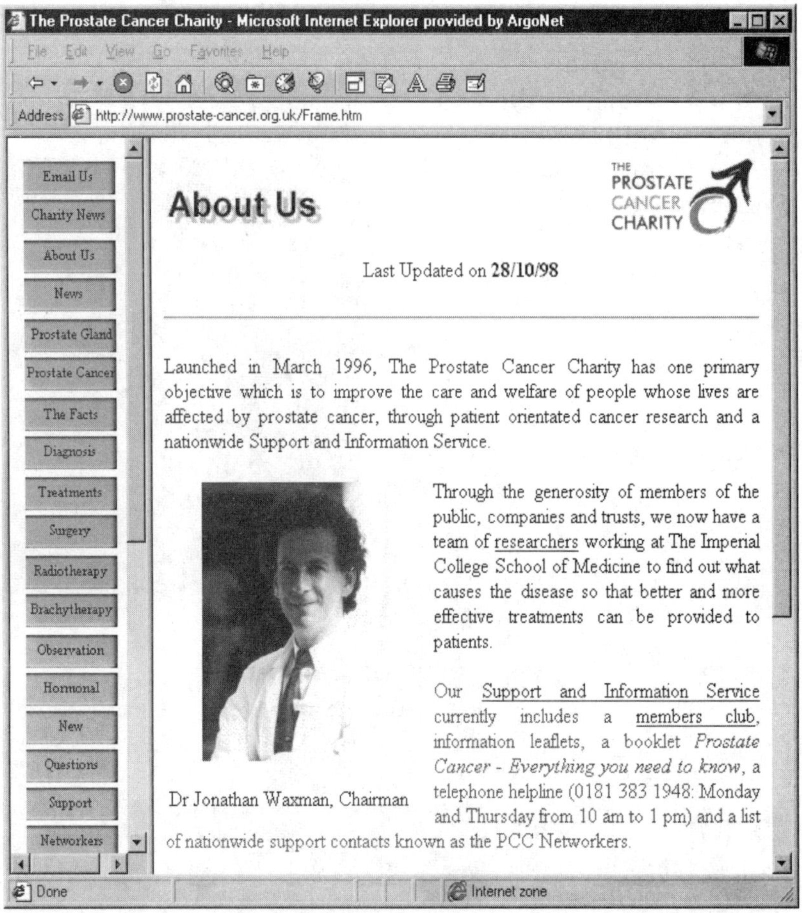
The Prostate Cancer Charity - Microsoft Internet Explorer provided by ArgoNet
File Edit View Go Favorites Help
Address http://www.prostate-cancer.org.uk/Frame.htm
Email Us
Charity News
About Us
News
Prostate Gland
Prostate Cancer
The Facts
Diagnosis
Treatments
Surgery
Radiotherapy
Brachytherapy
Observation
Hormonal
New
Questions
Support
Networkers
About Us
THE PROSTATE CANCER CHARITY
Last Updated on 28/10/98
Launched in March 1996, The Prostate Cancer Charity has one primary objective which is to improve the care and welfare of people whose lives are affected by prostate cancer, through patient orientated cancer research and a nationwide Support and Information Service.
Through the generosity of members of the public, companies and trusts, we now have a team of researchers working at The Imperial College School of Medicine to find out what causes the disease so that better and more effective treatments can be provided to patients.
Dr Jonathan Waxman, Chairman
Our Support and Information Service currently includes a members club, information leaflets, a booklet Prostate Cancer - Everything you need to know, a telephone helpline (0181 383 1948: Monday and Thursday from 10 am to 1 pm) and a list of nationwide support contacts known as the PCC Networkers.
Done
Internet zone

Prostate cancer is the most common male cancer, and has the highest mortality. Yet this cancer is often curable if caught in time. The trouble seems to be that men are just too shy or embarrassed to discuss the matter and so it gets left until it's too late. Find out more about prostate cancer at *http://www.prostate-cancer.org.uk.*

Testicular Cancer

The other scourge of the male population is testicular cancer. Again, it need not be fatal if treated in time. For more information go to *http://www.orchid-cancer.org.uk.*

Marie Curie

Along with the Macmillan Nurses, the Marie Curie Nurses and helpers are a special group of people who provide help and care to cancer patients and their families. They can provide anything from morning visits for medication to overnight stays for respite for families. Nothing is too much trouble.

The Marie Curie web site is at *http://www.mariecurie.org.uk*.

HANDY TIP **If you're considering donating to a charity, consider one of these.**

never say die
50 years of dedication
Marie Curie
Cancer Care
info@mariecurie.org.uk
21st September
Graham Currie,
Director of Research.
I had great news the other day - the Centre for Translational Research which we plan to build on site has cleared all the planning hurdles. Translational research is science which converts basic discoveries into useful applications - for example by developing new diagnostic methods, gene therapy or drugs.
We plan to exploit the discoveries made by the teams studying molecular mechanisms elsewhere in the Marie Curie Research
the charity
A brief introduction and overview of our work with details of how to get in touch.
how we care
Done
Internet zone

Smoking

Quit Smoking

As an ex-smoker, I'm amazed that anyone should want to start today. Since stopping over 15 years ago, I'm fitter and generally healthier. I've also saved a fortune.

BEWARE

It's also worth reading the health warning on cigarette packets.

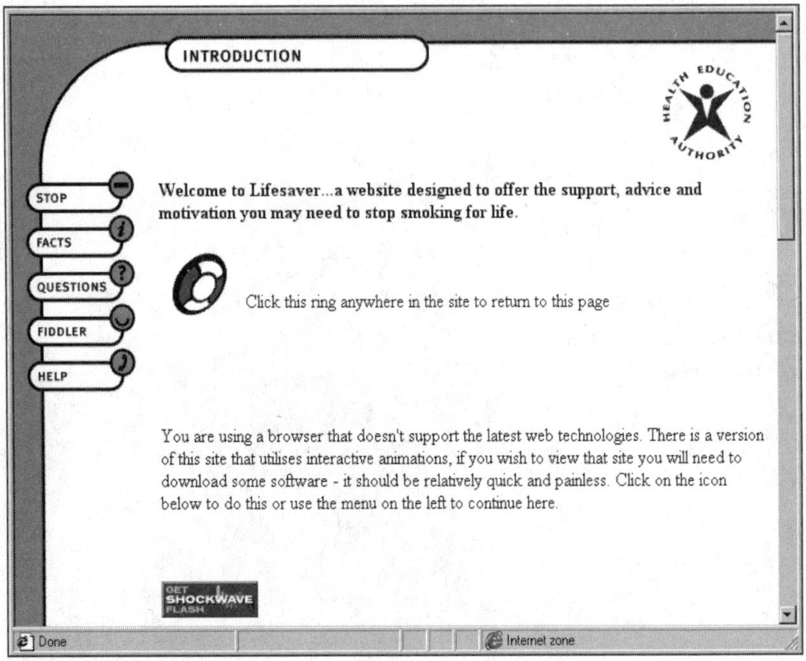
INTRODUCTION
HEALTH EDUCATION AUTHORITY
STOP
FACTS
QUESTIONS
FIDDLER
HELP
Welcome to Lifesaver...a website designed to offer the support, advice and motivation you may need to stop smoking for life.
Click this ring anywhere in the site to return to this page
You are using a browser that doesn't support the latest web technologies. There is a version of this site that utilises interactive animations, if you wish to view that site you will need to download some software - it should be relatively quick and painless. Click on the icon below to do this or use the menu on the left to continue here.
GET SHOCKWAVE FLASH
Done
Internet zone

Giving up cigarettes isn't easy, and the longer you've been smoking, the harder it is.

But it is possible, although it does take willpower and not just a quick visit to this site.

Once here you'll find practical advice as well as numerous facts about the effects of smoking so that if you were in any doubt about it, you won't be after reading it.

Personally, I found that any positive step towards stopping was a step in the right direction.

The Quit Smoking site can be found by going to (appropriately) *http://www.lifesaver.co.uk.*

Hay Fever

Fortunately I don't suffer with hay fever, although I know several people who do. It can be quite miserable when the pollen count is high.

To find out more about hay fever, go to *http://www.personal.u-net.com/~bev.*

HANDY TIP

Use these sites to find ways of learning to live with Hay Fever and Migraine.

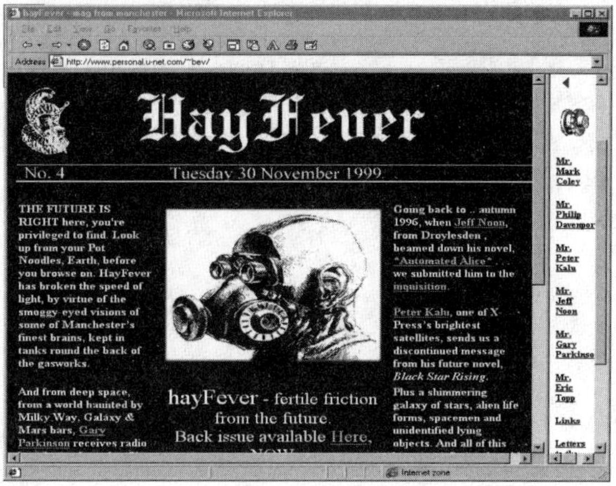

Migraine

A headache can be bad, but migraine is quite different. For those millions who, like me, suffer with migraines, any help which is available will be welcome. This site offers practical help for sufferers so they may at least learn to live with migraine. Visit the migraine site at *http://www.migraine.org.uk.*

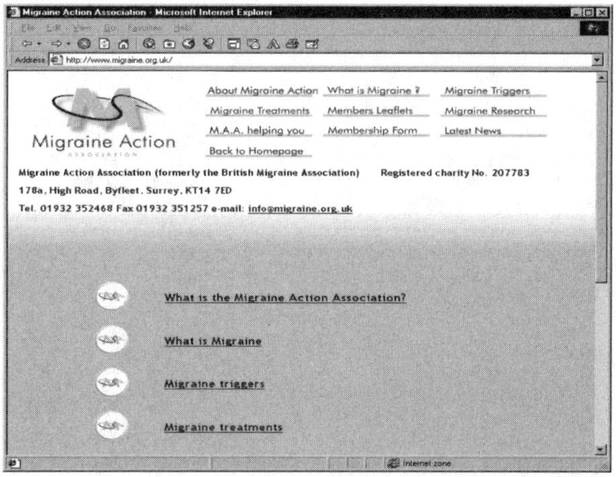

Other Healthy sites

Parents Place – *http://www.parentsplace.com/readroom/dr_answers.html*

Ask an Expert – *http://www.askanexpert.com/askanexpert/cat/hea.html*

Dr Greene's House Calls – *http://www.drgreene.com/topic.html*

HANDY TIP

Yahoo lists lots of health related web sites.

Health Clinic – *http://www.healthy.net/clinic*

The Vegetarian Pages – *http://www.veg.org*

Health & Nursing – *http://www.shef.ac.uk/~nhcon/nunews.htm*

Acupuncture – *http://www.flojo.demon.co.uk*

Homeopathy – *http://www.homeopathyhome.com* and *http://www.efn.org/~cblack/homeopathy.html*

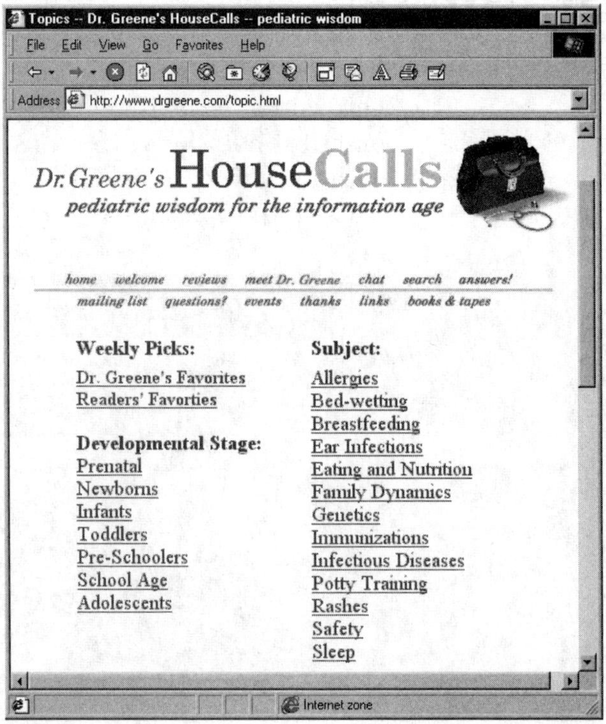

Chapter Six

Children's web sites

The Internet can be an unsuitable place to leave children. Sadly there is too much inappropriate material which children should not be subjected to. This chapter lists some sites that not only welcome children, but have been designed for the young, or the young at heart.

Covers

Argosphere

It is often said that the first is the best. If that is true, then never was is more so than with Argosphere. This site was a first of its type, and in my opinion, has yet to be bettered.

It was conceived and written by the brilliant Mike Matson – the driving force behind a great number of educational software programs. What Argosphere offers is a really well produced and safe site which kids (and adults) will enjoy strolling around. There are a variety of interactive tasks and exercises which can be either worked on on-line, or downloaded and used off-line with any Java script Internet browser. The topics are diverse and sometimes slightly off-beat like the Llama page which contains just about everything you would want to know about Llamas.

HANDY TIP

You'll need to register so, choose a password that your children will remember.

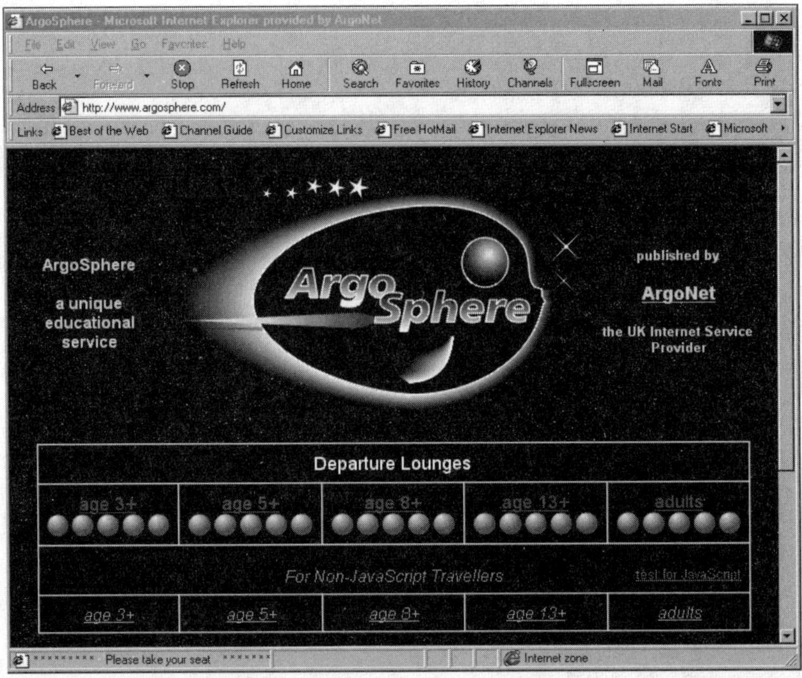

There are educational activities which will help your child. One section generates sums for children to work through. You can select the number range and the arithmetic signs used to suit your child. It will even produce an answer sheet for you.

REMEMBER **Most of the activities can be run off-line which will reduce the phone bill.**

You will have to register the first time you use this site and you will need to provide a username and a password which you will be required to enter on each subsequent visit to the site. Argosphere is currently free to anyone, although it may soon be free only to Argonet subscribers.

Connect to Argosphere at *http://www.argosphere.com.*

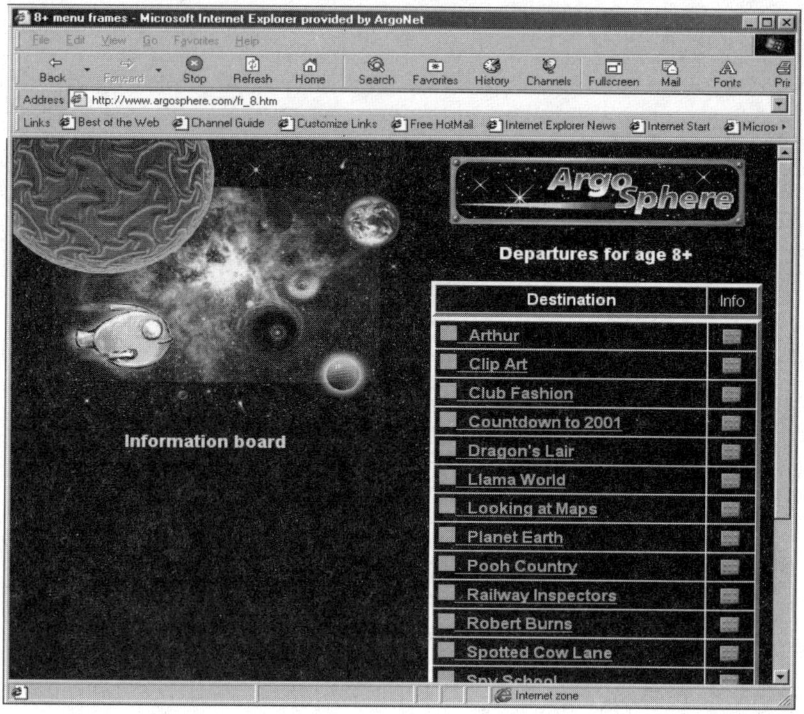

Toy Town

HANDY TIP **If you can't think what to buy for a present, look no further.**

Still on the theme of safe sites, although this time with a commercial bias, Toy Town is a lovely site for children of all ages. Once the site has been accessed, there are links to Games, Educational Toys, Outdoor Toys and Activities, Tots Toys and a miscellaneous assortment entitled Favourites which includes Winnie the Pooh and Barney Bear.

Toy Town is at *http://www.toytown.co.uk.*

Tamagotchi

Tamagotchi is Japanese for little egg. There are two stories about how they came to be. The first claims that they were invented as an alternative to pets. Apparently there is so little space in downtown Tokyo that many children cannot have pets. These were thought to be an alternative. The second, and even less likely tale, is that they were given to young school girls to show them how much time needs to be devoted to babies – presumably in the hope that they'd think twice before starting a family.

Whatever the reason, they caught on and made the manufacturers a fortune. You have to play with it, feed it, clean it and generally nurture it so that it grows up to be a likeable Tamagotchi and not a hooligan.

At their zenith, queues were forming outside toy shops waiting for the next delivery. The web site gives owners and prospective owners an insight into the company and its products, which are now numerous including versions that can 'talk' to each other.

BEWARE **These toys are not to everyone's taste.**

Tamagotchi Home page is at *http://members.hknet.com/~ada.*

Graveyard

Some people have claimed that Tamagotchi are harmless fun for kids, whilst others have banned them from schools. Some have even claimed that the death of a Tamagotchi leads to the stresses normally associated with the death of a relative! I don't believe it either but there is a virtual cemetery for dead Tamagotchi so when your beloved one finally passes to that electronic warehouse in the sky, you can leave a few thoughts and memories in this virtual graveyard. Typical of the epitaphs is 'You started smoking just after I connected you to the mains.....'

BEWARE **Don't try this at home. It's not to be taken seriously!**

Virtual Graveyard for Tamagotchi is at *http://www.netzon.com/tamagotch/lament.html.*

Meccano

When Frank Hornby invented Meccano, he launched an engineering system that would retain its popularity for decades.

The clever system of beams, brackets, bolts, nuts and washers continues to maintain its popularity with middle-aged children, but the rise in popularity of plastics has meant that some of the more recent construction products have taken a substantial proportion of Meccano's market.

MECCANO
The ISM Meccano WebSite
INTERNATIONAL SOCIETY OF MECCANOMEN
Published by
The International Society of Meccanomen
If your browser does not support frames, you may have difficulty viewing the following pages.
The latest versions of both Netscape and Internet Explorer are suitable.
Continue
Meccano is a registered trademark of Meccano SA, Avenue de Saint Exupéry, 62100 CALAIS-FRANCE
Many models and component parts incorporate original designs which are protected by copyrights, trademarks or design legislation.
No material from this WebSite may be reproduced or published in any form for public use without the permission of the editor. If permission to reproduce or publish is granted, then full acknowledgement of the source must accompany the material.
Done
Internet zone

BEWARE

Don't tread on any of the pieces in your bare feet.

In spite of this, Meccano continues to sell in large quantities and has a loyal following amongst would-be engineers of all ages. Cleverly, Meccano frequently showed pictures of fantastic creations in their advertising campaigns to demonstrate what could be done. Some models would probably require a small mortgage to buy all the parts required to build them.

This site puts you in touch with other enthusiasts so you can share ideas and buy or swap parts so that you too can build one of the amazing models.

SM Meccano Site is at *http://www.dircon.co.uk/meccano/m1/contents.htm.*

Teddy Bears

If you go down to the woods today, you're sure of a big surprise. If you go to one of their web sites, you're in for another surprise. My daughter's eyes lit up when she saw this beautifully presented site of the English Teddy Bear Company. The graphics are superb and the text is easy to access.

HANDY TIP **Save these sites in your Favourites folder.**

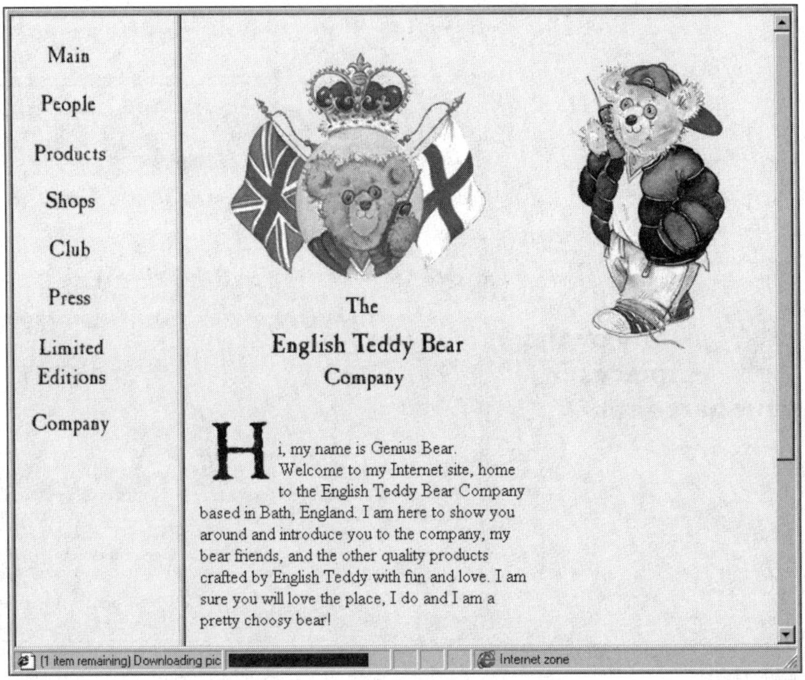
Main
People
Products
Shops
Club
Press
Limited Editions
Company
The
English Teddy Bear
Company
Hi, my name is Genius Bear. Welcome to my Internet site, home to the English Teddy Bear Company based in Bath, England. I am here to show you around and introduce you to the company, my bear friends, and the other quality products crafted by English Teddy with fun and love. I am sure you will love the place, I do and I am a pretty choosy bear!
(1 item remaining) Downloading pic
Internet zone

English Teddy Bear Company is at *http://www.teddy.co. uk.*

Some other bear-related sites are:

The Bear Shop – *http://www.c-vision.u-net.com/bearshop. htm*

Peter Rabbit and Friends – *http://www.wwwebguides. com/ companies/shops/retail/peter.html*

Sherwood Bear Clinic – *http://www.barrack.ndirect.co. uk/ bearclinic/index.htm*

Lego

When I was 8, I wanted a garage for Christmas. What Father Christmas bought me was one of the first Lego sets – an Esso Garage which I built so many times, I could do it by heart. I could probably still do it today!

Like many kids who are given Lego, more and more bits were added until I had a fair size town. When my children were old enough, we bought them Lego and we all still play with it.

This site gives all the information, history and help you'll need. For example, did you know there are over 80 billion Lego bricks in the world today? I wonder who counted them all?

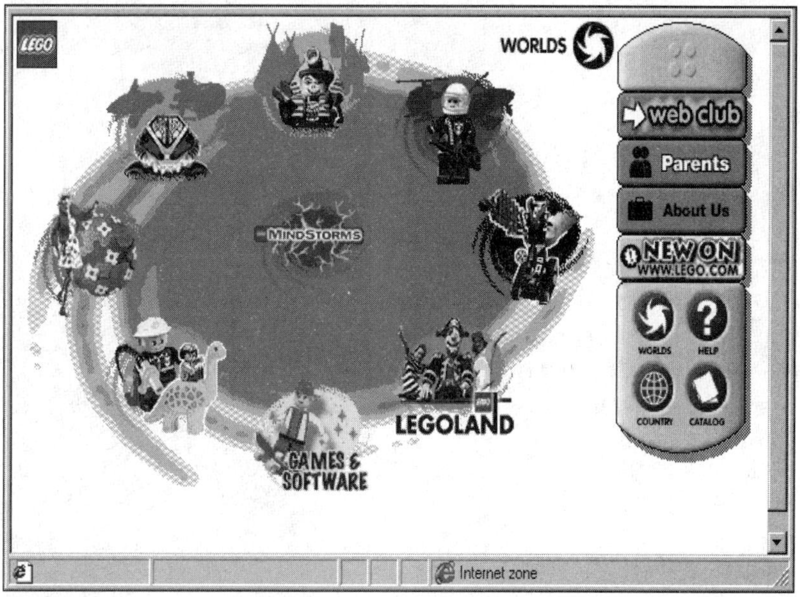

Adults could get hooked on this site too.

The main Lego site is at *http://www.lego.com/worlds.asp* but there is also a link Legoland Windsor at *http://www.lego.com/legoland/windsor/default.asp.*

Fibblesnork Lego Fan Page is also worth visiting at *http://www.fibblesnork.com/lego/guide.*

Model Cars

Scalextric

Slot car racing started in the mid 1950's and reached its height of popularity in the 1960's. At that time there were countless manufacturers of slot car sets for the home. Today, very few remain and Scalextric is probably the largest, certainly in this country.

The web site details the models, the sets and even offers limited edition cars that cannot be purchased anywhere other than on the Scalextric web site.

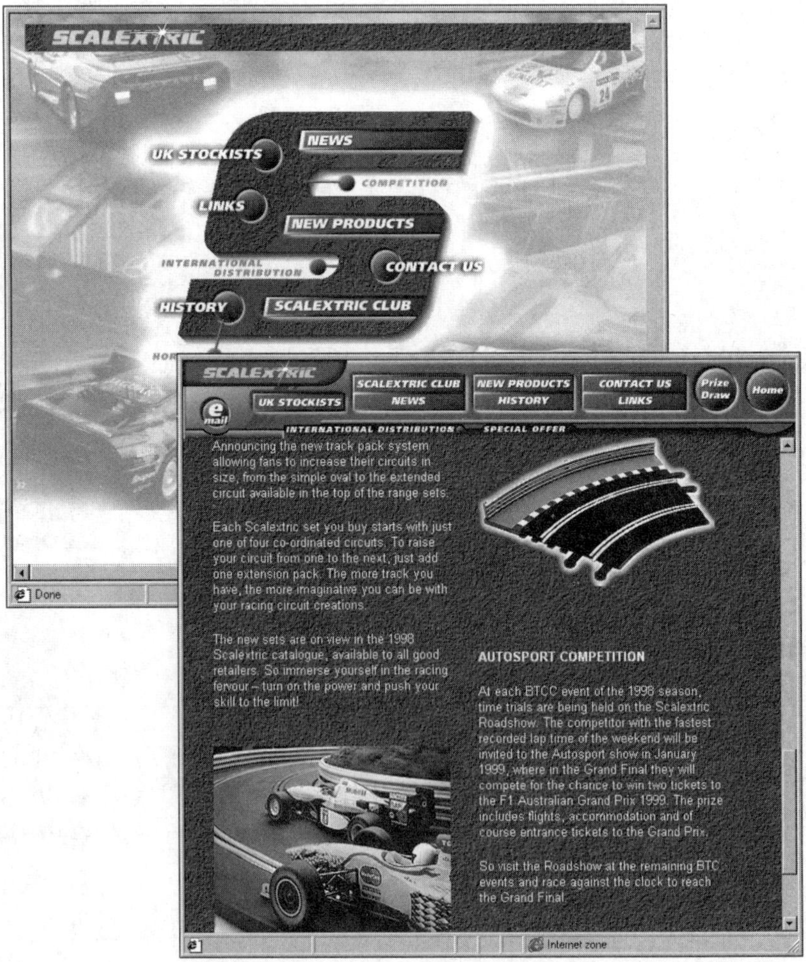

SCALEXTRIC
UK STOCKISTS
NEWS
COMPETITION
LINKS
NEW PRODUCTS
INTERNATIONAL DISTRIBUTION
CONTACT US
HISTORY
SCALEXTRIC CLUB
Done
SCALEXTRIC
SCALEXTRIC CLUB
NEW PRODUCTS
CONTACT US
Prize Draw
Home
UK STOCKISTS
NEWS
HISTORY
LINKS
e mail
INTERNATIONAL DISTRIBUTION
SPECIAL OFFER
Announcing the new track pack system allowing fans to increase their circuits in size, from the simple oval to the extended circuit available in the top of the range sets.
Each Scalextric set you buy starts with just one of four co-ordinated circuits. To raise your circuit from one to the next, just add one extension pack. The more track you have, the more imaginative you can be with your racing circuit creations.
The new sets are on view in the 1998 Scalextric catalogue, available to all good retailers. So immerse yourself in the racing fervour – turn on the power and push your skill to the limit!
AUTOSPORT COMPETITION
At each BTCC event of the 1998 season, time trials are being held on the Scalextric Roadshow. The competitor with the fastest recorded lap time of the weekend will be invited to the Autosport show in January 1999, where in the Grand Final they will compete for the chance to win two tickets to the F1 Australian Grand Prix 1999. The prize includes flights, accommodation and of course entrance tickets to the Grand Prix.
So visit the Roadshow at the remaining BTC events and race against the clock to reach the Grand Final.
Internet zone

REMEMBER There are lots of electronic gadgets to make it even more fun.

Scalextric is at *http://www.scalextric.co.uk*.

Model Railways

Hornby

Apparently, when I was born and my father told his brother that he had a nephew, his response was, "Oh good, we can buy him a train set!"

Five years on, I got my train set, but didn't get much of a look in for some time. When my son was born, it was a similar story but regrettably the pull of computers, Star Wars and other modern pastimes meant that railways didn't get a look in. I suppose it's largely because, having never seen a steam engine in service on a regular basis, having a model of one did not really appeal to him.

If the bug bites, a train set can take up an enormous amount of space.

Hornby is still going strong and has a constantly changing catalogue of steam, diesel and electric trains with a large selection of rolling stock and track.

Their web site is rather like an extension to their catalogue, with copious pictures of engines, and carriages and goods wagons. There is a news page and a very interesting section outlining the history of the company.

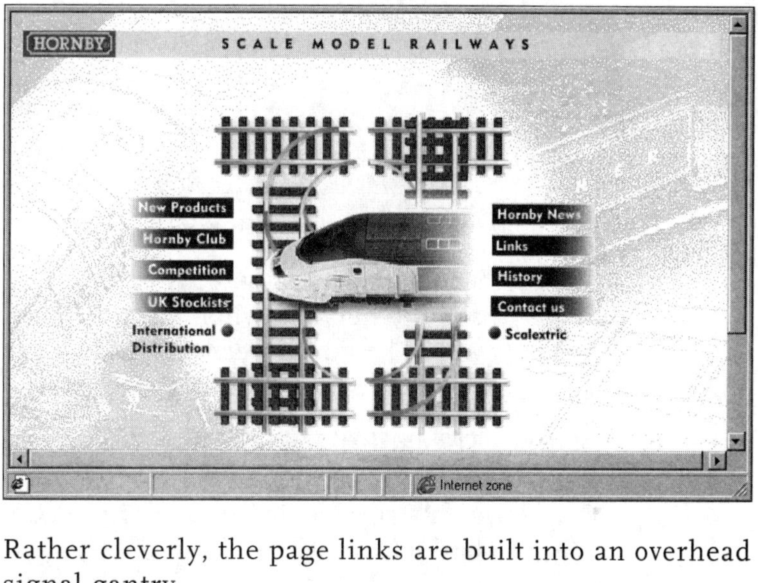

Rather cleverly, the page links are built into an overhead signal gantry.

Hornby is at *http://www.hornby.co.uk.*

Dolls

Barbie

Any web site designed for children but offering advice for parents gets my vote. The famous doll that most girls seem to own has her own web site laid out, appropriately, in candy colours.

HANDY TIP

Read the section for adults.

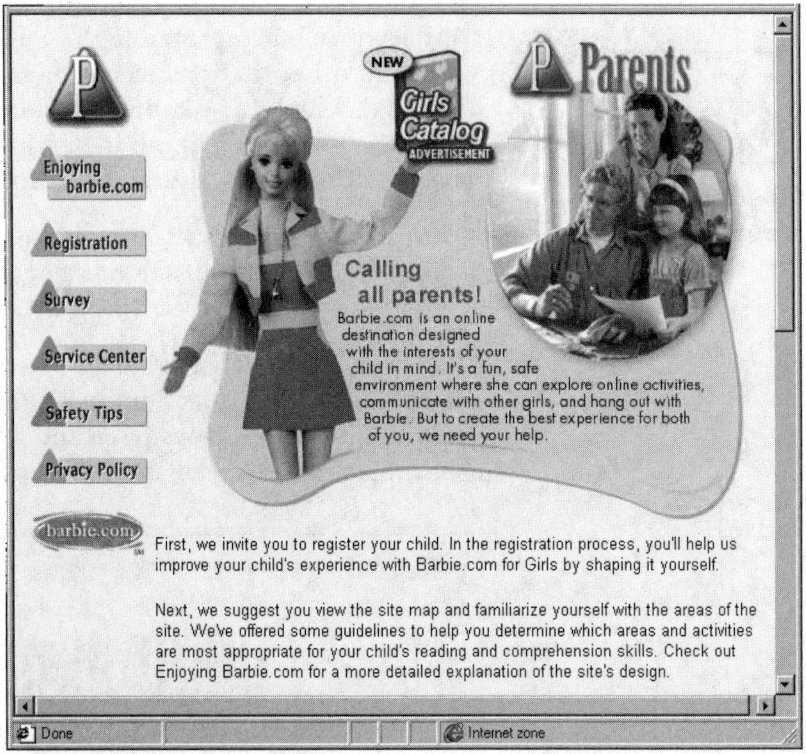
Parents
NEW
Girls Catalog
ADVERTISEMENT
Enjoying barbie.com
Registration
Survey
Service Center
Safety Tips
Privacy Policy
barbie.com
Calling all parents!
Barbie.com is an online destination designed with the interests of your child in mind. It's a fun, safe environment where she can explore online activities, communicate with other girls, and hang out with Barbie. But to create the best experience for both of you, we need your help.
First, we invite you to register your child. In the registration process, you'll help us improve your child's experience with Barbie.com for Girls by shaping it yourself.
Next, we suggest you view the site map and familiarize yourself with the areas of the site. We've offered some guidelines to help you determine which areas and activities are most appropriate for your child's reading and comprehension skills. Check out Enjoying Barbie.com for a more detailed explanation of the site's design.
Done
Internet zone

The part that caught my eye was the advice for parents about when and when not to allow their children to use the web. The advice seems sound and is worth reading, even if you don't read anything else on this site.

The Barbie Doll site does contain an on-line catalogue where you can view Barbie's wardrobe, but there are also safety tips, registration and a section entitled Enjoying barbie.com which gives some useful advice about using the site.

Barbie Doll is at *http://www.barbie.com.*

Reading

The Children's Bookshop

Children should be encouraged to read and this site will help as it contains details of most children's books. Carefully divided into reading ages, books can be searched by author or title. The files are in text format and can be searched off-line.

When you've found what you're looking for, you can place an order there and then.

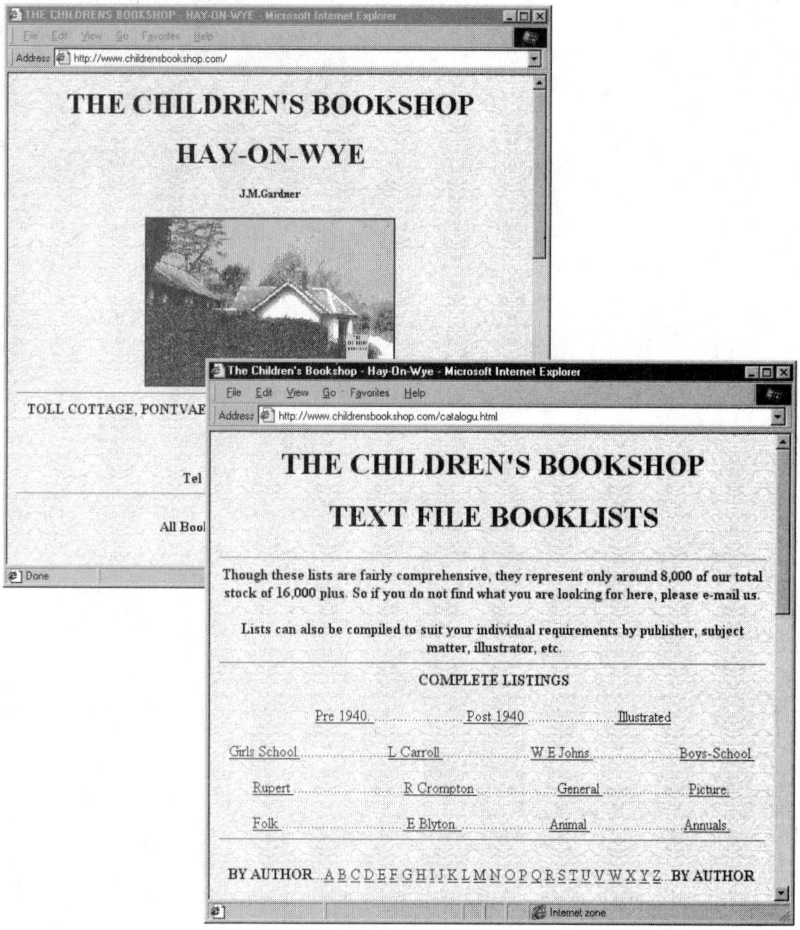

The Children's Bookshop is at *http://www.childrensbookshop.com.*

Outings

Kennedy Space Center

The web allows us to visit places we might not otherwise be able to physically go to. One of the most popular sites to visit is the home of space travel: the Kennedy Space Center at *http://www.kennedyspacecenter.com.* Another popular site is Disney at *http://www.disney.com.*

Summer Fun

How many times do we hear the kids say "I'm bored"? During school holidays and those long winter evenings, they can often find themselves lacking something to do. Summer Fun is at *http://www.ok.bc.ca/summer.*

Also try *http://freeweb.pdq.net/headstrong*

A Night Out

The Blacktie Company

Finding a suitable venue for young teenagers to have fun is no easy task. On one hand you want them to enjoy themselves, but on the other hand you need to be sure they are safe and are not coming into contact with either alcohol or cigarettes or worse.

HANDY TIP

This makes an ideal birthday or Christmas gift.

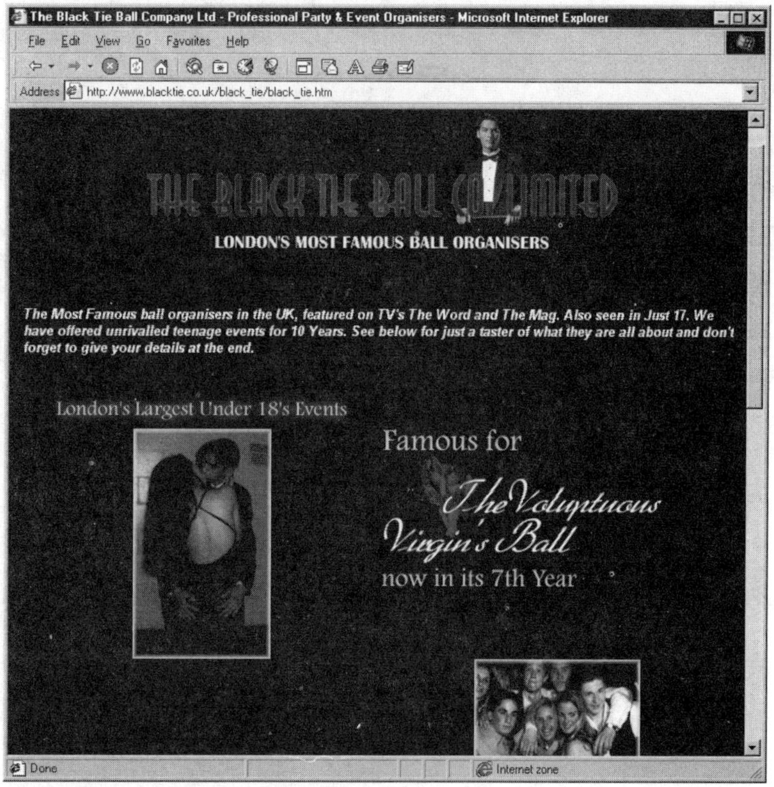
The Black Tie Ball Company Ltd - Professional Party & Event Organisers - Microsoft Internet Explorer
File Edit View Go Favorites Help
Address http://www.blacktie.co.uk/black_tie/black_tie.htm
THE BLACK TIE BALL CO LIMITED
LONDON'S MOST FAMOUS BALL ORGANISERS
The Most Famous ball organisers in the UK, featured on TV's The Word and The Mag. Also seen in Just 17. We have offered unrivalled teenage events for 10 Years. See below for just a taster of what they are all about and don't forget to give your details at the end.
London's Largest Under 18's Events
Famous for
The Voluptuous Virgin's Ball
now in its 7th Year
Done
Internet zone

The Blacktie Ball Company Ltd have been organising events for under 18's for over 10 years. They are well attended and relatively cheap. You don't have to live in a big city either as they are organised at small local venues around the country.

The events are well organised and are well staffed by responsible adults.

For further information, visit the Blacktie Ball Company at *http://www.blacktie.co.uk.*

On a serious note

BritKid

This site is quite unlike any other. It's intended to make kids think about the world around them. It confronts racism and racial issues in a way in which they can understand. There are situations to resolve and descriptions to get you thinking.

This site is well worth visiting, and not just by children.

HANDY TIP **Try to spend time with your child going through this site.**

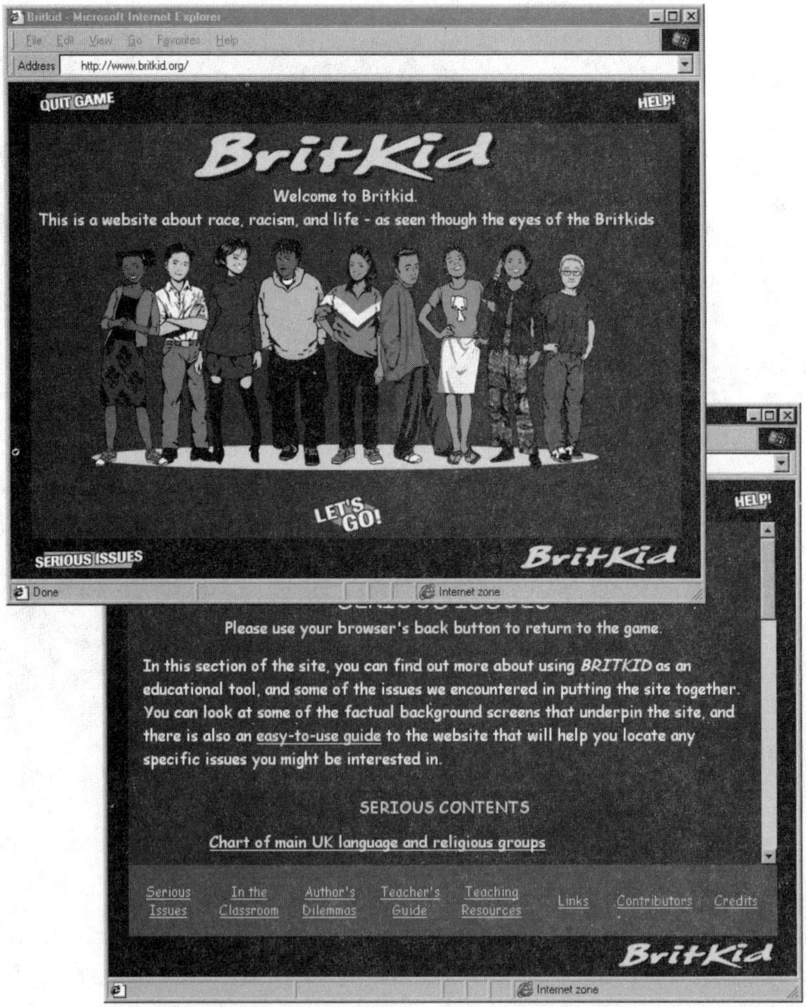
Britkid - Microsoft Internet Explorer
File Edit View Go Favorites Help
Address http://www.britkid.org/
QUIT GAME
HELP!
BritKid
Welcome to Britkid.
This is a website about race, racism, and life - as seen though the eyes of the Britkids
LET'S GO!
SERIOUS ISSUES
BritKid
Done
Internet zone
HELP!
Please use your browser's back button to return to the game.
In this section of the site, you can find out more about using BRITKID as an educational tool, and some of the issues we encountered in putting the site together. You can look at some of the factual background screens that underpin the site, and there is also an easy-to-use guide to the website that will help you locate any specific issues you might be interested in.
SERIOUS CONTENTS
Chart of main UK language and religious groups
Serious Issues
In the Classroom
Author's Dilemmas
Teacher's Guide
Teaching Resources
Links
Contributors
Credits
BritKid
Internet zone

Britkid is at *http://www.britkid.org.*

Chapter Seven

Education

Education is at a major crossroads. The Internet has opened up huge possibilities, but is the expertise available to take advantage of it?

The educational Internet sites can be roughly divided into two categories: those for teachers and those for learners.

Covers

SHA

The Internet is not short of pages for teachers, but I suppose I'd better start at the top with Headteachers.

The Secondary Heads Association (SHA) have their own web site and it is here that Heads (and anyone else) can look to clarify points of law, as well as to read about the latest initiatives.

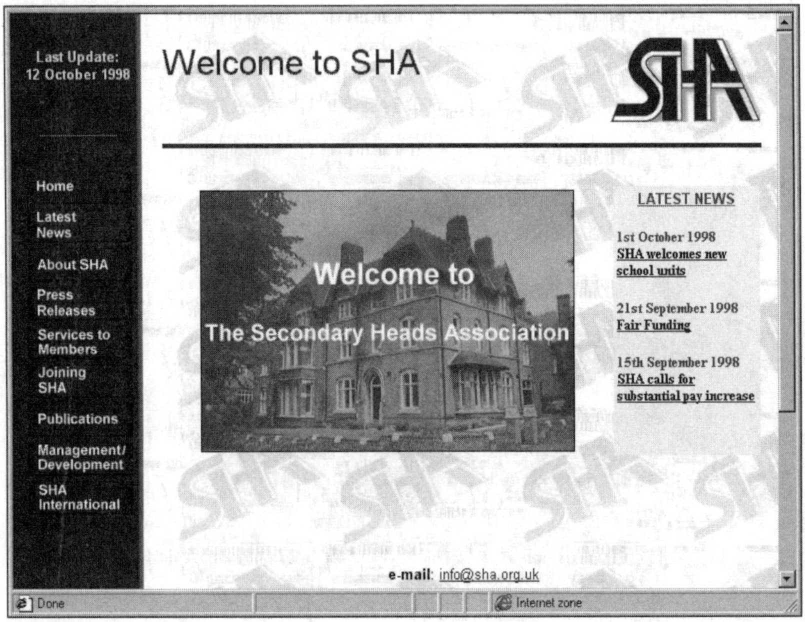

Parents can use this site too.

Also contained within this site are a variety of statistics relating to all manner of issues and initiatives.

SHA is at *http://www.sha.org.uk.*

OFSTED

The name guaranteed to turn most Heads' hair grey, OFSTED (Office for Standards in Education) regularly inspects schools to ensure standards are maintained. They can be found at *http://www.ofsted.gov.uk/*

To access the database of school reports you'll need Adobe Acrobat reader which can be downloaded from this site.

DfEE

The Department for Education and Employment is the body set up to, amongst other things, monitor and improve standards in schools.

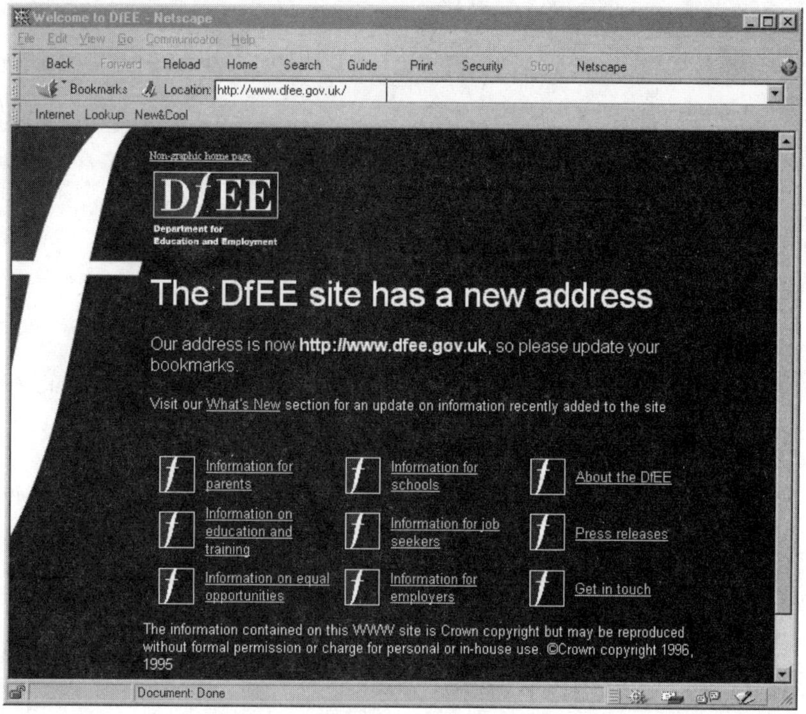

The site contains information for schools and colleges to help them raise achievement and improve standards. As well as information about the DfEE, there are numerous press releases to look up and there is a feedback service.

But the site is not there just for teachers. There are many pages which are primarily for parents so they can understand what is happening with their children's education.

Literacy and numeracy are high on the Government's list of improvements and there are pages to help parents help their children in these important areas of their education.

DfEE *is at http://www.dfee.gov.uk.*

BECTa

Formerly NCET (the National Council for Education Technology), the primary aim of BECTa (British Educational Communications and Technology agency) is to ensure that technology supports the DfEE's drive to raise educational standards.

BECTa is at *http://www.becta.org.uk.*

Welcome to BECTa - Microsoft Internet Explorer
Welcome to Becta Home Page
Information
Projects
Resources
Support Providers
What's New?
About Becta
Press Information
Archive
Site Map
Search
Copyright
Web Keeper
BECTa
British Educational
Communications
and Technology agency
NGfL
VTC

NGfL Consortium

The NGfL Consortium was formed as a response to the government's request for companies to deliver integrated Information and Communications Technology solutions for education. The site has links to the major NGfL partners.

NGfL is at *http://www.ngfl.org.uk.*

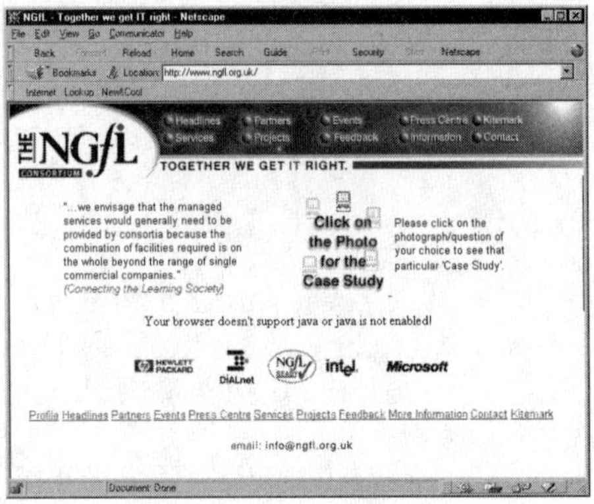
NGfL - Together we get IT right - Netscape
THE NGfL CONSORTIUM
TOGETHER WE GET IT RIGHT.
"...we envisage that the managed services would generally need to be provided by consortia because the combination of facilities required is on the whole beyond the range of single commercial companies."
(Connecting the Learning Society)
Click on the Photo for the Case Study
Please click on the photograph/question of your choice to see that particular 'Case Study'.
Your browser doesn't support java or java is not enabled!
DiALnet
intel
Microsoft
email: info@ngfl.org.uk

UCAS

The Universities and Colleges Admission Service is a centralised organisation which processes university and college applications for a variety of full-time courses.

If you are considering a particular course, this site will search out all of the universities and colleges currently offering the course, giving entry requirements and qualifications.

HANDY TIP

This site is probably the easiest way to access any of the UK universities' web sites, enabling would-be students to order prospectuses.

The search is started by choosing the initial letter of the subject. Next select the subject from the list, enter the level you wish to study to, then choose the entry requirements (A level, HNC etc). You may also choose whether to display all colleges and universities or just those in a particular area.

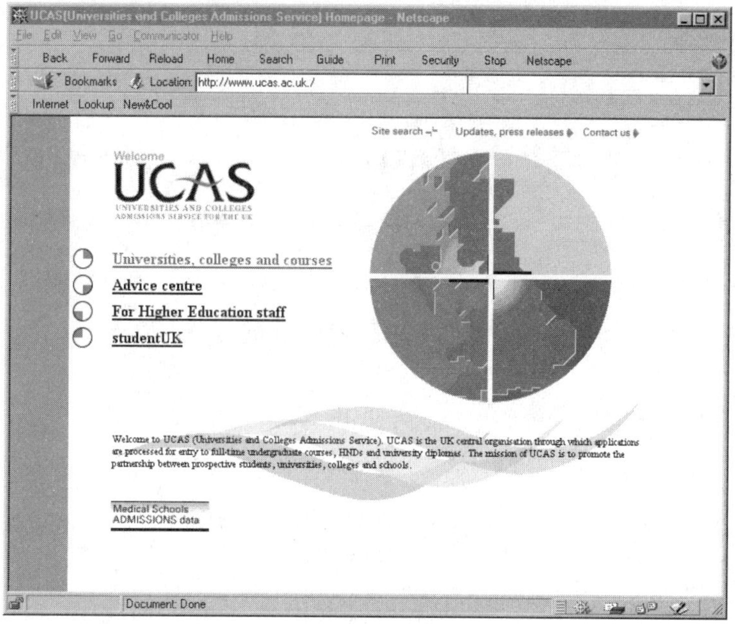

The site can also be searched for a specific university which will enable would-be students to find out what their local university is offering. Again, begin by choosing the initial letter of the university and then choosing the university from the list.

UCAS is at *http://www.ucas.ac.uk.*

Other Sites for Teachers

Advisory Unit – *http://www.advisory-unit.org.uk*

BBC Education – *http://www.bbc.co.uk/cbbc/cbbc.html*

Campus Connect – *http://www1.btconnect.com*

Campus World – *http://www.campus.bt.com*

Chemistry Teaching Resources – *http://www.anachem.umu.se/cgi-bin/pointer.exe?Graphics*

Education Extra – *http://www.educationextra.org.uk*

Education Management Information Exchange – *http://www.nfer.ac.uk/emie/index.htm*

Education Network – *http://www.ednet.org.uk.*

Educational Reports – *http://www.niss.ac.uk*

European Education – *http://www.eurydice.org*

Excellence for All – *http://www.open.gov.uk*

National Governors' Council – *http://www.ngc.org.uk*

NFER – *http://www.nfer.ac.uk*

SENCO Information Exchange – *http://www.ncet.org.uk/senco*

UKTeachernet – *http://www.ukteachernet.co.uk/default_ie3.htm*

National Union of Teachers – *http://www.teachers.org. uk/home.htm*

Association of Teachers and Lecturers – *http://www.atl.org.uk*

Teacher Resources – *http://www.siec.k12.in.us/~west/ed*

Pathways to School Improvement – *http://www.ncrel.org/sdrs/pathwayg.htm*

Education-Quest

Education-Quest is one of the newest education sites and was set up by Questions Publishing.

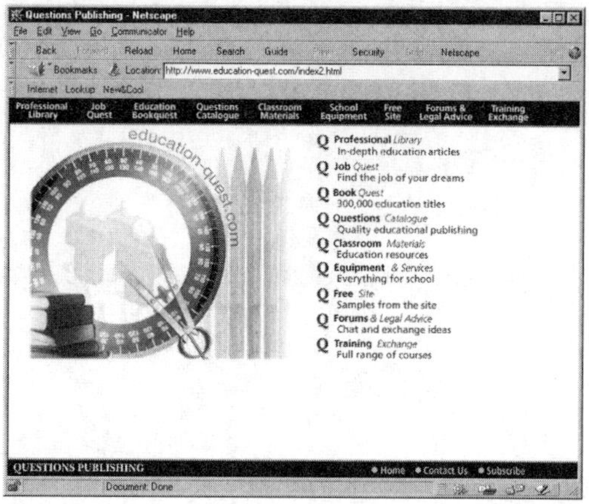
Questions Publishing - Netscape
File Edit View Go Communicator Help
Back Forward Reload Home Search Guide Print Security Stop Netscape
Bookmarks Location: http://www.education-quest.com/index2.html
Internet Lookup New&Cool
Professional Library Job Quest Education Bookquest Questions Catalogue Classroom Materials School Equipment Free Site Forums & Legal Advice Training Exchange
education-quest.com
Q Professional Library
In-depth education articles
Q Job Quest
Find the job of your dreams
Q Book Quest
300,000 education titles
Q Questions Catalogue
Quality educational publishing
Q Classroom Materials
Education resources
Q Equipment & Services
Everything for school
Q Free Site
Samples from the site
Q Forums & Legal Advice
Chat and exchange ideas
Q Training Exchange
Full range of courses
QUESTIONS PUBLISHING
Home Contact Us Subscribe
Document: Done

When the title page has loaded, there is the opportunity to go in one of two directions: Education Services, which came on-line in November 1998, and Teaching Today which came on line in January 1999.

Once into the Education Services section, there is a wealth of material to help the teacher in the classroom. Some of the material is free, some has to be paid for but there is the facility to trial a part of it before deciding to buy.

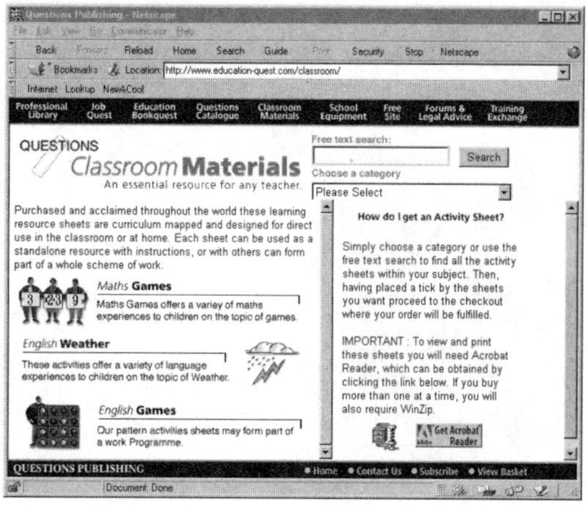
Questions Publishing - Netscape
Back Forward Reload Home Search Guide Print Security Stop Netscape
Bookmarks Location: http://www.education-quest.com/classroom/
Internet Lookup New&Cool
Professional Library Job Quest Education Bookquest Questions Catalogue Classroom Materials School Equipment Free Site Forums & Legal Advice Training Exchange
QUESTIONS
Classroom Materials
An essential resource for any teacher.
Free text search:
Search
Choose a category
Please Select
Purchased and acclaimed throughout the world these learning resource sheets are curriculum mapped and designed for direct use in the classroom or at home. Each sheet can be used as a standalone resource with instructions, or with others can form part of a whole scheme of work.
Maths Games
Maths Games offers a variety of maths experiences to children on the topic of games.
English Weather
These activities offer a variety of language experiences to children on the topic of Weather.
English Games
Our pattern activities sheets may form part of a work Programme.
How do I get an Activity Sheet?
Simply choose a category or use the free text search to find all the activity sheets within your subject. Then, having placed a tick by the sheets you want proceed to the checkout where your order will be fulfilled.
IMPORTANT : To view and print these sheets you will need Acrobat Reader, which can be obtained by clicking the link below. If you buy more than one at a time, you will also require WinZip.
Get Acrobat Reader
QUESTIONS PUBLISHING
Home Contact Us Subscribe View Basket
Document: Done

Education-Quest is at *http://www.education-quest.com.*

Booksearch

Books provide a great deal of pleasure for people of all ages. There is a huge amount of information on the web about all sort of books.

To find the exact book you want, go to *http://www.nwnet.co.uk/BFG*, the home page of Bookfinder General. There is a very friendly search facility that will help you locate your book.

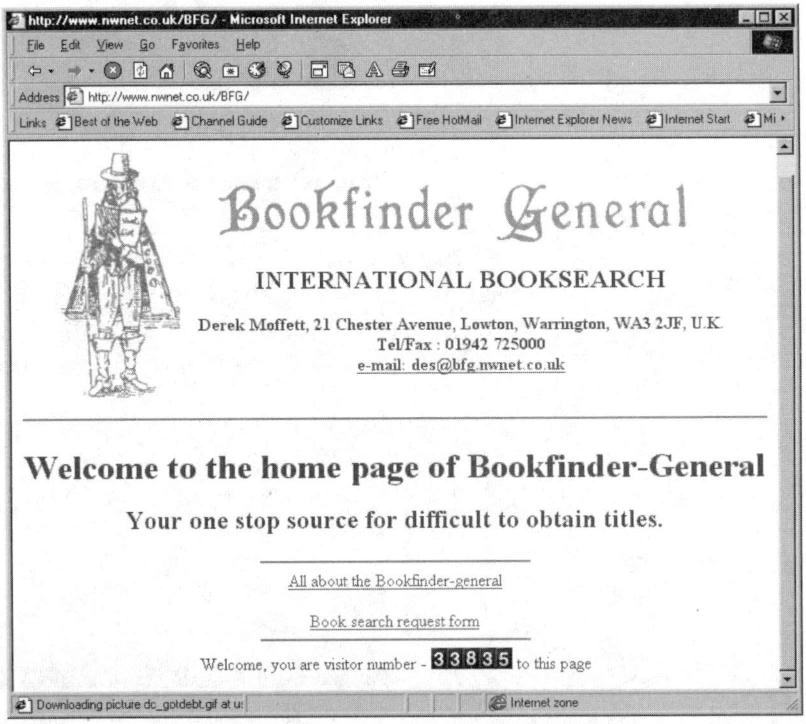

New York Times Books – *http://www.nytimes.com/books*

REMEMBER

This is only a small sample of related web sites.

Computer Step – *http://www.computerstep.com*

Questions Publishing – *http://www.questpub.co.uk/index.htm*

Blackwell's – *http://www.blackwell.co.uk/bookshops*

Waterstones – *http://www.waterstones.co.uk*

Books.co.uk

Searching for books can be a little tiresome but this site can help. It has links into several major distributers with on-line ordering. Choosing and buying books has never been simpler.

Use this site to locate book retailers.

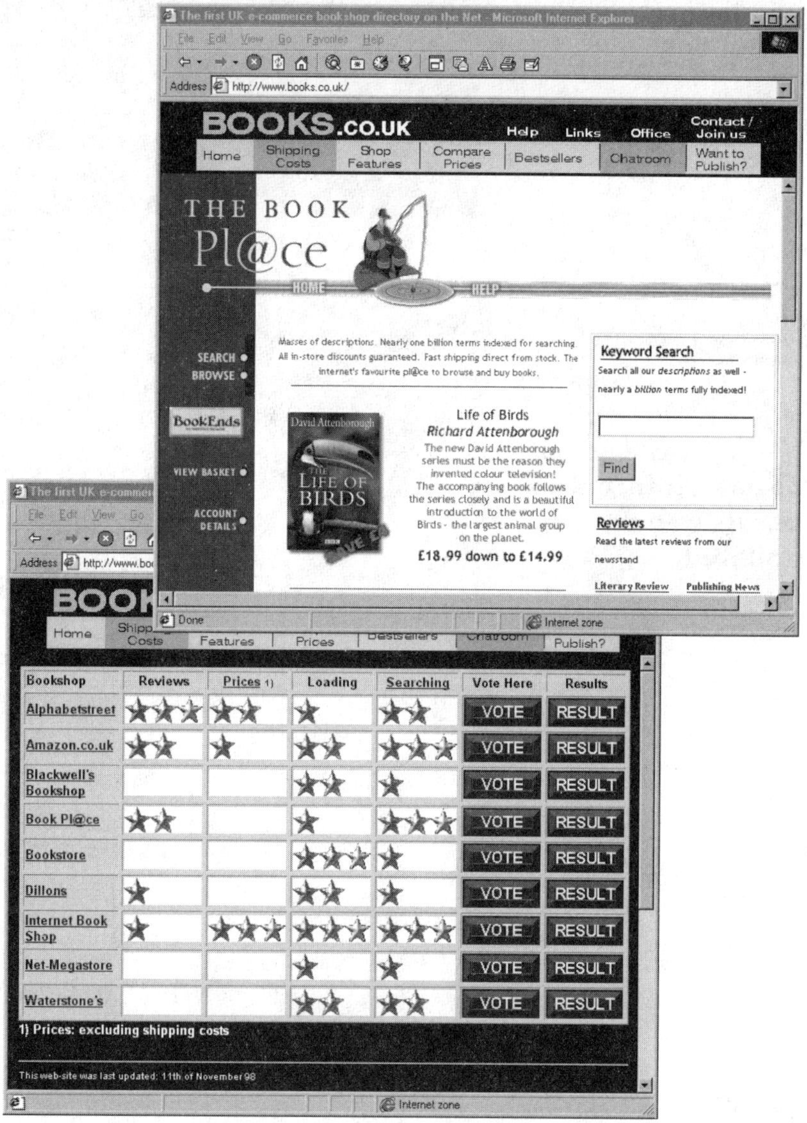

Books can be found at *http://www.books.co.uk.*

Encyclopedia Britannica

Probably the best known encyclopedia in the world is also on-line. To support their books and their CD ROMs, EB have this web site which contains a mine of fascinating information.

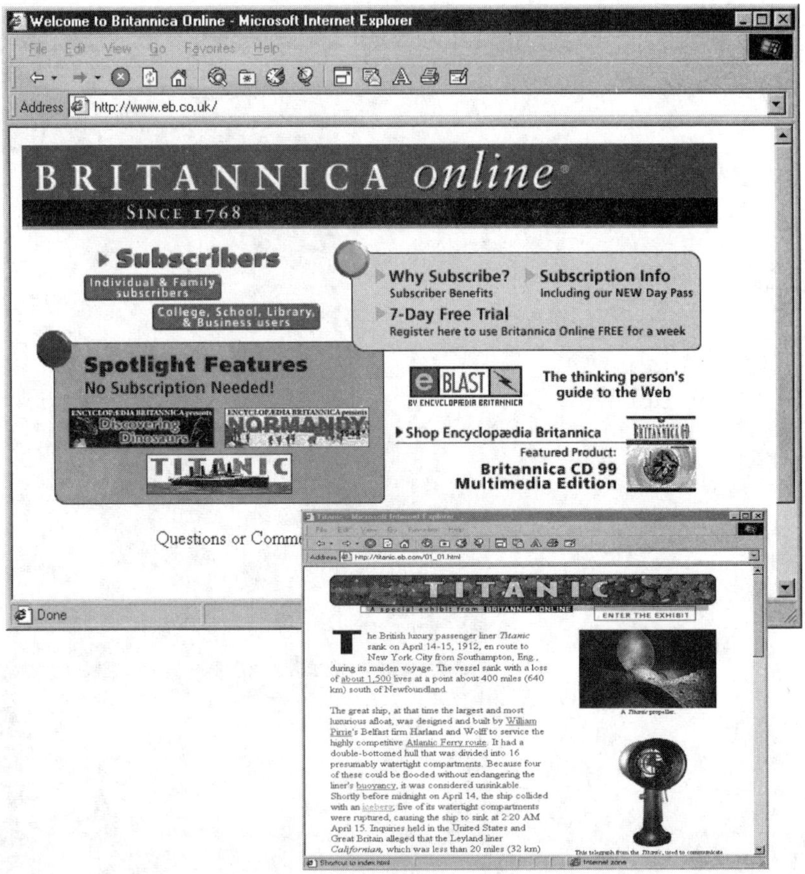

REMEMBER

The information in books can go out of date. Information on the web can be updated.

This site regularly hosts major features. At the time of writing, one of the current features was a study of the Titanic. As can be clearly seen from the screenshot, there are dozens of links to other pages covering every aspect of the ship, the incident and the aftermath, as well as detailed descriptions about related issues such as iceberg formation.

This is a truly excellent site and can be found at *http://www.eb.co.uk.*

The Book of Clichés

Just to underline the diversity of the Internet, we have clichés. Personally, I avoid clichés like the plague. A cliché to me is like a red rag to a bull. In fact, I go to the ends of the earth to avoid clichés. If you are of a different leaning, then this site will provide you with lots of 'off-the-cuff' clichés to amaze your friends and confound your enemies.

The address is rather long, but worth entering. It's *http://utopia.knoware.nl/users/sybev/cliche/cliche.htm.*

HANDY TIP

Use the favourites facility in your browser to avoid having to repeatedly type long web addresses.

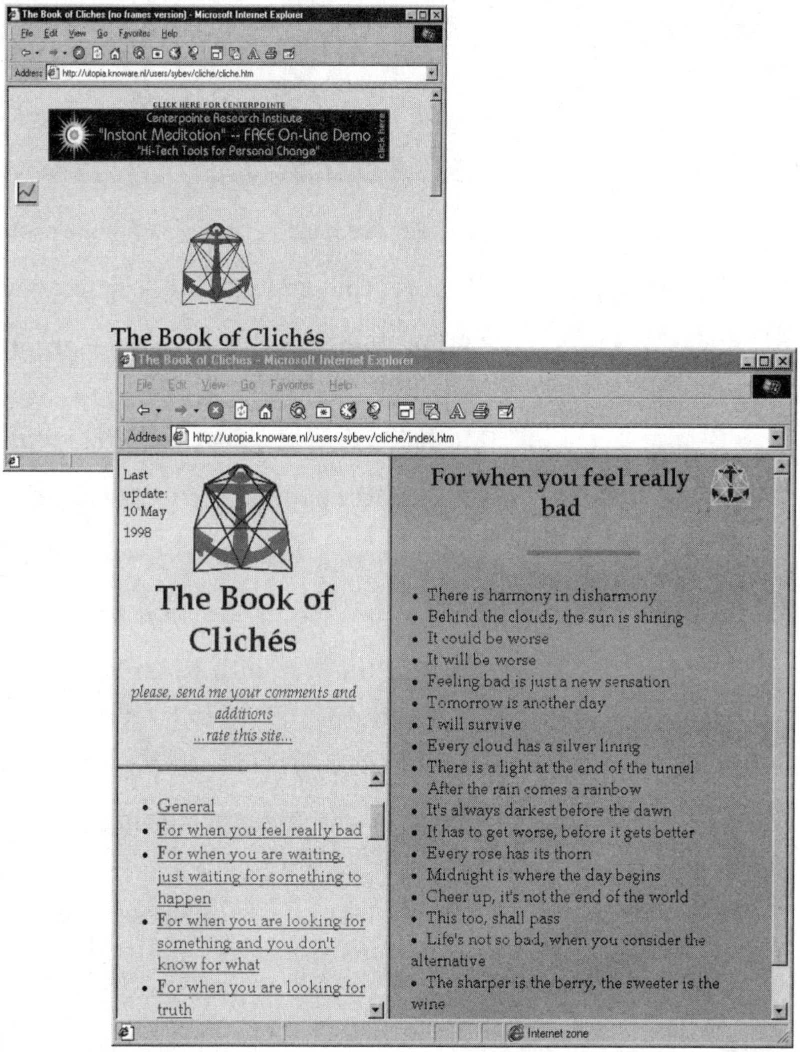

The Book of Cliches (no frames version) - Microsoft Internet Explorer
http://utopia.knoware.nl/users/sybev/cliche/cliche.htm
Centerpointe Research Institute
"Instant Meditation" -- FREE On-Line Demo
"Hi-Tech Tools for Personal Change"
The Book of Clichés
The Book of Cliches - Microsoft Internet Explorer
http://utopia.knoware.nl/users/sybev/cliche/index.htm
Last update: 10 May 1998
The Book of Clichés
please, send me your comments and additions
...rate this site...
General
For when you feel really bad
For when you are waiting, just waiting for something to happen
For when you are looking for something and you don't know for what
For when you are looking for truth
For when you feel really bad
There is harmony in disharmony
Behind the clouds, the sun is shining
It could be worse
It will be worse
Feeling bad is just a new sensation
Tomorrow is another day
I will survive
Every cloud has a silver lining
There is a light at the end of the tunnel
After the rain comes a rainbow
It's always darkest before the dawn
It has to get worse, before it gets better
Every rose has its thorn
Midnight is where the day begins
Cheer up, it's not the end of the world
This too, shall pass
Life's not so bad, when you consider the alternative
The sharper is the berry, the sweeter is the wine
Internet zone

Other Educational Sites

Arthur C Clarke Foundation – *http://www.acclarke.co.uk*

Chemistry – *http://www.chemistry.co.nz/chem.htm*

Chemist's Art Gallery – *http://www.csc.fi/lul/chem/graphics.html*

European History – *http://www.eurohistory.com*

Fractal Database – *http://spanky.triumf.ca/www/welcome1.html*

Guy Fawkes – *http://www.highdown.berks.sch.uk/subjects/history/guyfawkes/gfawkes.htm*

History – *http://www.thehistorynet.com*

History Search – *http://argos.evansville.edu*

History Search – *http://www.perseus.tufts.edu*

History Today Magazine – *http://www.historytoday.com*

Maths Websites – *http://www.argonet.co.uk/oundlesch/mlink.html*

Mathsnet – *http://www.anglia.co.uk/education/mathsnet*

Megamathematics – *http://www.c3.lanl.gov/mega-math*

Prehistoric Sites – *http://www.henge.demon.co.uk*

Religious Studies – *http://www.ajbird.demon.co.uk*

Surfing the Net with Kids: Volcanos – *http://www.surfnetkids.com/volcano.htm*

Tomorrow's World – *http://www.bbc.co.uk/tw*

Trinidad and Tobago – *http://anansi.mit.edu/tnt/ttdir/ttdir.html*

Violent Planet – *http://www.iwaynet.net/%7Ekwroejr/violent.html*

Chapter Eight

News and Information

People need to keep up to date with world events for a variety of different reasons, but it's not always easy to catch the latest news. The morning paper doesn't get delivered, your train is late so you miss the evening broadcast and all of a sudden you're behind the times. The Internet can help to keep you informed.

Covers

Newspapers

The Telegraph

Most newspapers have a web site. This is true not only in this country, but over much of the world. They are clearly very successful and are widely used. Frankly I find this rather surprising as I observe that in general, people still seem to prefer to read paper rather than screens.

The Telegraph is typical of these sites, being effectively an electronic version of the paper that comes through the letter box each morning.

It's not always as convenient as the traditional papers.

It has the usual mix of news, opinion and sport, together with interviews and articles of general interest.

What the electronic version offers that the hardcopy version doesn't is a search facility so that you can search for a specific story or article.

Daily Telegraph is at *http://www.telegraph.co.uk.*

The Mirror

The Mirror's web site is similar to the paper, being less 'heavy' and containing some interesting features such as a crossword puzzle. The Mirror Online is at *http://www.mirror.co.uk*.

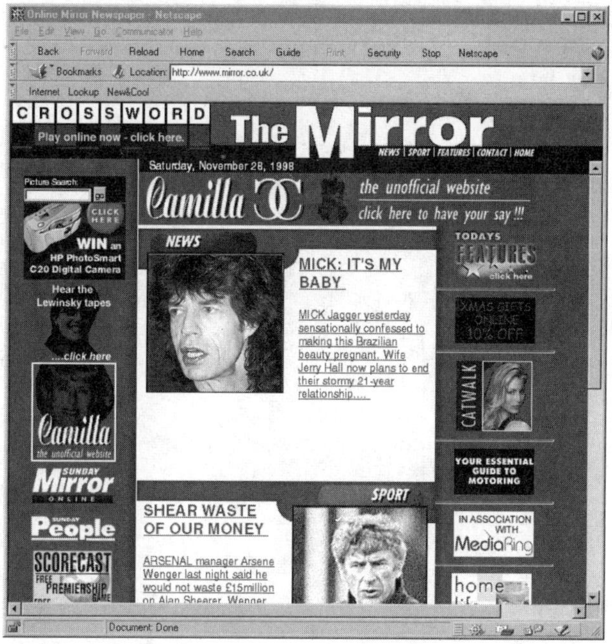

Other newspapers can be found at:

Daily Star – *http://www.megastar.co.uk/site/today/index.html*

Guardian – *http://go2.guardian.co.uk*

Independent – *http://www.independent.co.uk*

Jewish Chronicle – *http://www.jchron.co.uk*

Observer – *http://www.guardian.co.uk*

The Times – *http://www.the-times.co.uk*

Sunday Times – *http://www.sunday-times.co.uk*

Financial Times – *http://www.ft.com*

What's Going On

There are an increasing number of sites aimed at the local population, rather than aimed nationally. Typical of these is What's Going On which serves North London. The site is growing by the day and contains information about anything and everything in the North London area. Restaurants feature heavily and some offer as much as 15% discount if you provide them with a print out of the web advert.

HANDY TIP **Look out for other local area information services on the web.**

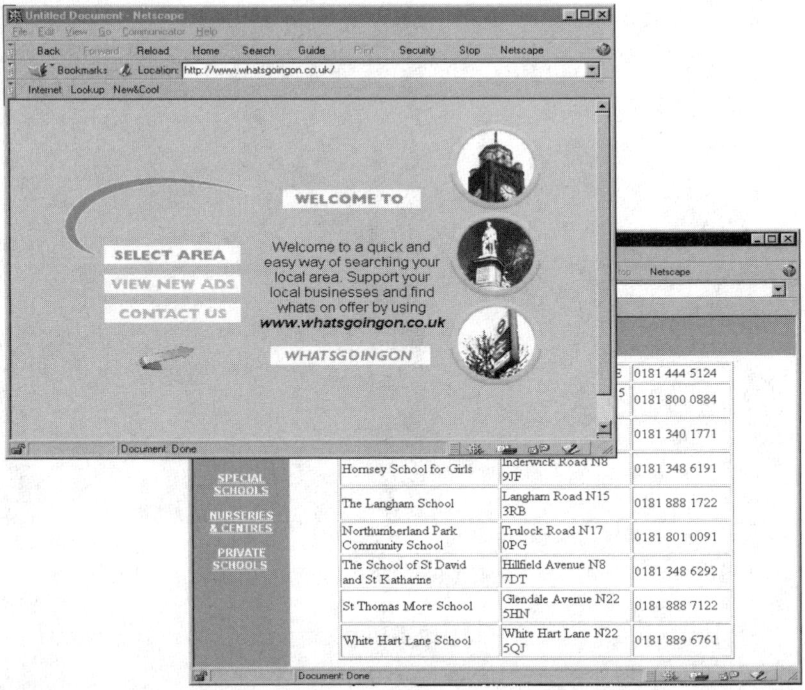

If you want to learn to drive, want details of the local schools, what's on at the cinemas or you just want to see what's happening in North London in preparation for a visit, this site is highly recommended.

Clearly What's Going On isn't going to be much use if you live in an area of the country other than North London, but enquiries in your local library could reveal other local sites.

What's Going On is at *http://www.whatsgoingon.co.uk.*

BBC News

The BBC are world famous for their efficient and unbiased delivery of news into our living rooms. The trouble is, if you don't happen to be at home at the right times, you won't get to hear what is happening.

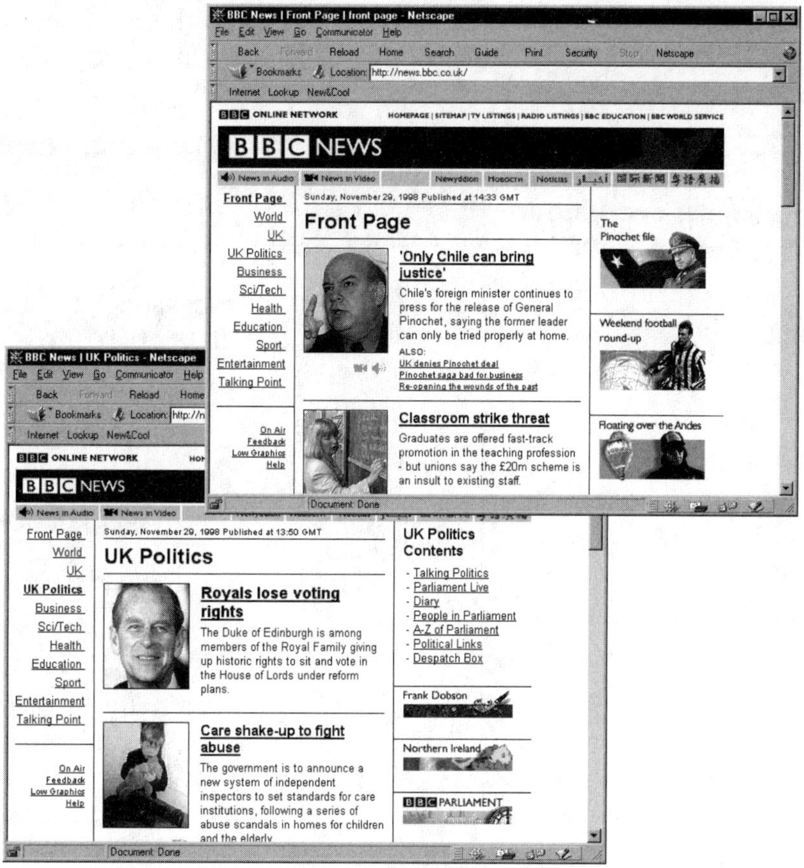

BBC News | Front Page | front page - Netscape
http://news.bbc.co.uk/
BBC ONLINE NETWORK
BBC NEWS
Front Page
World
UK
UK Politics
Business
Sci/Tech
Health
Education
Sport
Entertainment
Talking Point
Sunday, November 29, 1998 Published at 14:33 GMT
Front Page
'Only Chile can bring justice'
Chile's foreign minister continues to press for the release of General Pinochet, saying the former leader can only be tried properly at home.
Classroom strike threat
Graduates are offered fast-track promotion in the teaching profession - but unions say the £20m scheme is an insult to existing staff.
The Pinochet file
Weekend football round-up
Floating over the Andes
BBC News | UK Politics - Netscape
Sunday, November 29, 1998 Published at 13:50 GMT
UK Politics
Royals lose voting rights
The Duke of Edinburgh is among members of the Royal Family giving up historic rights to sit and vote in the House of Lords under reform plans.
Care shake-up to fight abuse
The government is to announce a new system of independent inspectors to set standards for care institutions, following a series of abuse scandals in homes for children and the elderly
UK Politics Contents
- Talking Politics
- Parliament Live
- Diary
- People in Parliament
- A-Z of Parliament
- Political Links
- Despatch Box
Frank Dobson
Northern Ireland
BBC PARLIAMENT
Document: Done

HANDY TIP

Unlike TV news, you can view web news whenever you want.

BBC Online News enables you to keep abreast of world developments at a time which suits yourself and not the programme planners.

The site is divided into categories so you can easily select the item you want, but if you prefer, there is a search facility which will track down a specific item for you.

BBC News is at *http://news.bbc.co.uk.*

Independent Radio News

Radio listeners will be familiar with Independent Radio News broadcasts. These hourly updates are also available on the web and take a similar format to the broadcast news: all the headlines first and then the details.

The web site opens with the headlines and a brief outline of the story. Clicking on the headline will take you to a page where there is a more detailed account of the story.

REMEMBER

This news is updated every hour.

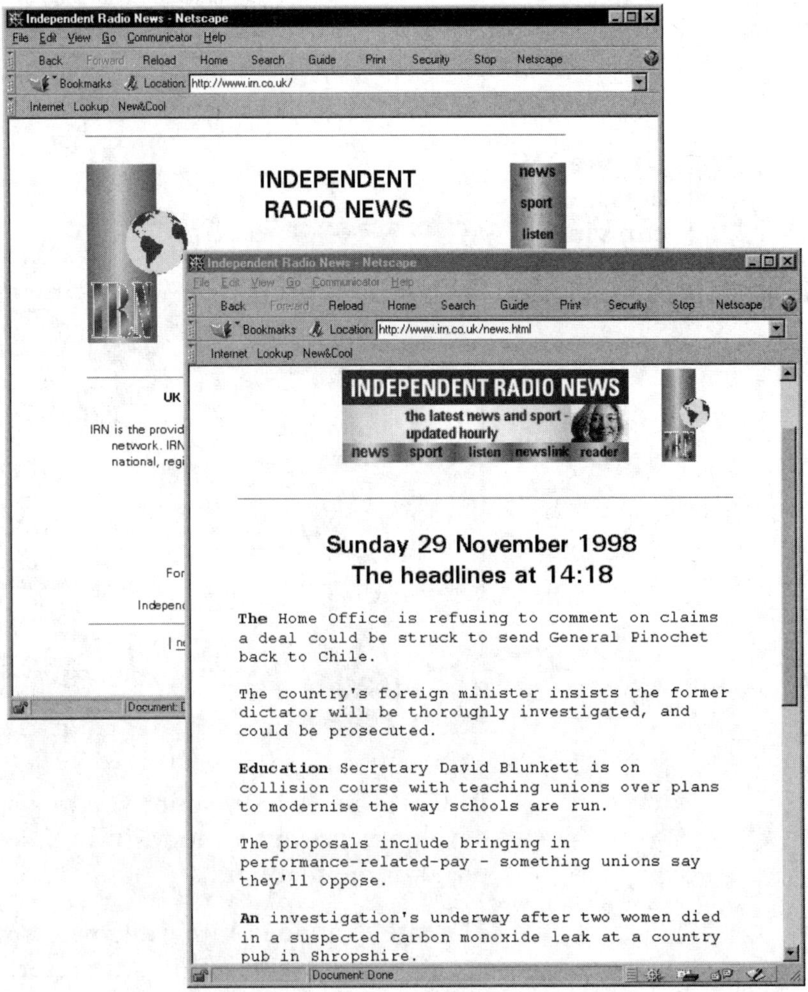

Independent Radio News - Netscape
File Edit View Go Communicator Help
Back Forward Reload Home Search Guide Print Security Stop Netscape
Bookmarks Location: http://www.irn.co.uk/
Internet Lookup New&Cool
INDEPENDENT RADIO NEWS
news
sport
listen
Independent Radio News - Netscape
File Edit View Go Communicator Help
Back Forward Reload Home Search Guide Print Security Stop Netscape
Bookmarks Location: http://www.irn.co.uk/news.html
Internet Lookup New&Cool
INDEPENDENT RADIO NEWS
the latest news and sport - updated hourly
news sport listen newslink reader
Sunday 29 November 1998
The headlines at 14:18
The Home Office is refusing to comment on claims a deal could be struck to send General Pinochet back to Chile.
The country's foreign minister insists the former dictator will be thoroughly investigated, and could be prosecuted.
Education Secretary David Blunkett is on collision course with teaching unions over plans to modernise the way schools are run.
The proposals include bringing in performance-related-pay - something unions say they'll oppose.
An investigation's underway after two women died in a suspected carbon monoxide leak at a country pub in Shropshire.
Document: Done

Independent Radio News is at *http://www.irn.co.uk.*

Daily Briefing

Daily Briefing allows you to build your own customised news broadcasts. You select the top stories in various categories and from various news services. A module is then downloaded into your computer which delivers your customised daily news briefing.

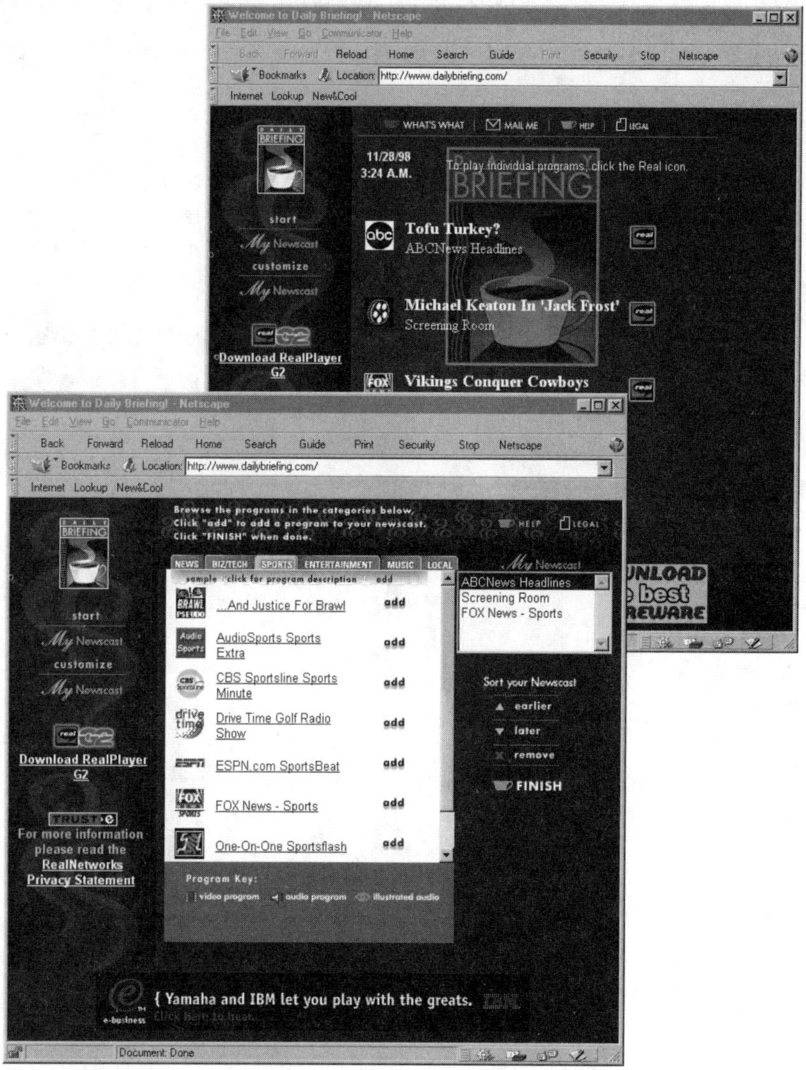

Daily Briefing is at *http://www.dailybriefing.com.*

Weather

UK Weather

A conversation without reference to the weather is almost unheard of. Phrases like 'miserable morning', 'should stay nice' and 'blowing up a bit' trip off our tongues almost daily. We Brits are preoccupied with the weather largely because we perceive it to be so changeable and unpredictable.

So it is therefore wholly appropriate that we should have so many sites dedicated to the changing state of our climate.

Whether they are more reliable than other means of ascertaining whether to take a brolly or not, I'll leave others to decide. All I'll add is that last winter I shovelled 3 inches of 'damp and slightly overcast' off my drive!

You can get local weather forecasts for any part of the country.

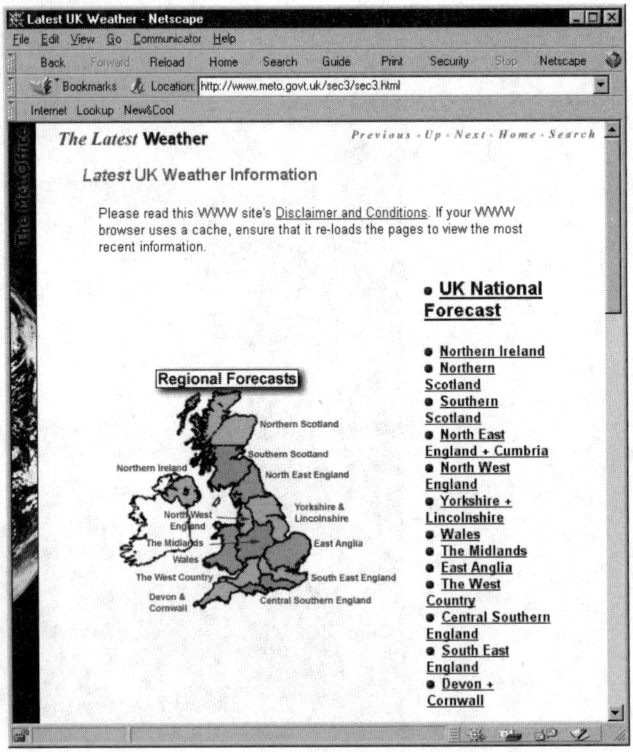

UK Weather is at *http://www.meto.govt.uk.*

Weather Post

For a broad view of the weather, including other parts of the world, Weather Post offers a good service. Of special note is the ice/snow forecast for skiers.

Weather Post is at *http://www.weatherpost.com.*

HANDY TIP

Check out this site before going on a skiing holiday.

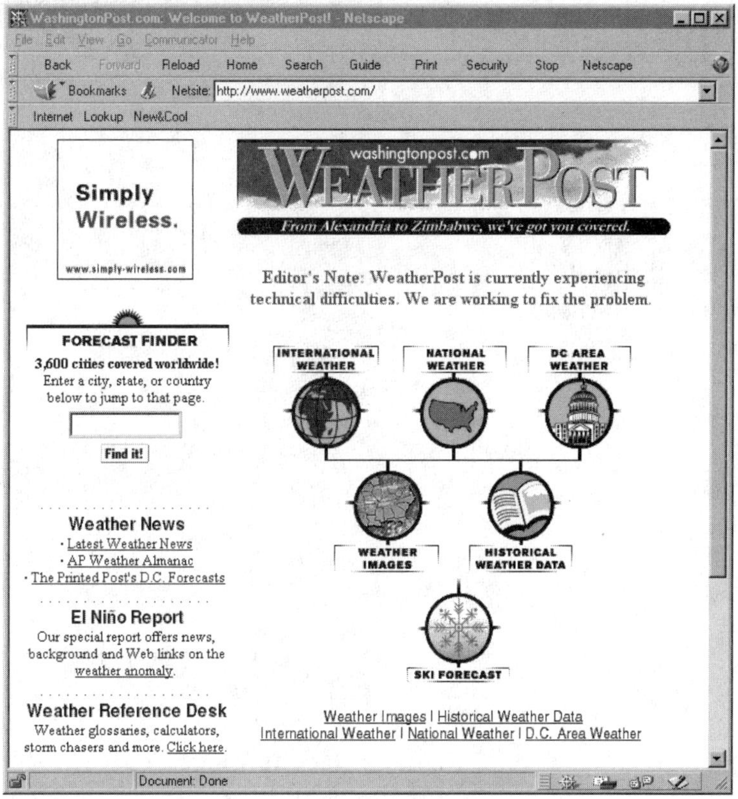

REMEMBER

These are just a few of the weather related web sites.

BBC Weather Centre – *http://www.bbc.co.uk/weather*

Dept of Meteorology – *http://www.met.rdg.ac.uk/~brugge*

The Mining Company – *http://weather.miningco.com/index.htm*

CNN Weather – *http://www.cnn.com/weather/cities/world.html*

Electronic Yellow Pages

Letting your fingers do the walking has a whole new meaning now that Yellow Pages is on the web.

I think it's fair to say that many electronic versions of age-old technology are certainly not an advancement in terms of ease of use.

HANDY TIP

Throw away the book version.

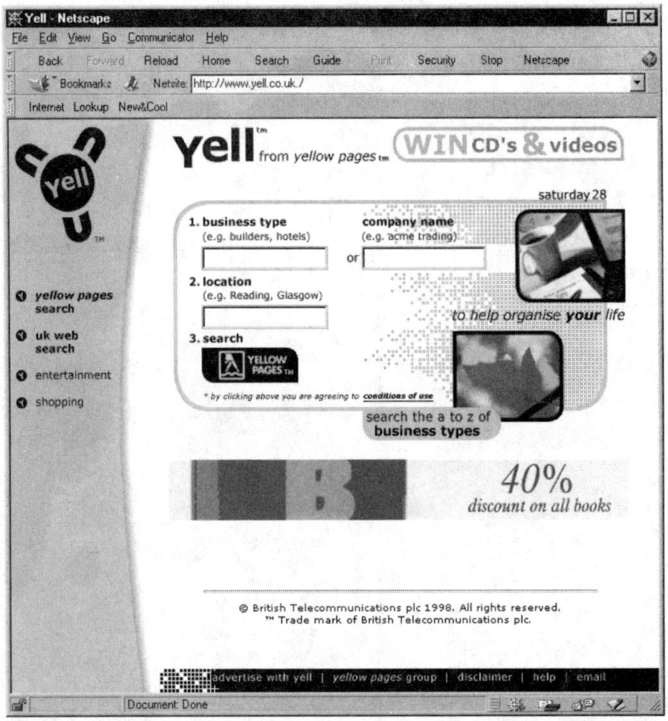

This is not the case with Yellow Pages. I can't imagine why anyone would want to use the book version if they have access to this. You want a plumber? In box 1, type in 'plumber', in box 2 type in the area and click on the Yellow Pages logo.

Within seconds a list of plumbers for the specified area is displayed. For good measure, you also get the option of displaying associated businesses.

Electronic Yellow Pages is at *http://www.yell.co.uk* and Thompson Pages are at *http://www.thomweb.co.uk.*

Job Search UK

HANDY TIP

If you have a vacancy, place details of it on this web site.

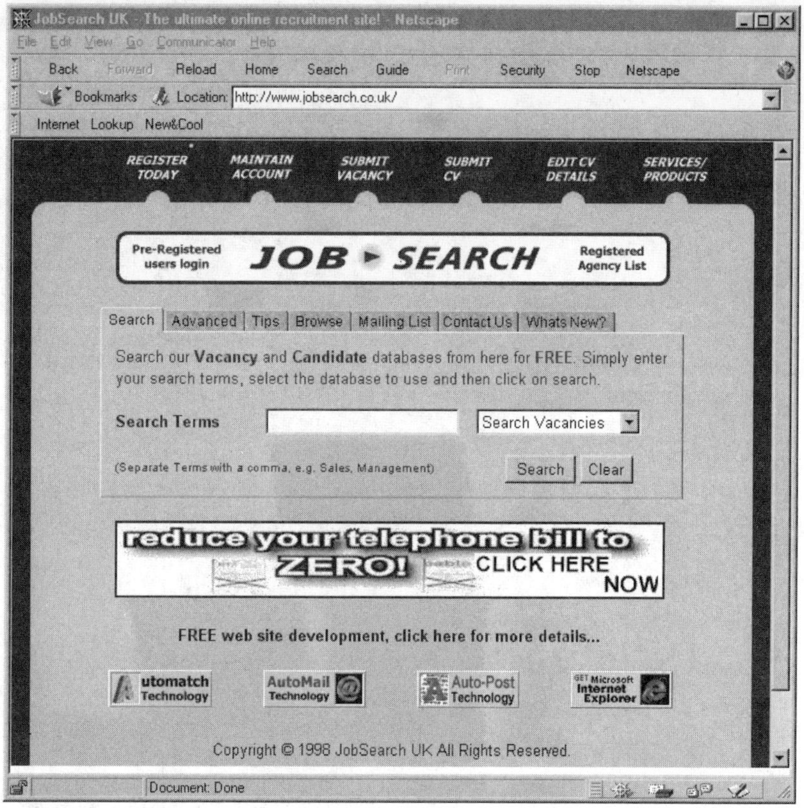

For job-hunters of all ages, Job Search UK could provide some help. The site has two ways of searching which could help you land the right job. You may either enter a job title or search through the vacancies. Help is available to ensure you enter the information in the correct format.

However you choose to search, you will be presented with a list of jobs and selecting one of them will display more information about it.

Job Search UK is at *http://www.jobsearch.co.uk.*

The RAC

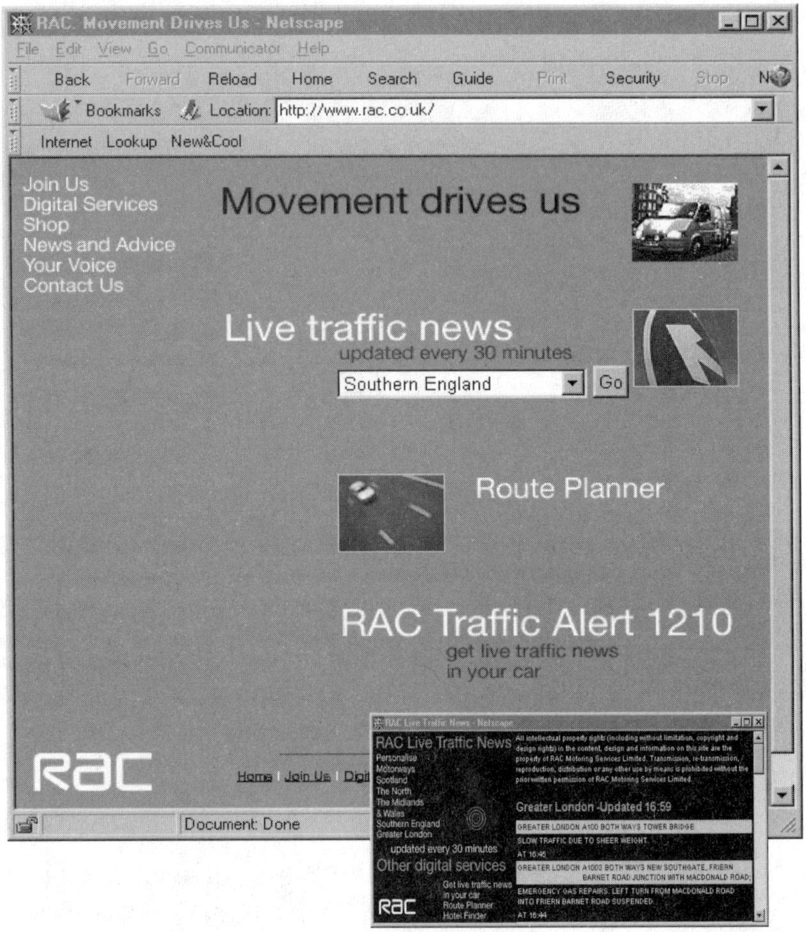

HANDY TIP

Check out this site before going on a car journey.

The web site for the Royal Automobile Club is a site well worth visiting before any car journey beyond the local shops. First, it is updated every 30 minutes so you can be sure the information is recent and relevant. Second, it has some features which will make driving a lot more pleasurable and consequently safer.

The section headed Local Traffic News is just that. Live information about news in your immediate area. After choosing the area you are currently in, the information is quickly returned about accidents, road works or any other hold up.

Journey planning is vital for a safe journey. It's never a good idea to just point your car in about the right direction and hope that you can work it out as you go.

The Route Planner requires you to enter your starting location and your destination, which can be names of towns or just postcodes. You also have the opportunity of entering a location to travel through (perhaps for a stop-over), and the choice of whether you want the fastest route or the shortest. When that information has been entered, type in your email address and press the 'submit' button.

If you have a laptop computer and the facility to access the internet on the move, refer to this site frequently.

You'll be emailed your route from door to door taking into account local road and traffic conditions.

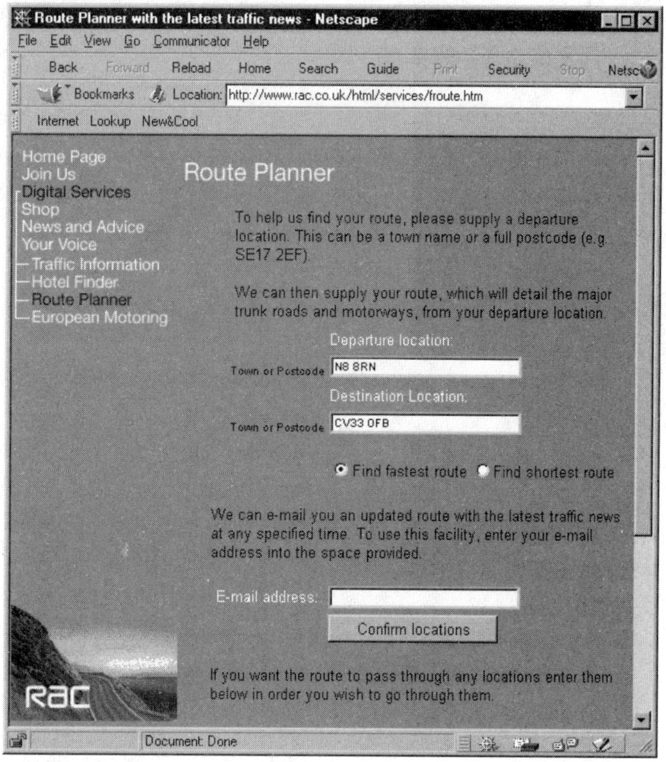

The RAC are at *http://www.rac.co.uk* and the AA are at *http://www.theaa.co.uk.*

Chat Lines

This is on-line, real-time chat, or perhaps type (as in touch type). Join a chat line and you need never be lonely again.

The Yahoo chat line is typical of the hundreds available. You first need to register and then you can take part in discussions about pre-selected topics either as part of a group, privately between yourself and one other, or if your typing is really good, both together.

Select the topic you wish to discuss from the list and begin chatting. If you want to chat to an individual, click on their name and continue the conversation in private.

This is a great way to get questions answered, keep up to date with a particular story or practice a foreign language.

Yahoo chat is at *http://chat.yahoo.com.*

Newsgroups

You won't know what information overload is unless you've subscribed to a newsgroup.

A newsgroup is an assortment of people's questions and answers on a specific topic. The articles are rather like emails except that generally everyone can read them and contribute to the group.

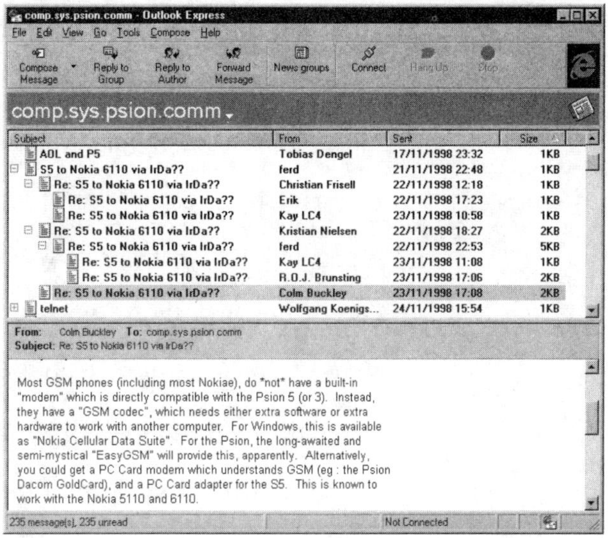

Your Internet Service Provider keeps a datafile of articles which it updates regularly. The list will be downloaded when you first log on and you can choose to subscribe to whichever ones you wish to. Later, the list of newsgroups may be updated and you can subscribe or unsubscribe to any.

The comp.sys.psion.comm newsgroup (*shown above*) is currently involved in a discussion about the viability of connecting a Psion Series 5 computer to a Nokia 6110 mobile phone via the infrared ports featured on both items. (If nothing else, the topics are specific.)

There are over 30,000 newsgroups on every imaginable subject, so there's bound to be something of interest to everyone.

Other News Sites

News Page – *http://www.newspage.com*

NewsBytes News Network – *http://www.nbnn.com*

Reuters – *http://www.reuters.com*

The Press Association – *http://www.pa.press.net*

The Sporting Life – *http://www.sporting-life.com*

This is London – *http://www.thisislondon.co.uk*

Anorak – *http://www.anorak.co.uk*

FutureNet – *http://www.futurenet.com*

FT Briefing – *http://www.briefing.FT.com/ms/intro.htm*

What's New – *http://www.whatsnew.com/msie/intro*

List of On-line Papers – *http://www.webwombat.com.au*

Newspaper Society – *http://www.newspapersoc.org.uk*

The Church Times – *http://www.churchtimes.co.uk*

Times Educational Supplement – *http://www.tes.co.uk*

Discovery – *http://www.discovery.com*

Media UK – *http://www.mediauk.com/directory*

London City News – *http://www.citynews.co.uk*

The PRnet Newswire – *http://www.prnet.co.uk*

Other Information Sites

Skeptics Society – *http://www.skeptic.com*

IGC Headline News – *gopher://gopher.igc.apc.org/11/headlines*

HM Treasury – *http://www.hm-treasury.gov.uk*

Chapter Nine

Organisations

This section includes mainly Religious, Environmental and Humanitarian organisations, although there are also some other organisations.

Covers

Religion

There are web sites for every religion, although only a few can be described as 'official' sites. The chances are the address of an 'official' site will end with 'org.uk'.

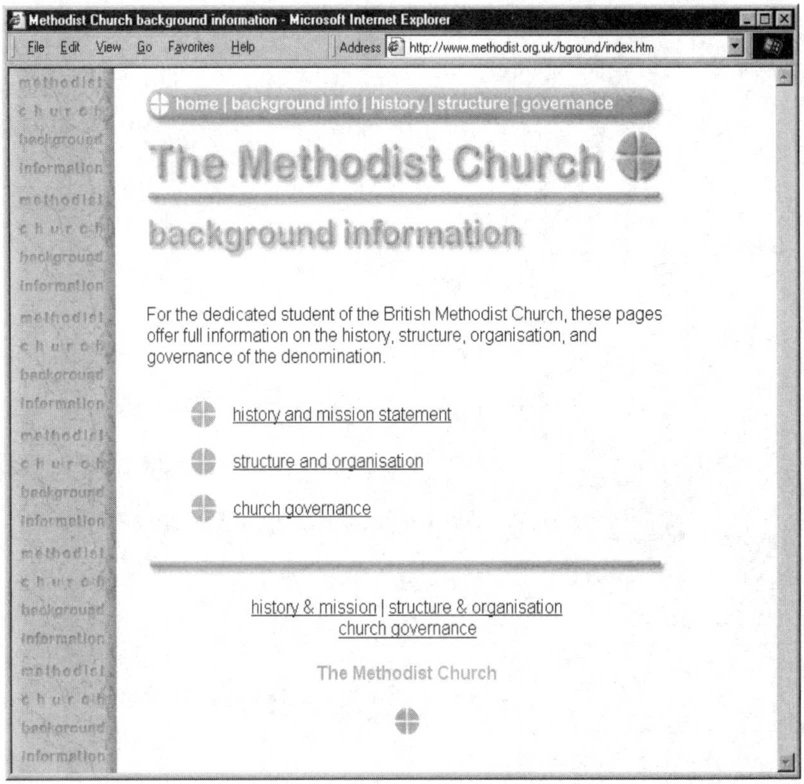

REMEMBER

Most religions have web sites.

Apart from a base from which to convey a religious message, many of these sites offer an insight into the particular religion, including information about the internal organisation.

Although many sites are primarily for students of the particular religion, they do offer everyone a way in. Some sites even include links to local fellowships.

The Methodist web site is at *http://www.methodist.org.uk*.

The Baptist web site is at *http://www.baptist.org.uk*.

Help the Aged

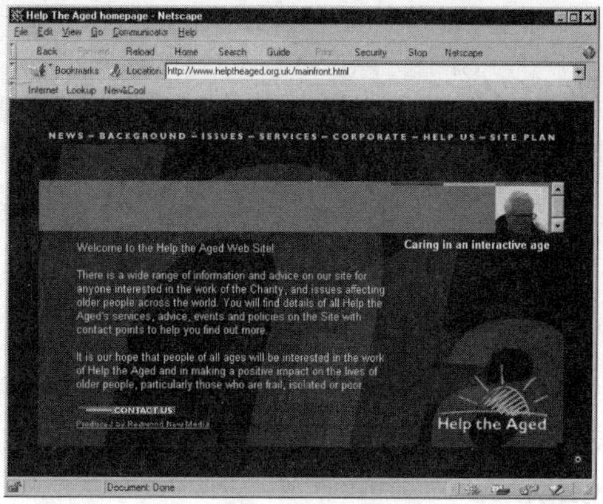
Help The Aged homepage - Netscape
http://www.helptheaged.org.uk/mainfront.html
NEWS – BACKGROUND – ISSUES – SERVICES – CORPORATE – HELP US – SITE PLAN
Caring in an interactive age
Welcome to the Help the Aged Web Site!
There is a wide range of information and advice on our site for anyone interested in the work of the Charity, and issues affecting older people across the world. You will find details of all Help the Aged's services, advice, events and policies on the Site with contact points to help you find out more.
It is our hope that people of all ages will be interested in the work of Help the Aged and in making a positive impact on the lives of older people, particularly those who are frail, isolated or poor.
CONTACT US
Help the Aged
Document: Done

It's a sad but true fact that over one third of our senior citizens live alone. These are the people who have worked hard all their lives, even fought for our country and yet have to struggle to keep warm.

Help the Aged is at *http://www.helptheaged.org.uk.*

One World

http://www.oneworld.org/
oneworld
a community of over 200 leading global justice organisations under one roof
supported by BT
26 November 1998
CRIMINAL LAW
Dictator in the dock?
In an historic step towards ending impunity five UK Law Lords have ruled that Augusto Pinochet is not immune from prosecution. The former Chilean dictator now faces an extradition battle with Spain in the UK courts. Will Pinochet finally stand trial for crimes against humanity or successfully fight extradition and walk away a free man? It's not all over yet.
NEWS HEADLINES
Iranian opposition figures killed
Refugees head homewards
news
Today's Headlines
This Week
By Country
By Theme
Special Reports
Radio News Service
themes
Guides
Analysis
Think Tank
European Perspectives
Education
BLAST
INDIGENOUS RIGHTS
Oldman of the woods
Document: Done

HANDY TIP **This site has links to other humanitarian sites.**

One World is an appropriate title for this site which looks at a variety of humanitarian issues from around the world. Apart from its own pages, there are links to most of the humanitarian organisations.

One World is at *http://www.oneworld.org.*

Greenpeace

We didn't inherit the earth from our parents, we are minding it for our children. The earth has paid a huge price for 20th Century technology: we take from the Earth and then spew back the waste with little regard for the long or short term consequences. Greenpeace brings the world's attention to what we our doing to our planet. Its web site outlines many of the key issues.

REMEMBER

Earth is only home we have and it's got to last a long time.

Greenpeace International Homepage - Netscape
File Edit View Go Communicator Help
Back Forward Reload Home Search Guide Print Security Stop Netscape
Bookmarks Location: http://www.greenpeace.org/
Internet Lookup New&Cool
GREENPEACE.ORG information inter@ct join search help
GREENPEACE.ORG
Headline . . .
Toxics
Ship industry ignores EU law saddling Asia with Toxic Waste
Search . . .
Campaign Events . . .
Toxics
Toys R Us reacts to Greenpeace demands but most soft PVC Toys are still on sale
Play Safe
BUY PVC FREE
Genetic Engineering
"The latest survey shows an on-going collapse of public support for biotechnology and GM foods", says a recent Monsanto study, leaked to Greenpeace. Click here to read what they know but don't want you to know.
Join Greenpeace
Become a member
join
press releases
climate toxics nuclear oceans genetic engineering ocean dumping forests
Document: Done

Greenpeace is at *http://www.greenpeace.org.*

Friends of the Earth

Like Greenpeace, Friends of the Earth are concerned with environmental issues. Their web site also outlines some of the major environmental problems.

Friends of the Earth is at *http://www.foe.co.uk.*

Amnesty International

Not all countries have a justice system based on a fair trial. As a result there are countless people throughout the world who have been imprisoned for political reasons and many are living in appalling conditions.

Amnesty International speaks out for all people who are oppressed for whatever reason.

REMEMBER

This is a good site for discussion groups at school.

The site contains a great deal of information about Amnesty International, including details of current campaigns throughout the world of which, tragically, there are many.

As can be seen from the picture, the site is updated daily with news about current issues from around the world.

The library section details past campaigns that Amnesty International has worked on, and also gives a list of other humanitarian organisations with hotlinks to take you straight to their sites.

Amnesty International is at *http://www.amnesty.org.*

Samaritans

Modern living certainly does not suit everyone. For some, it's all too much and for one reason or another, the situation appears unresolvable. Desperation then takes over, sometimes with tragic consequences.

Help is at hand from probably the best known counselling organisation in the world: The Samaritans.

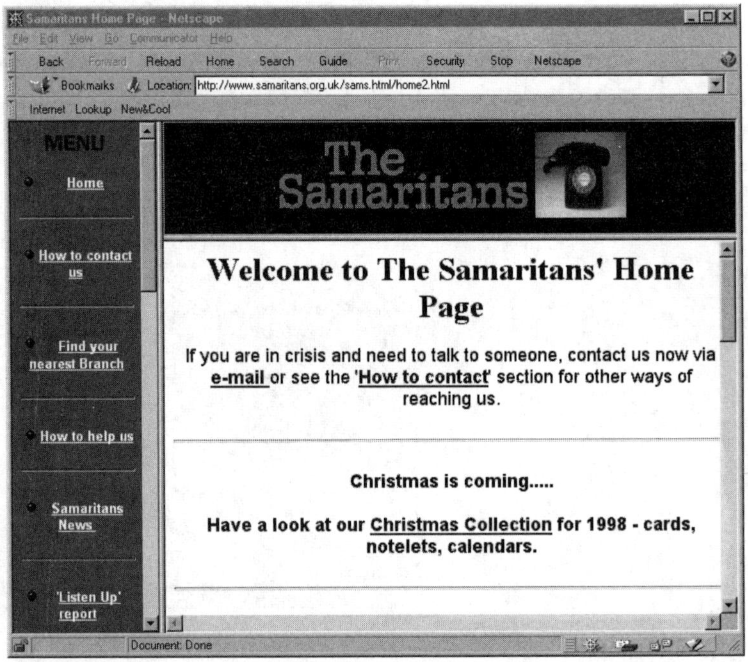
Samaritans Home Page - Netscape
Back Forward Reload Home Search Guide Print Security Stop Netscape
Bookmarks Location: http://www.samaritans.org.uk/sams.html/home2.html
Internet Lookup New&Cool
MENU
Home
How to contact us
Find your nearest Branch
How to help us
Samaritans News
'Listen Up' report
The Samaritans
Welcome to The Samaritans' Home Page
If you are in crisis and need to talk to someone, contact us now via e-mail or see the 'How to contact' section for other ways of reaching us.
Christmas is coming.....
Have a look at our Christmas Collection for 1998 - cards, notelets, calendars.
Document: Done

It is now possible to email the Samaritans as well as telephone for confidential counselling. There are many centres across the country and they are all included here for those who might wish to contact them in the traditional manner, rather than electronically. Full contact details are provided.

Their web site also includes current news about The Samaritans and some practical advice about how you can help.

The Samaritans web site is *http://www.samaritans.org.uk*.

Christian Aid

Christian Aid is one of the best known charities in the world. Its work in war-torn areas and scenes of natural disaster is well known to all of us.

The Christian Aid web site brings some of the good work to our homes, including a selection of links to other sites.

Christian Aid helps all people, regardless of their religion. It may be contacted at *http://www.christian-aid.org.uk.*

Save the Children

Another great humanitarian organisation that does so much good throughout the world. Save The Children also has an excellent web site which contains a great deal of information about the plight of some of the children throughout the world.

Its web site is at *http://www.savethechildren.org.uk* although it may also be accessed via the One World web site at *http://www.oneworld.org.*

HANDY TIP

This is another great web site for use in schools.

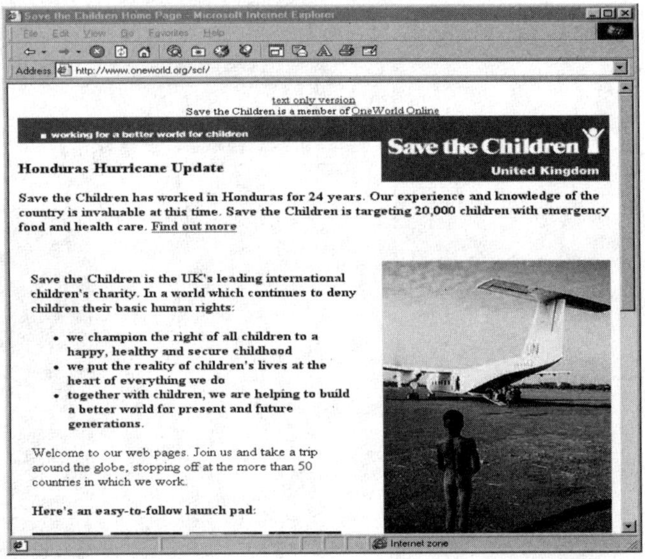

Save the Children Home Page - Microsoft Internet Explorer
Address http://www.oneworld.org/scf/
text only version
Save the Children is a member of OneWorld Online
working for a better world for children
Save the Children
United Kingdom
Honduras Hurricane Update
Save the Children has worked in Honduras for 24 years. Our experience and knowledge of the country is invaluable at this time. Save the Children is targeting 20,000 children with emergency food and health care. Find out more
Save the Children is the UK's leading international children's charity. In a world which continues to deny children their basic human rights:
we champion the right of all children to a happy, healthy and secure childhood
we put the reality of children's lives at the heart of everything we do
together with children, we are helping to build a better world for present and future generations.
Welcome to our web pages. Join us and take a trip around the globe, stopping off at the more than 50 countries in which we work.
Here's an easy-to-follow launch pad:
Internet zone

Other Organisations

Government Information Service – *http://www.open.gov.uk*

New Deal – *http://www.newdeal.gov.uk*

RSPCA On-line – *http://www.rspca.org.uk*

Institute for Global Communications – *http://www.igc.org*

The New Internationalist – *http://oneworld.org/ni/index.html*

Cyber Law Centre – *http://www.cyberlawcentre.org.uk*

Chapter Ten

Technology

What materialistic people we are! This chapter is devoted to some of the technology we have surrounded ourselves with.

Covers

Automotive

Some of the best designed web sites are those owned by manufacturing companies who seem to have large quantities of money to throw at web designers.

Searching for web sites about cars is made easier using Yahoo's listings of Automotive makes and models at *http://www.yahoo.com/recreation/automotive/makes_and_models/*

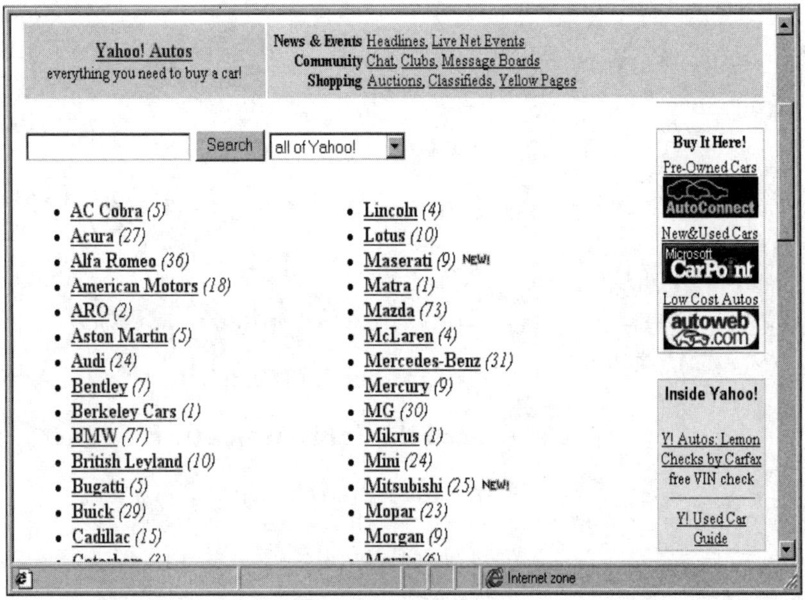

HANDY TIP

If you own a classic car, it's worth searching for a related web site.

Many of the automotive web sites are the official manufacturers' sites, but not all. There are countless 'unofficial' sites representing individuals' own personal love affairs. Some sites are best described as being in between the official and the unofficial sites. These are the pages constructed by the various owners clubs around the world.

If you own a classic car, or just an old car, it's worth seeking out the web sites relating to it as they will contain a wealth of information. If nothing else, it could point you in the right direction of some cheap spare parts. Even if you have a newer car, Owners Club pages are worth checking out.

Typical of the enthusiasts' web sites is the MG site which contains information about almost every car that ever carried an MG badge. The home page lists all of the MG models over the years and clicking on one of the links will take you to a pages of further information about that particular model. There are also links to other MG related sites where you can read the news and get the views about MG.

HANDY TIP **There are lots of clubs run by enthusiasts and many of these have web sites.**

There is also a guide to various meetings and competitions held throughout the year.

To find out more, go to *http://www.mgcars.org.uk.*

For collectors of miscellaneous facts, The Rolls Royce facts site at *http://www.darkforce.com/royce/facts.htm* is full of interesting off-beat snippets. Nothing to do with the Rolls Royce company, just an individual who likes 'Rollers'. Or is it 'Royces'?

Mail Order Car Parts

HANDY TIP **There are many sites that offer mail order. Look at the section on shopping.**

If you own a Land Rover, (including Range Rover, Discovery and Freelander) then this award winning site is a must. The small independent Land Rover Specialist, Duncan Mansfield, scooped the prestigious e-business Award for small businesses.

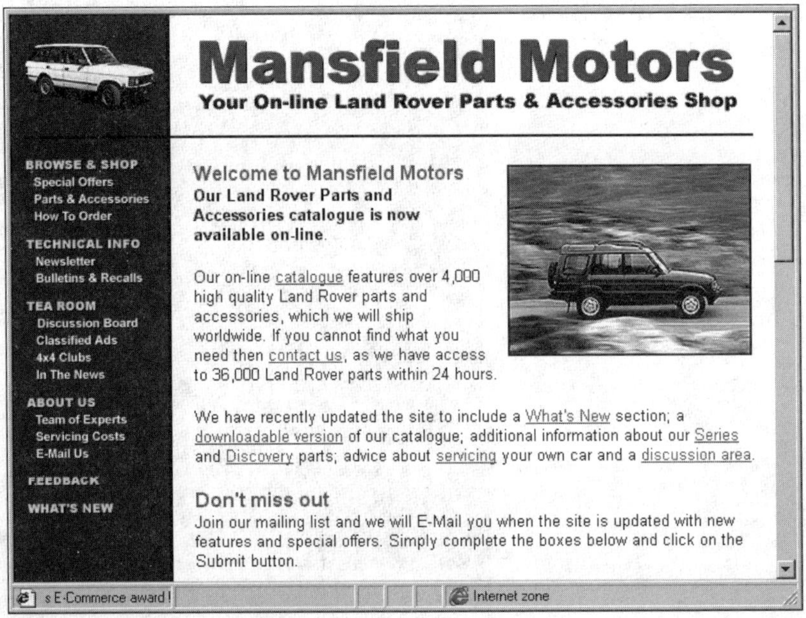
Mansfield Motors
Your On-line Land Rover Parts & Accessories Shop
BROWSE & SHOP
Special Offers
Parts & Accessories
How To Order
TECHNICAL INFO
Newsletter
Bulletins & Recalls
TEA ROOM
Discussion Board
Classified Ads
4x4 Clubs
In The News
ABOUT US
Team of Experts
Servicing Costs
E-Mail Us
FEEDBACK
WHAT'S NEW
Welcome to Mansfield Motors
Our Land Rover Parts and Accessories catalogue is now available on-line.
Our on-line catalogue features over 4,000 high quality Land Rover parts and accessories, which we will ship worldwide. If you cannot find what you need then contact us, as we have access to 36,000 Land Rover parts within 24 hours.
We have recently updated the site to include a What's New section; a downloadable version of our catalogue; additional information about our Series and Discovery parts; advice about servicing your own car and a discussion area.
Don't miss out
Join our mailing list and we will E-Mail you when the site is updated with new features and special offers. Simply complete the boxes below and click on the Submit button.
s E-Commerce award!
Internet zone

It is incredible just how the web can help small businesses. About 20% of all parts sold by Mansfield Motors are now on-line orders.

Look at the chapter on shopping for more about on-line sales.

Visit this site at *http://www.mansfield-motors.com.*

Another source of information about the cars is Team.Net Automotive Webs at *http://www.team.net.*

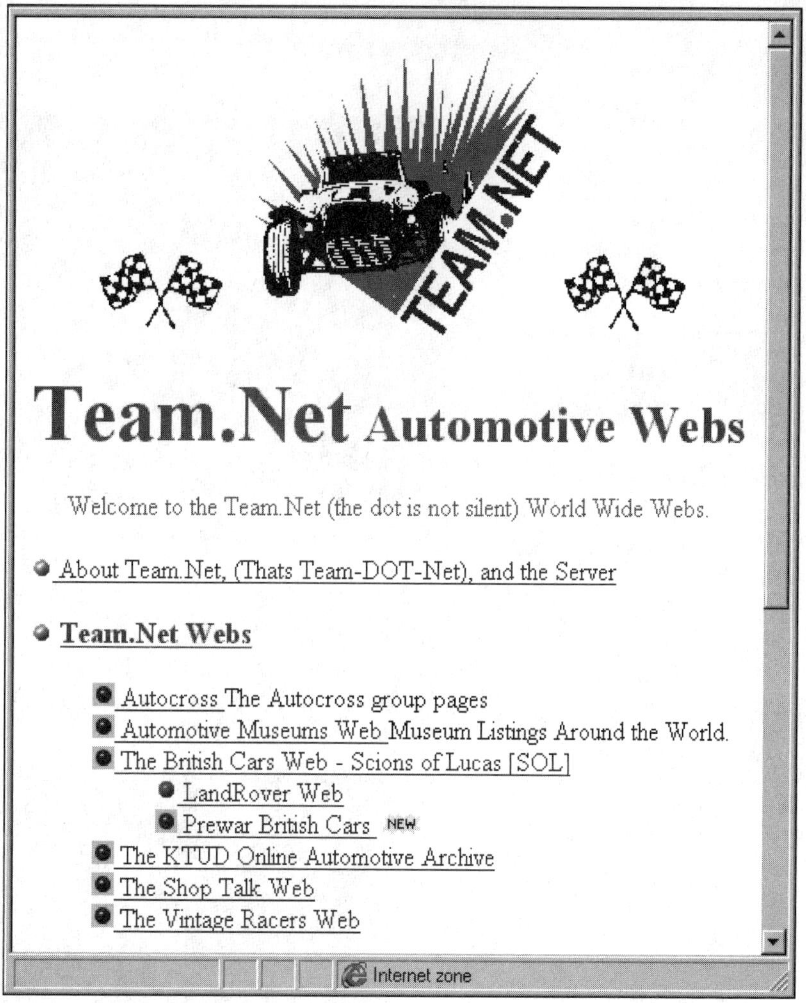

BEWARE

Many of the sites are not the 'official' ones but are run by individuals.

Use this site to access information about all manner of diverse motor related topics including motor sports, pre-war British cars, museums and chatlines. If I were lucky enough to own a vintage car, the last thing I would want to do is risk wrecking it by entering it into a race. If you feel differently, you can also access the Vintage Racers Web from this page.

Official Sites

Almost all of the major motor manufacturers throughout the world have their own sites. Most are used to advertise their products, and to announce the arrival of new models in the range.

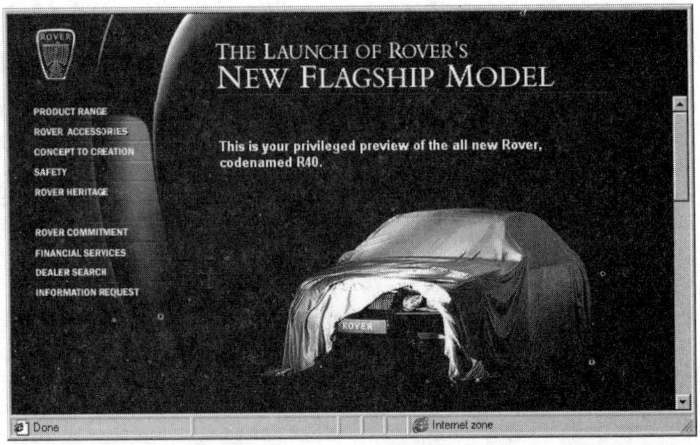

HANDY TIP The automotive web sites are some of the best around.

The majority require no more than to prefix the name of the company with *www.* and to suffix it with *.com*. Opposite though is a list of some of the official automotive web sites. Rover Cars are at *http://www.rovercars.com.*

Manufacturer's Web Sites

Alfa Romeo – *http://www.alfaromeo.com*

Aston Martin – *http://www.astonmartin.com*

Audi – *http://www.audi.com*

BMW – *http://www.bmw.com*

Citroen – *http://www.citroen.com*

Ferrari – *http://www.ferrari.com*

Fiat – *http://www.fiat.com*

Ford – *http://www.ford.co.uk*

Jaguar – *http://www.jaguar.com*

McLaren – *http://www.mclaren.co.uk*

Mercedes Benz – *http://www.mercedes-benz.co.uk*

Mini – *http://www.mini.co.uk*

Morgan – *http://www.morgan-motor.co.uk*

Nissan – *http://www.nissan-usa.com*

Peugeot – *http://www.peugeot.com*

Porsche – *http://www.porsche.com*

Renault – *http://www.renault.com*

Rolls Royce – *http://www.rolls-royce.com*

Saab – *http://www.saab.com*

Subaru – *http://www.subaru.com*

TVR – *http://www.tvr-eng.co.uk*

Vauxhall – *http://www.vauxhall.co.uk*

Volkswagon – *http://www.vw.com*

Volvo – *http://www.volvo.com*

Individuality

Not long ago I could identify any car just by looking at it. Now, I have to read the name badge. The constraints of profit have meant that cars tend to look very similar. Certainly the cars that most people can afford seem to be a product influenced more by the corporate parts bin rather than the designer.

Born out of a need to satisfy people's desire for individuality, there are numerous companies producing after-sales bolt-on goodies.

Always inform your insurance company if you intend modifying your car in any way.

SW Autodesigns (*http://www.swautodesigns.co.uk*) fit wheels, spoilers and suspension modifications to a range of UK, European and Japanese cars, whilst Momo (*http://www.momo.it*) are one of the top manufacturers of alloy wheels for road and race cars.

Registrations

Ever since the registration number RR1 was sold in a blaze of publicity, personalised registrations have become a peculiarly British love. Registration Transfers (*http://www.regtransfers.co.uk*) have a huge selection of numbers and the facilities to transfer one to your vehicle with a minimum of fuss.

RT Registration Transfers
CLICK HERE to enquire about 'T-Registrations' NOW
TI GER
SIMPLY THE BEST AT WHAT WE DO !

REMEMBER

We never stop learning to drive.

Advanced Driving

Passing the driving test should not be regarded as the ultimate accolade. Further tuition should be sought especially if you're considering driving a high performance car. The Institute of Advanced Motorists (*http://www.iam.org.uk*) will provide some useful tips and even a test.

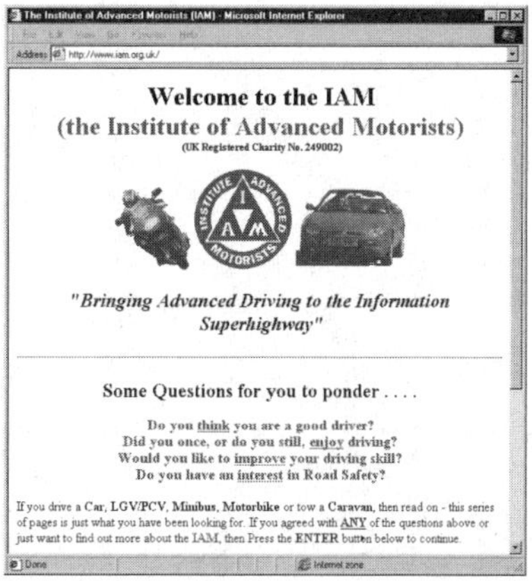
Welcome to the IAM
(the Institute of Advanced Motorists)
"Bringing Advanced Driving to the Information Superhighway"
Some Questions for you to ponder . . . .
Do you think you are a good driver?
Did you once, or do you still, enjoy driving?
Would you like to improve your driving skill?
Do you have an interest in Road Safety?

Computers

It would be difficult to write a book such as this without at least a passing reference to web sites associated with the computer industry. There are a huge number of sites relating to computers: some for hardware; some for software; some provide help; others are somewhere in between.

Networking

If more than half a dozen computers are in the same place, the chances are that linking them together would prove beneficial. First, it enables users to share resources – rather than each person having their own printer (all of which would be idle for most of the time) you can provide one really good printer and let everyone share it. The second major advantage of networking is that people will be able to access their work from any of the computers.

HANDY TIP

For more information on networking, see the appropriate title from the 'in easy steps' series table on the inside-back cover of this book.

But modern network design and construction is a specialist task and needs to be carried out by specialists. One of the top names in the business is Atomwide and as well as advising, designing and constructing networks, they can tailor them to very specific requirements both in business and educational environments.

Atomwide are at *http://www.atomwide.co.uk.*

Psion

REMEMBER **This site contains software upgrades that can be freely downloaded.**

Portable computing is very much the order of the day for business people on the move. A computer that runs on batteries frees the user from the desk and enable him or her to work at times when they would otherwise be passing the time of day, possibly being bored. A train journey is a typical example.

One of the companies at the forefront of personal mobile computing is Psion and their web site is a mine of information about their products, both hardware and software and importantly the ability to link their computer to others. Psion plc is at *http://www.psion.com/*

Apart from the official Psion site which is run by the company, there are others run by third party software houses as well as individuals for whom mobile computing appears to be their hobby.

HANDY TIP **It's also worth looking at Geofox (www.geofox.com) who make portable computers using the Psion operating system.**

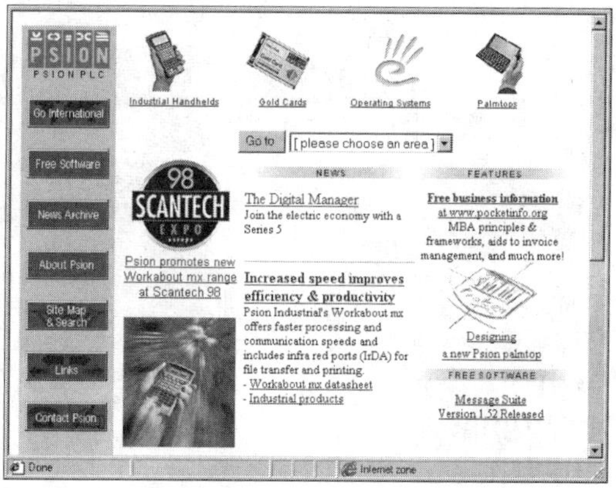
PSION
PSION PLC
Industrial Handhelds
Gold Cards
Operating Systems
Palmtops
Go International
Free Software
News Archive
About Psion
Site Map & Search
Links
Contact Psion
Go to
[please choose an area]
NEWS
FEATURES
98
SCANTECH
EXPO
The Digital Manager
Join the electric economy with a Series 5
Free business information
at www.pocketinfo.org
MBA principles & frameworks, aids to invoice management, and much more!
Psion promotes new Workabout mx range at Scantech 98
Increased speed improves efficiency & productivity
Psion Industrial's Workabout mx offers faster processing and communication speeds and includes infra red ports (IrDA) for file transfer and printing.
- Workabout mx datasheet
- Industrial products
Designing
a new Psion palmtop
FREE SOFTWARE
Message Suite
Version 1.52 Released
Done
Internet zone

HANDY TIP **See 'Psion 5 in easy steps' for more information on this particular product.**

Palmtop NV and Purple Software are two of the top names in the Psion world and their sites are at *http://www.palmtop.nl* and *http://www.purplesoft.com* respectively.

Psion info at *http://www.pocketinfo.org* contains a great deal of material for Psion users and the 3-Lib Library at *http://3lib.ukonline.co.uk* is the largest shareware software library for Psion users.

If you own a printer, you'll need a printer driver. These are frequently updated by the printer manufacturers and are available on the web as free downloads. All of the major printer manufacturers put their drivers onto the web and also supply a lot of other material including download instructions, product information and company details.

HANDY TIP **Look out for job opportunities frequently advertised in computer web sites.**

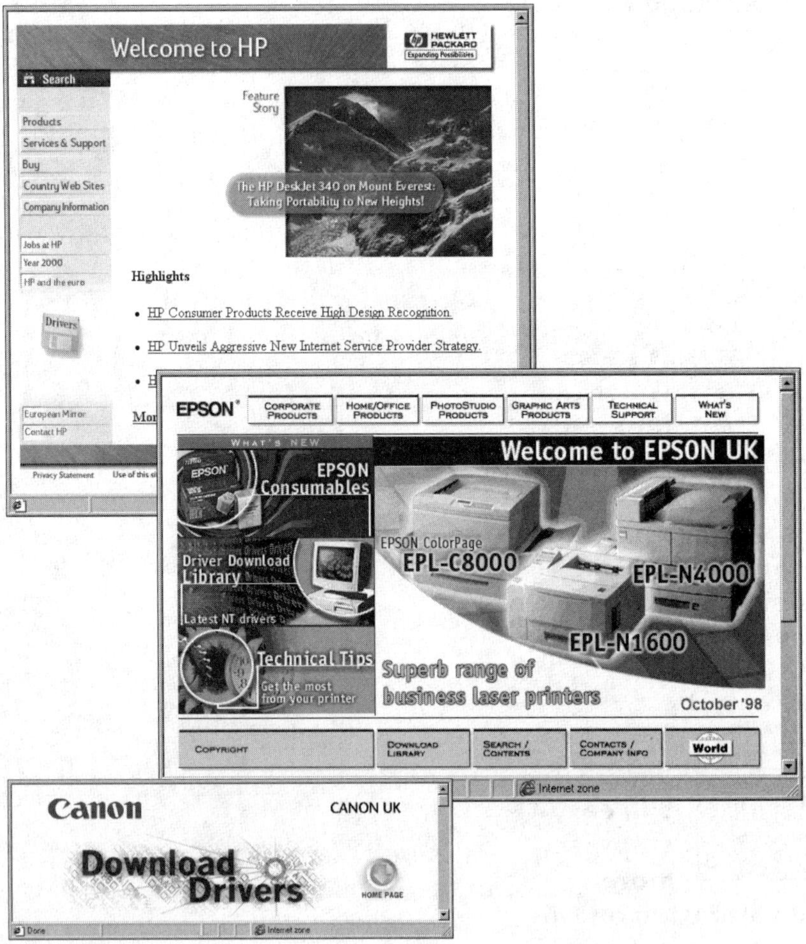

HANDY TIP **When down loading printer drivers, it's often best to choose to download in modules that can then be stored on floppy disc.**

Canon – *http://www.canon.com*

Epson – *http://www.epson.com*

Hewlett Packard – *http://www.hp.com*

REMEMBER **You can get all of the original Spectrum software to run on your PC.**

Some individuals apparently prefer looking back rather than forward. In these days where 64MBytes is the norm, and 32 bit operating systems with 300MHz processors is regarded as a minimum requirement, the Spectrum site takes us back to the early 1980s when the 8bit Sinclair Spectrum with 48Kbytes of memory and 8 colours was everyone's dream. I had one, and most of my friends had one. If you were involved in computing in any form at that time, chances are you had one too.

The Spectrum site offers news, views and general enthusiasm about this great little computer as well as providing all the software ever published for it. No, you don't need a tape recorder to load it, you can save it all onto disc and install the purpose-built ZX Emulator to run it on your PC.

HANDY TIP **Check out the FTP directory listing ftp://ftp.gns.getronics.nl/pub/os/sinclair/games.**

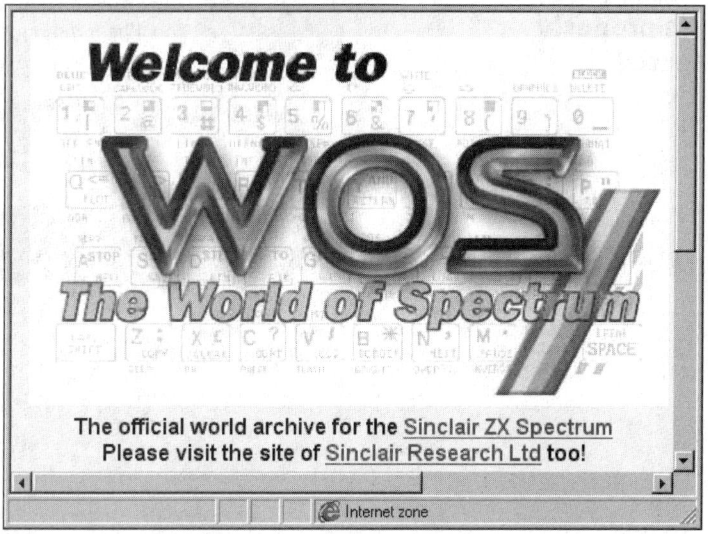
Welcome to
WOS
The World of Spectrum
The official world archive for the Sinclair ZX Spectrum
Please visit the site of Sinclair Research Ltd too!
Internet zone

An emulator basically fools a computer into thinking that it's something it isn't. In this case, your PC is fooled into thinking it's a 48K Spectrum (which I would have thought must be a fairly traumatic experience for the PC).

The World of Spectrum is at *http://www.void.demon.nl/spectrum.html.*

Anti Virus software

I often wonder if the same people who write the anti-virus software are actually responsible for some of the viruses in the first place! Now there's a thought.

It's a great shame that so many intelligent people feel the need to apply their skills in such a negative way. But, viruses exist and so you need to be protected against them, especially when downloading files from the Internet.

The Virus Information site will help you sort out what you've got and what you need to get rid of it and stay rid of it.

Check this site out very carefully and make sure you're properly protected.

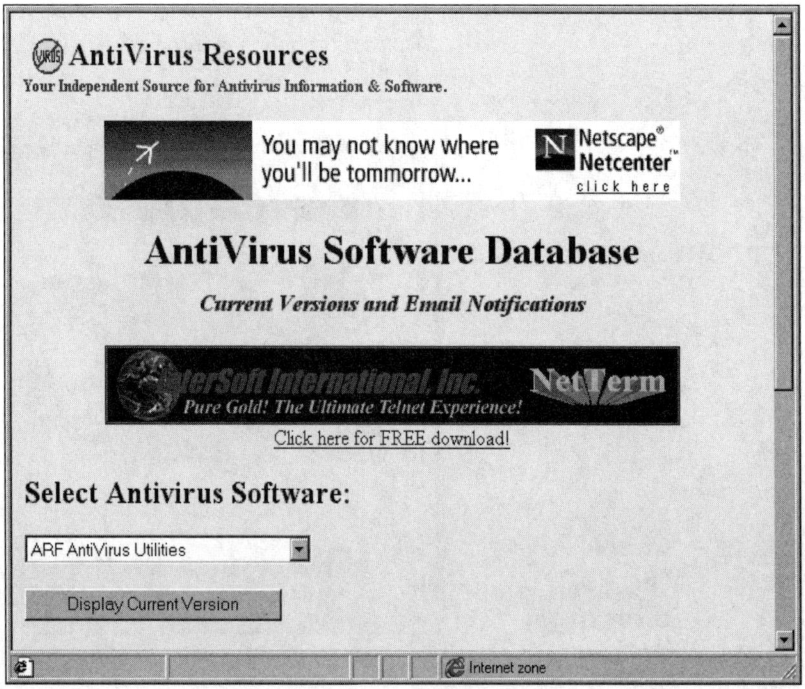

Apart from the information about the various viruses, there is also free software to download. The web site is at *http://www.hitchhikers.net/antivirus/antivirus-dis.phtml*.

Also look at Symantec at *http://www.symantec.com*

CD-ROM Reviews

CD ROMs were the computer revolution of the early 1990s but with the advent of the Internet, they seem to have slipped into the background.

There are a huge number of CD ROMs for all ages and this site gives unbiased views and information on the major releases.

HANDY TIP **Check out this site before buying a CD ROM.**

Visit *http://www.roundo.demon.co.uk/cd.htm* to get a roundup of all the top CD ROMs.

Check out some of these sites for information about the top names in the computer world.

Adobe – *http://www.adobe.com*

AIMS Lab Web – *http://www.aimslab.com/welcome.html*

Apple – *http://www.apple.com*

Casio – *http://www.casio.com*

Citizen – *http://www.citizen.co.uk*

Compaq – *http://www.compaq.com*

IBM – *http://www.ibm.com*

Intel – *http://www.intel.com*

HANDY TIP **There's free software at:** http://www.hotfiles.zdnet.com.

Iomega – *http://www.iomega.com*

Microsoft – *http://www.microsoft.com*

Microsoft Info – *http://www.microsoft.com/ie/ie40*

Silicon Graphics – *http://www.sgi.com*

Sun Microsystems – *http://www.sun.com*

WinZip – *http://www.teleport.com/support/utilities/winzip95.htm*

Xara – *http://www.xara.com*

Computer Supplies

The cost doesn't end when you buy a computer. If nothing else, you'll need paper. You may also require hardware add-ons and other consumables like floppy discs.

The rise of the home computer has also seen the rise of companies offering peripherals and consumables. Like Action (*http://www.action.com*) many now have their own web site from which on-line ordering is possible. On-line ordering is frequently faster, but it can take longer to fill out the on-line order form. Also check out Misco (*http://www.misco.co.uk*) and Viking (*http://www.vikingdirect.com*).

HANDY TIP

It's worth shopping around to get the best prices.

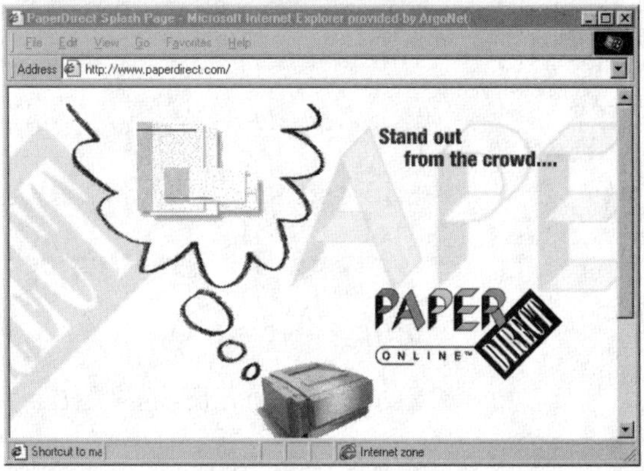

Paper Direct (*http://www.paperdirect.com*) supply a range of pre-printed papers onto which you add the text. It's a sort of ready-made corporate image.

Computer Help

With computer software becoming evermore sophisticated, and manuals becoming evermore sketchy, computer assistance has become big business. There are countless sites offering on-line help, advice and support on a wide range of software and hardware.

BEWARE

It's sometimes quicker to sort out the problem yourself.

http://www.pchelponline.com/
"The PC Information you need to get the answers you want"
New & Improved
Target Your Job Search
What's New?
PC-Help
PC-Vendors
PC-Software
PC-Hardware
PC-Resources
PC-Feedback
PC-Search
PC-Sponsors
PC-Submit
About Us
[Online]
Welcome:
The purpose of this site is to avoid searching all over the Internet trying to locate a specific company or information to cure your PC woes. We have organized all the PC information online that we could find and made it easy for you to get to it.
We have searched the individual company web pages listed here so you do not have to. This way, you spend less time downloading irrelevant information and looking for those high quality sites. PC-Users, such as yourself, are what help make the links on PC-Help Online the best that there are.
To join the PC-Help Mailing List please enter your email below.
Internet zone
Help-Site Computer Manuals - Main Index - Microsoft Intern
http://help-site.com/
Mind Share.
Planet IT
Help-Site.com
Help-Site computer manuals
Search
options
Main Index
Categories
DOS
Hardware
Internet
Mac
Network
OS/2
Programming
Unix
VAX/VMS
Windows 95 / 98
Windows 98 only
Windows NT
Linking to Help-Site
New Links Report
Other Sites
Done
Internet zone

HANDY TIP

You will find the solution to many of your computer problems in the appropriate title from the 'in easy steps' series. See the inside-back cover for details.

Ask the Experts – *http://www.zdnet.com/zdhelp*

Experts Exchange – *http://www.experts-exchange.com*

Help Site – *http://help-site.com*

No Wonder – *http://www.nowonder.com*

PC Help Online – *http://www.pchelponline.com*

Support Help – *http://www.supporthelp.com*

Mobile Communications

If the 1980s was the decade of the rise of personal computing, then the 1990s will surely be seen as the advent of mass mobile communications.

Personal mobile phones are now as commonplace as calculators and digital watches.

The major providers of mobile phone services have established themselves: Cellnet, One-to-One, Orange and Vodafone.

BEWARE

Selecting the best service is not easy. Use these sites to help you decide.

The Vodafone Group
Financial
Press Releases
International
vodafone
Environment
Career Opportunities
NEW!
What's New
GSM World
Globalstar
The Vodafone Network
The Mobile Office
Paging
Data Networks
SHOP
Buying a Phone
Welcome to the Vodafone Group Home Page. Vodafone Group Plc. is a world leader in mobile communication offering a range of mobile services to suit every need. Whether you are already a Vodafone customer or would like to know more about us, simply select one of the options above. To find a particular subject, you can use our search engine.
Internet zone

Vodafone provide several 'value-added' services like traffic news and you can find out more about these services and about Vodafone as a company from the Vodafone web site.

Cellnet – *http://www.cellnet.co.uk*

One-to-One – *http://www.one2one.co.uk*

Orange – *http://www.uk.orange.net*

Vodafone – *http://www.vodafone.co.uk*

Just as the service providers have established themselves in the relatively new market, so too have the manufacturers of the actual phones.

As with all microelectronics, advances in technology have enabled the phones to become so small they can now fit into a shirt pocket or a handbag with ease.

Manufacturing companies like Nokia continue to take full advantage of all technological innovations, but also take the time to style the phone so that it is no longer a purely functional rectangle, but a form which is actually pleasant to look at and comfortable to use.

REMEMBER

These sites are run by mobile phone manufacturers.

Ericsson – *http://www.ericsson.com*

Motorola – *http://www.mot.com*

Nokia Phones – *http://www.nokia.com*

Global Positioning

A few years ago the US Military launched a constellation of satellites which now orbit the Earth. At any time and at any place on Earth, at least three of these satellites will be 'visible'. With the right hardware and software it is possible for anyone to establish their own exact position (including altitude) and speed.

HANDY TIP

This site gives more information about global positioning.

This is the Global Positioning System and Garmin are one of the major manufacturers of GPS receivers which may be either self-contained handsets about the size of a mobile phone with keypad and screen, or it may be just a receiver which can be connected to a portable computer. GPS is of limited use in a car in this country as the signposts and maps are more than adequate. But in the air, on water or on a road in another country, this is an excellent method of preventing yourself from becoming lost.

Garmin's website is at *http://www.garmin.com* where you can find out more about GPS and about Garmin's products.

Watches

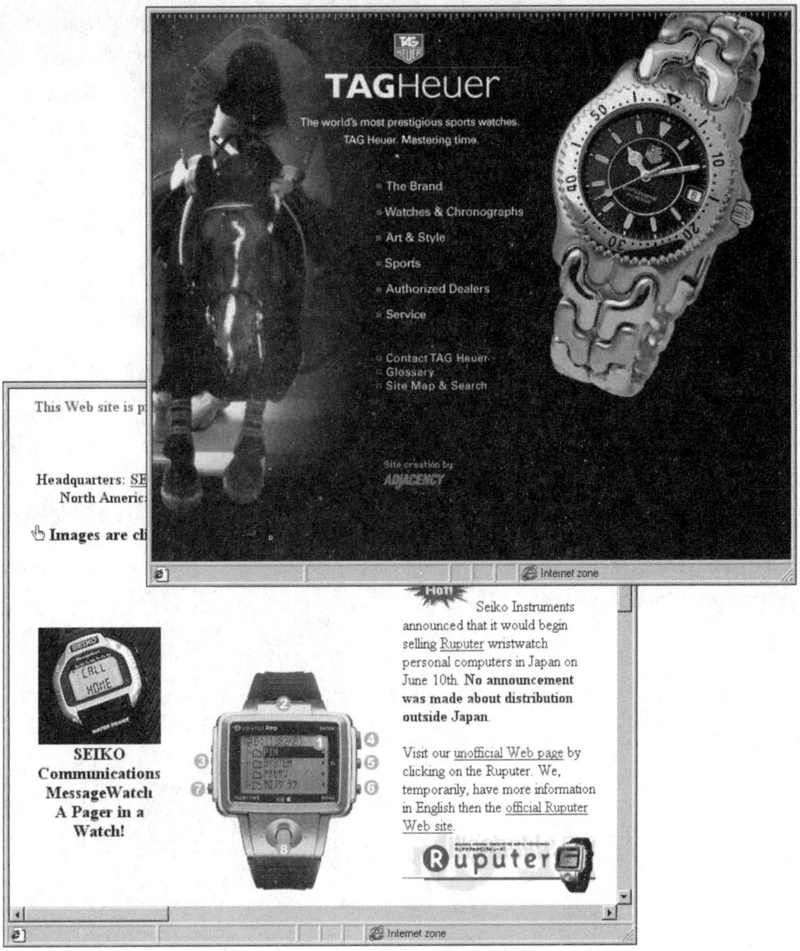
TAGHeuer
The world's most prestigious sports watches.
TAG Heuer. Mastering time.
The Brand
Watches & Chronographs
Art & Style
Sports
Authorized Dealers
Service
Contact TAG Heuer
Glossary
Site Map & Search
Site creation by
ADJACENCY
Internet zone
Hot!
Seiko Instruments announced that it would begin selling Ruputer wristwatch personal computers in Japan on June 10th. **No announcement was made about distribution outside Japan.**
Visit our unofficial Web page by clicking on the Ruputer. We, temporarily, have more information in English then the official Ruputer Web site.
SEIKO Communications MessageWatch A Pager in a Watch!
Ruputer
Internet zone

These are primarily commercial sites although they frequently contain some interesting facts.

Manufacturers of wrist watches have also realised the benefits of the web to advertise their wares. Check out the sites below, one of which contains a surprise.

Citizen – *http://www.citizenwatch.com*

Seiko – *http://www.seiko.com*

Sekonda – *http://www.sekonda.com*

TAG Heuer – *http://www.tagheuer.com*

Timex – *http://www.timex.com*

HiFi

Consumer electronics have come a long way since Akia Morita exported tape recorders under the name Sony. More than any other Japanese manufacturer, Sony dispelled the image of Japanase goods being cheap imitations of European products.

The web sites of these companies primarily exist to advertise their products, but they are slick works of art that are a pleasure to navigate.

REMEMBER

Although these sites are frequently little more than catalogues, they are always up to date.

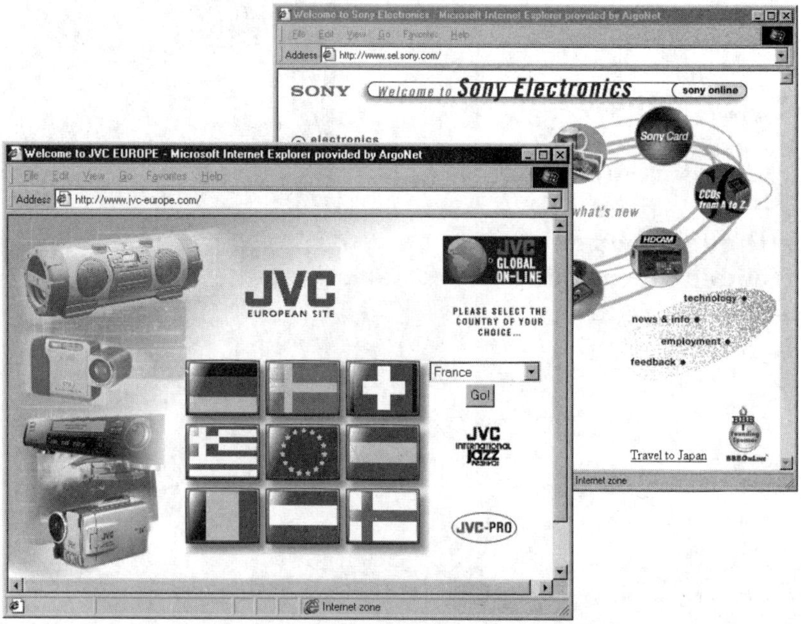

Akai – *http://www.akai.com*

Alpine – *http://www.alpine-europe.com*

Hitachi – *http://www.hitachi.com*

JVC – *http://www.jvc-europe.com*

Sharp – *http://www.sharp.co.jp/index-e.html*

Sony – *http://www.sony.com*

Technics – *http://www.technics.com*

Cameras

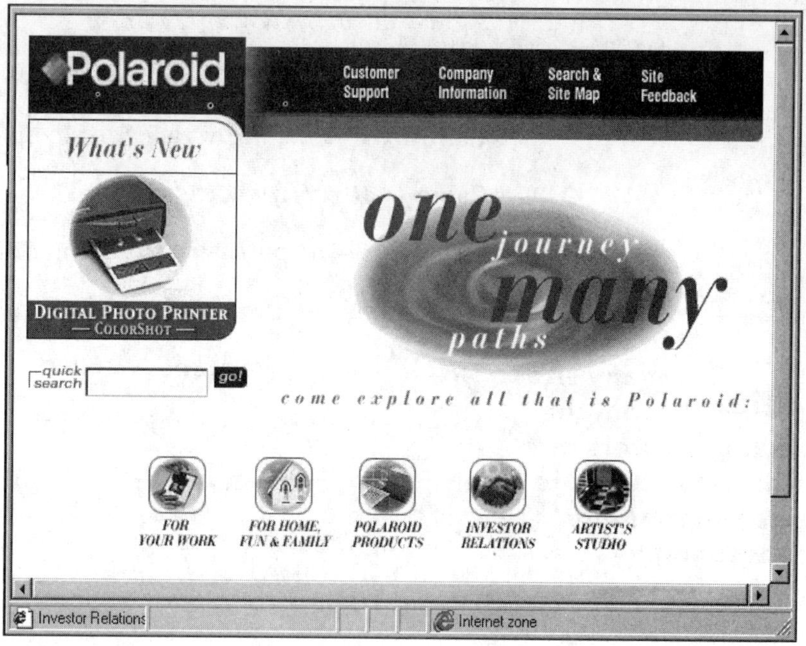

Polaroid's site not only contains information about their range of cameras, but also about the technology behind the cameras invented by Dr Edwin Land, that develop the film themselves and spit out finished photographs.

This technology was leading edge when a marketable Land camera was launched in the 1960s. In the late 1990s digital cameras are rapidly gaining ground.

A digital camera records the image not on film, but onto a small floppy disc, or more recently directly into memory. The image can then be displayed on a television or a computer, can be printed and can even be stored on a recordable CD ROM.

For the more adventurous, the pictures can be loaded into a photo retouching program for some fancy effects to be added.

Only time will tell whether digital cameras will totally replace conventional cameras which use rolls of film and expensive processing.

Photographic Web Sites

Not only are there many sites from the manufacturers of cameras, there are also sites about photography.

Agfa – *http://www.agfa.com*

Professional Photography – *http://www.bipp.com*

Canon UK – *http://www.canon.co.uk*

Casio – *http://www.casio.co.uk*

Fuji Film – *http://www.fujifilm.com*

Holography – *http://www.holograms.co.uk*

Kodak – *http://www.kodak.co.uk*

Minolta – *http://www.minolta.co.uk*

Olympus – *http://www.olympus-europa.com*

Olympus Digital – *http://www1.olympusdigital.co.uk*

Pentaprism – *http://www.pentaprism.com*

Pentax – *http://www.pentax.co.uk*

Polaroid – *http://www.polaroid.com*

Ricoh – *http://www.ricoh-cameras.co.uk*

Royal Photographic Society – *http://www.rps.org*

Time Lapse Photography – *http://www.gn.apc.org/maxim*

Ultimate Camera Page – *http://szym.com/cameras*

WebCam Central – *http://www.camcentral.com*

Chapter Eleven

Travel and Tourism

We pack as many of our belongings as we can into a case that we can only just carry, and then get someone to take us to the railway station. Once there we wait for hours because the train has been cancelled. Eventually we get to the airport for another interminable wait before being marched onto an aeroplane to be whisked to another part of the world. Meanwhile, scores of equally mad foreign individuals have done exactly the same to get to the place we've just left!

Covers

Getting there

Travelling to a holiday destination can be one of the most stressful activities we voluntarily inflict upon ourselves. Pre-planning your journey can relieve much of the stress.

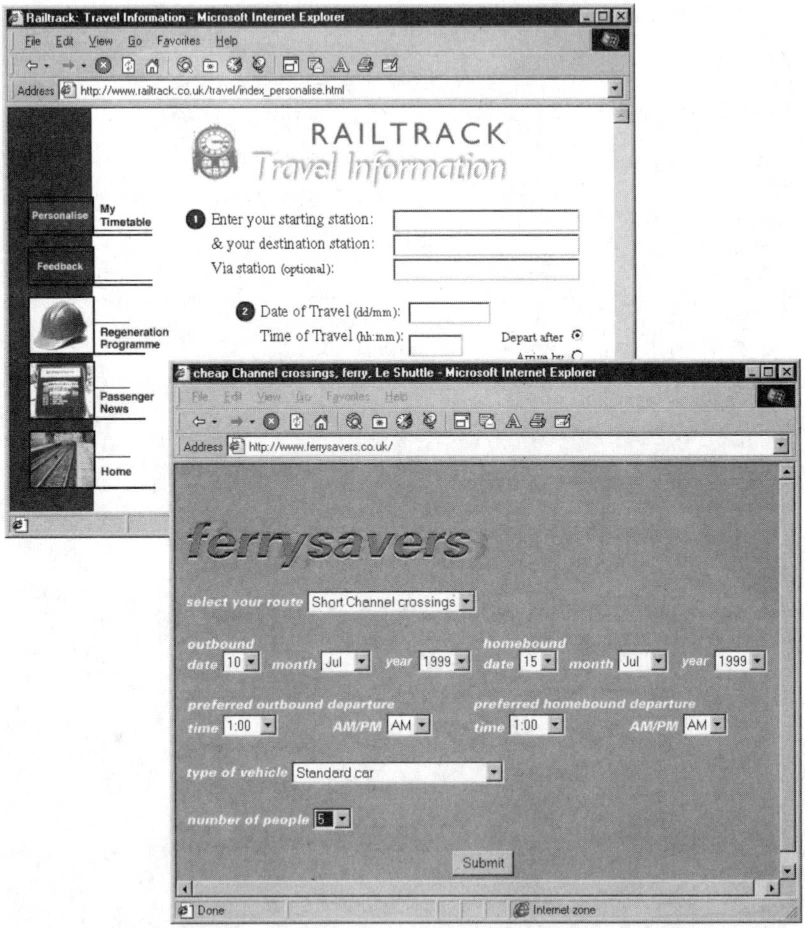

Plan well ahead to avoid delays and disappointments.

There are two web sites which should be of use when planning your journey. The first is a railway planner, the second is a ferry planner. Both work in much the same way: enter the date and time of your journey and they will give you all the information you need to book.

Railtrack is at *http://www.railtrack.co.uk/travel* whilst Ferrysavers is at *http://www.ferrysavers.co.uk.*

Holidays can be an expensive business, especially if you've got a couple of children to take. One way of cutting the cost of international travel is to go to a company that specialises in discount tickets. Cheapflights is one such company. Their web site lists thousands of seats on hundreds of flights. Cheapflights can be found at *http://www.cheapflights.co.uk.*

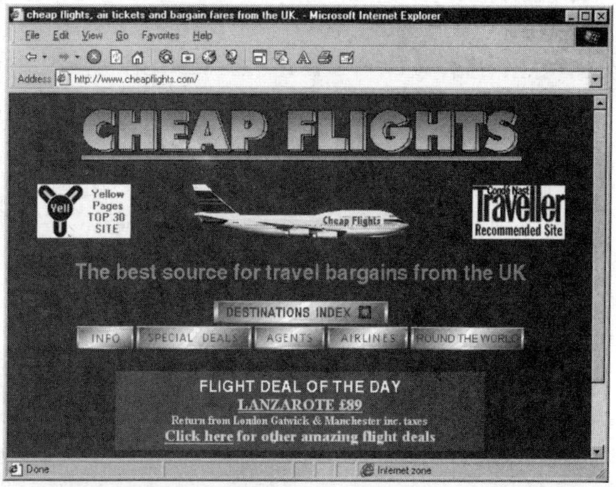
cheap flights, air tickets and bargain fares from the UK. - Microsoft Internet Explorer
http://www.cheapflights.com/
CHEAP FLIGHTS
Yellow Pages TOP 30 SITE
Traveller Recommended Site
The best source for travel bargains from the UK
DESTINATIONS INDEX
INFO
SPECIAL DEALS
AGENTS
AIRLINES
ROUND THE WORLD
FLIGHT DEAL OF THE DAY
LANZAROTE £89
Return from London Gatwick & Manchester inc. taxes
Click here for other amazing flight deals

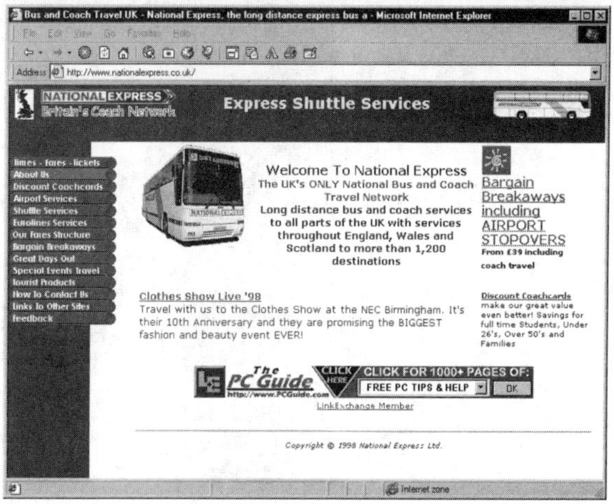
Bus and Coach Travel UK - National Express, the long distance express bus a - Microsoft Internet Explorer
http://www.nationalexpress.co.uk/
NATIONAL EXPRESS
Britain's Coach Network
Express Shuttle Services
Welcome To National Express
The UK's ONLY National Bus and Coach Travel Network
Long distance bus and coach services to all parts of the UK with services throughout England, Wales and Scotland to more than 1,200 destinations
Bargain Breakaways including AIRPORT STOPOVERS
Clothes Show Live '98
Travel with us to the Clothes Show at the NEC Birmingham. It's their 10th Anniversary and they are promising the BIGGEST fashion and beauty event EVER!
Discount Coachcards
CLICK FOR 1000+ PAGES OF:
FREE PC TIPS & HELP
Copyright © 1998 National Express Ltd.

HANDY TIP

Modern coaches are equipped with video to keep the kids and the parents amused.

For UK travel, what better than to sit on a coach and get taken across the country. It's not all motorways – you get to see some of the countryside too. National Express can be found at *http://www.nationalexpress.co.uk.*

Places to stay

Eurocamp

REMEMBER **Camping isn't necessarily sleeping on cold damp grass.**

Personally I've never liked sleeping under canvas, especially when I wake up freezing cold in the middle of the night and remember I've got a perfectly good bed 500 miles away. But with Eurocamp you don't have to stay under canvas, although if you do it's much more pleasurable. They have a great many camp sites throughout Europe which offer mobile homes and chalets.

The term 'mobile' is something of a misnomer because there isn't anything mobile about it other than the fact that it can be moved around the site with a great deal of effort and a rather powerful crane. These are extremely comfortable homes that just happen to be on wheels and should not be confused with a caravan that can be towed by the family car.

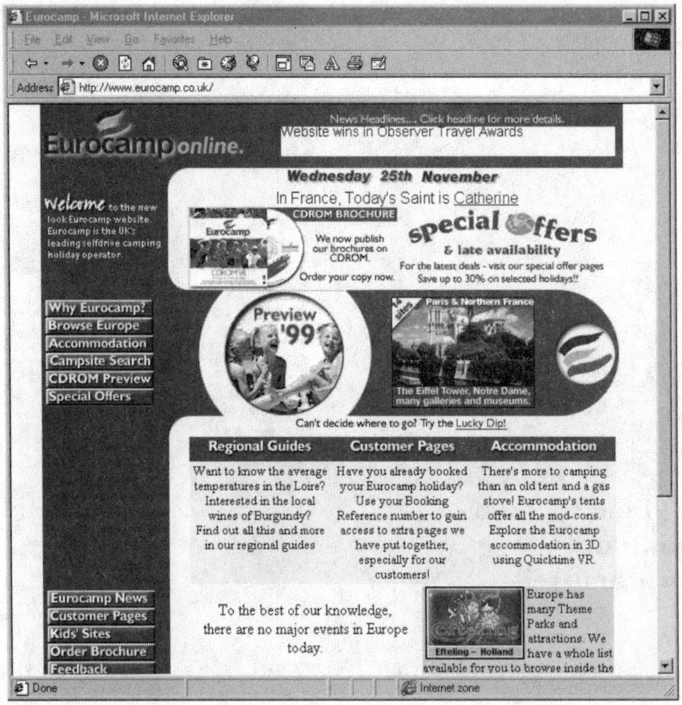
Eurocamp - Microsoft Internet Explorer
Address http://www.eurocamp.co.uk/
News Headlines.... Click headline for more details.
Eurocamp online.
Website wins in Observer Travel Awards
Wednesday 25th November
In France, Today's Saint is Catherine
CDROM BROCHURE
We now publish our brochures on CDROM.
Order your copy now.
special offers
& late availability
For the latest deals - visit our special offer pages
Save up to 30% on selected holidays!!
Why Eurocamp?
Browse Europe
Accommodation
Campsite Search
CDROM Preview
Special Offers
Preview '99
Paris & Northern France
The Eiffel Tower, Notre Dame, many galleries and museums.
Can't decide where to go? Try the Lucky Dip!
Regional Guides
Customer Pages
Accommodation
Want to know the average temperatures in the Loire? Interested in the local wines of Burgundy? Find out all this and more in our regional guides
Have you already booked your Eurocamp holiday? Use your Booking Reference number to gain access to extra pages we have put together, especially for our customers!
There's more to camping than an old tent and a gas stove! Eurocamp's tents offer all the mod-cons. Explore the Eurocamp accommodation in 3D using Quicktime VR.
Eurocamp News
Customer Pages
Kids' Sites
Order Brochure
Feedback
To the best of our knowledge, there are no major events in Europe today.
Efteling - Holland
Europe has many Theme Parks and attractions. We have a whole list available for you to browse inside the
Done
Internet zone

The Eurocamp web site is at *http://www.eurocamp.co.uk.*

Bowhills

An alternative to a campsite is a villa or a gite: a house for one or more families in a picturesque part of France either by the sea or inland.

HANDY TIP **These are great for two families to take a joint holiday.**

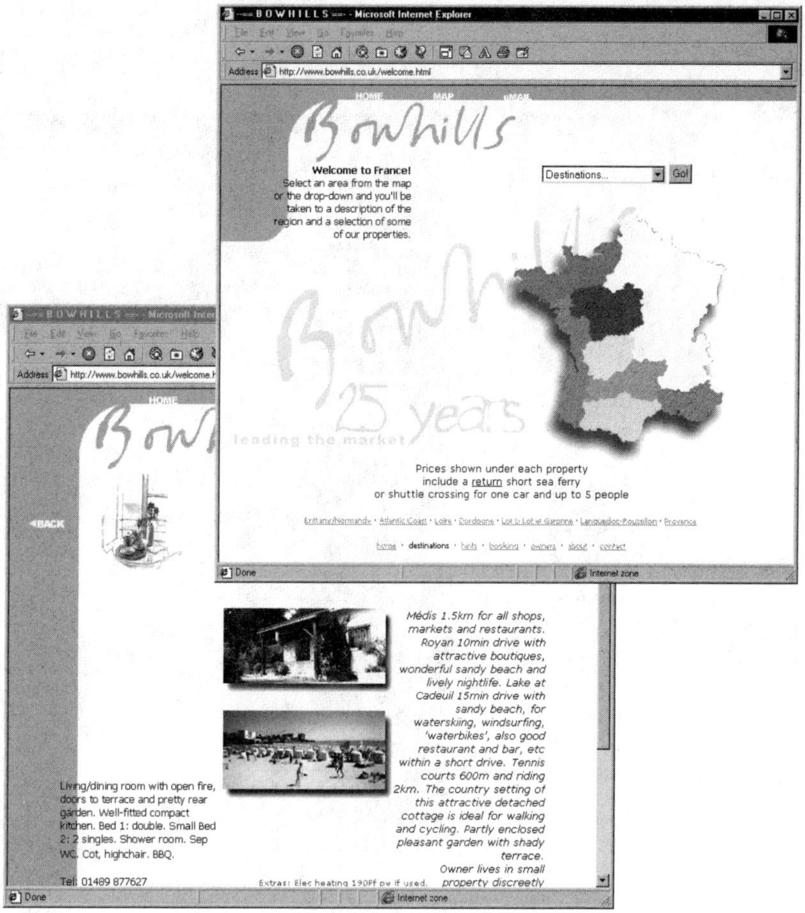

---B O W H I L L S---- Microsoft Internet Explorer
Address http://www.bowhills.co.uk/welcome.html
Welcome to France!
Select an area from the map or the drop-down and you'll be taken to a description of the region and a selection of some of our properties.
Destinations...
Go!
25 years
leading the market
Prices shown under each property include a return short sea ferry or shuttle crossing for one car and up to 5 people
Done
Internet zone
Address http://www.bowhills.co.uk/welcome.h
HOME
BACK
Médis 1.5km for all shops, markets and restaurants. Royan 10min drive with attractive boutiques, wonderful sandy beach and lively nightlife. Lake at Cadeuil 15min drive with sandy beach, for waterskiing, windsurfing, 'waterbikes', also good restaurant and bar, etc within a short drive. Tennis courts 600m and riding 2km. The country setting of this attractive detached cottage is ideal for walking and cycling. Partly enclosed pleasant garden with shady terrace. Owner lives in small property discreetly
Living/dining room with open fire, doors to terrace and pretty rear garden. Well-fitted compact kitchen. Bed 1: double. Small Bed 2: 2 singles. Shower room. Sep WC. Cot, highchair. BBQ.
Tel: 01489 877627
Extras: Elec heating 190Ff pw if used.
Done
Internet zone

BEWARE **It two families are holidaying together, they need to get on really well.**

Bowhills specialises in renting villas and gites and their web site lists many. After opening the site, the first major page contains a map of France with a description about each area. Click on the area of France you're interested in and you get a list of villas with a description and price for each.

The Bowhills web site is at *http://www.bowhills.co.uk.*

Hotels

If you feel you're past the age where laying on damp grass is seen as an adventure and you want something a little more up-market, then clearly you're looking for a hotel. Booking hotels in advance can be difficult and time consuming if you don't know what is available in the place you're heading to.

If you're planning a business trip, take a look at this site first.

Hotel World lists all the major hotels throughout the world. A hotel can be searched for by either name or location and can then be booked on-line. Many of the hotels have quite a lengthy editorial about them and the web site features special discounts and offers on specific hotels at particular times.

Hotel World can be found at *http://www.hotelworld.com.*

Hotels on the Web offer similar services and are at *http://www.all-hotels.com.*

Bed and Breakfast

B&B allows you to plan your day to suit yourself, not the set mealtimes of the guest house.

There is something peculiarly British about Bed & Breakfast. Other countries have the equivalent, but when one thinks of B&B it immediately conjures up pictures of seaside towns and little old ladies locking the front door at 10:30 and serving bacon and eggs for breakfast.

To find out more about what B&B is really like, visit *http://www.beduk.co.uk* or *http://www.visitus.co.uk.*

Planning and booking

HANDY TIP **Look through this site carefully before making any plans.**

Epicurious

Some people love shopping around for their holiday, buying a bit here and bit there. If you have neither the time nor inclination to operate this way and want to get the whole holiday from one place, take a trip to Epicurious Travel.

You can choose your location, make your travel plans and even chat to other would-be holiday makers in the Forum section. Whether it's a family holiday or a romantic weekend for two, Epicurious Travel is likely to have something to suit at *http://travel.epicurious.com.*

a2b Travel

This is a service which allows customers to find the times of trains, planes and ferries and then to book them.

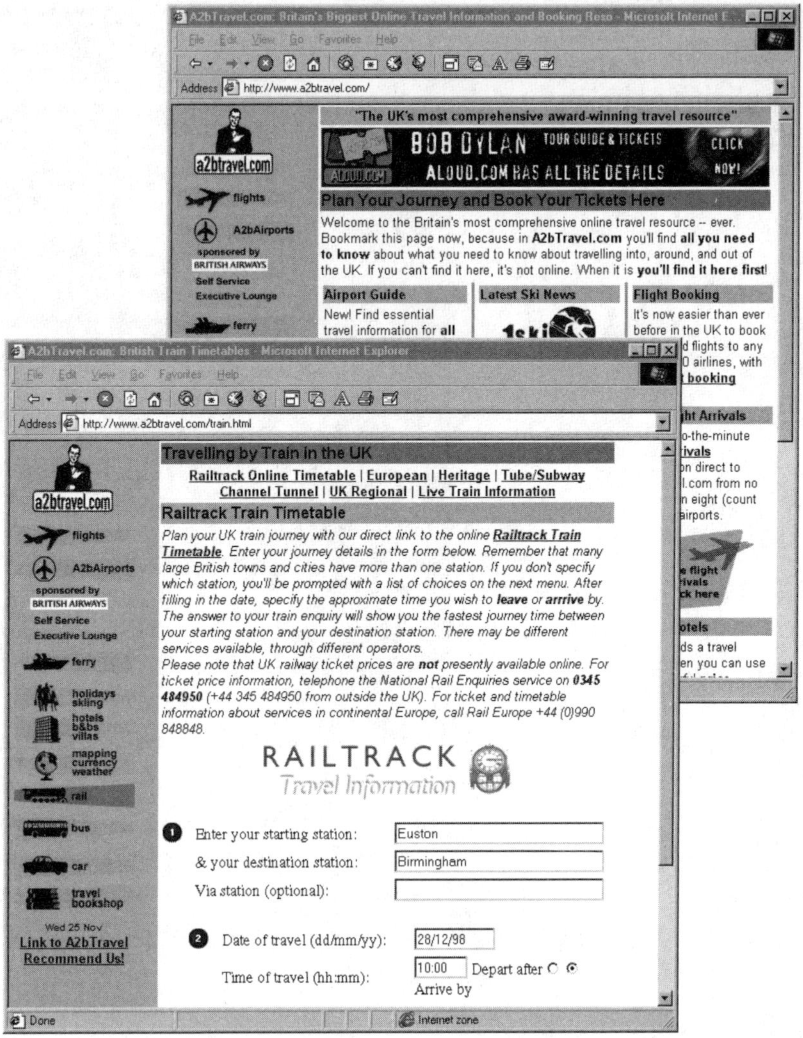

A2bTravel.com: Britain's Biggest Online Travel Information and Booking Reso - Microsoft Internet E
File Edit View Go Favorites Help
Address http://www.a2btravel.com/
"The UK's most comprehensive award-winning travel resource"
BOB DYLAN TOUR GUIDE & TICKETS CLICK NOW!
ALOUD.COM HAS ALL THE DETAILS
Plan Your Journey and Book Your Tickets Here
Welcome to the Britain's most comprehensive online travel resource -- ever. Bookmark this page now, because in A2bTravel.com you'll find all you need to know about what you need to know about travelling into, around, and out of the UK. If you can't find it here, it's not online. When it is you'll find it here first!
Airport Guide
New! Find essential travel information for all
Latest Ski News
Flight Booking
It's now easier than ever before in the UK to book
a2btravel.com
flights
A2bAirports
sponsored by BRITISH AIRWAYS
Self Service
Executive Lounge
ferry
A2bTravel.com: British Train Timetables - Microsoft Internet Explorer
Address http://www.a2btravel.com/train.html
Travelling by Train in the UK
Railtrack Online Timetable | European | Heritage | Tube/Subway
Channel Tunnel | UK Regional | Live Train Information
Railtrack Train Timetable
Plan your UK train journey with our direct link to the online Railtrack Train Timetable. Enter your journey details in the form below. Remember that many large British towns and cities have more than one station. If you don't specify which station, you'll be prompted with a list of choices on the next menu. After filling in the date, specify the approximate time you wish to leave or arrrive by. The answer to your train enquiry will show you the fastest journey time between your starting station and your destination station. There may be different services available, through different operators.
Please note that UK railway ticket prices are not presently available online. For ticket price information, telephone the National Rail Enquiries service on 0345 484950 (+44 345 484950 from outside the UK). For ticket and timetable information about services in continental Europe, call Rail Europe +44 (0)990 848848.
RAILTRACK
Travel Information
Enter your starting station: Euston
& your destination station: Birmingham
Via station (optional):
Date of travel (dd/mm/yy): 28/12/98
Time of travel (hh:mm): 10:00 Depart after Arrive by
holidays skiing
hotels b&bs villas
mapping currency weather
rail
bus
car
travel bookshop
Wed 25 Nov
Link to A2bTravel
Recommend Us!
Done
Internet zone

REMEMBER

The information in these sites is updated very regularly which means it should be very accurate.

But it's not just travel, you can also book complete holidays on the internet as well as accommodation. You can even get the local weather report. To find a2b Travel enter *http://www.a2btravel.com.*

Preparation

My late uncle had the notion that if you want to make yourself understood in foreign parts, you just have to speak slowly and loudly.

HANDY TIP

Don't assume everyone speaks English. Make an effort to speak their language.

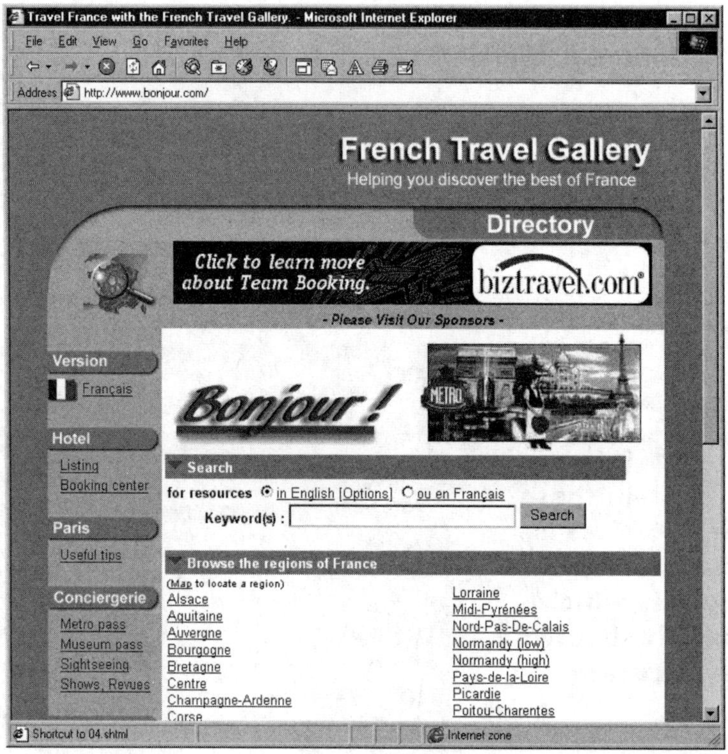

If you're thinking of travelling to France for a holiday or just to get the shopping, first take the time to visit Bonjour! This site contains a huge amount about France, including places to stay, customs and language help.

Similar sites exist for most European countries...

Spain – *http://www.spanishabroad.com/spain.htm*

Italy – *http://www.mi.cnr.it/WOI/woiindex.html*

France – *http://www.bonjour.com*

Holland – *http://www.visitholland.com*

TravLang

If you're going to travel abroad, one should make some effort to communicate in the native language and not just assume everyone will speak English – even though they probably do.

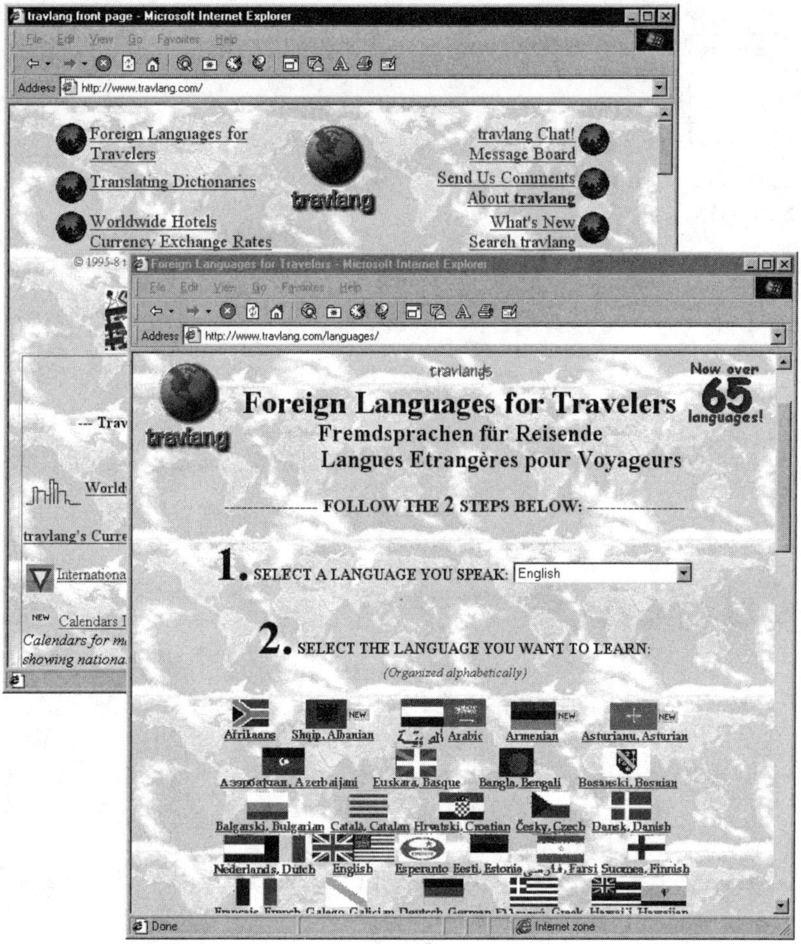

REMEMBER

You don't have to take a full course. There are sections for tourists.

TravLang offer would-be visitors to foreign parts a great deal of help with language. You don't have to embark on a complete course, there is a really handy section especially for travellers. TravLang may be found at *http://www.travlang.com/languages.*

Cruises

If all this seems too tourist oriented, and the prospect of fighting for a plot on an over-crowded and over-heated beach is too much, then how about a cruise?

P&O have a web site at which you can find out about their cruises, from short breaks to lengthy world cruises. P&O Cruises are at *http://www.pocruises.com.*

REMEMBER

Ensure you have currency for every country you expect to visit.

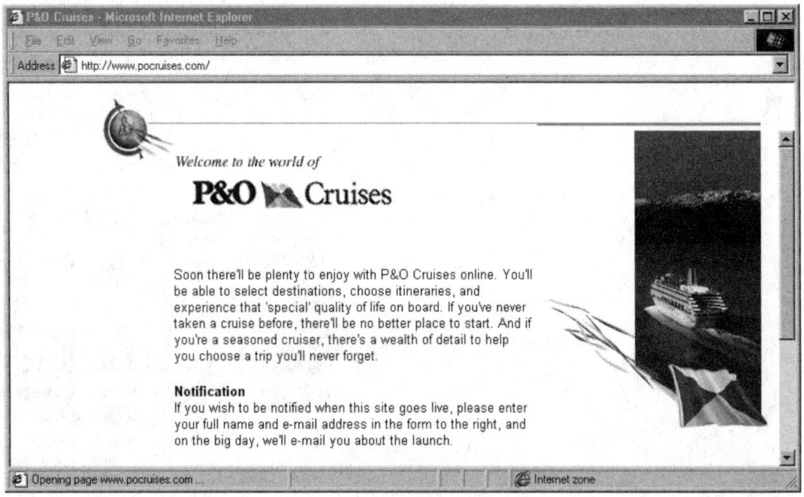
P&O Cruises - Microsoft Internet Explorer
File Edit View Go Favorites Help
Address http://www.pocruises.com/
Welcome to the world of
P&O Cruises
Soon there'll be plenty to enjoy with P&O Cruises online. You'll be able to select destinations, choose itineraries, and experience that 'special' quality of life on board. If you've never taken a cruise before, there'll be no better place to start. And if you're a seasoned cruiser, there's a wealth of detail to help you choose a trip you'll never forget.
Notification
If you wish to be notified when this site goes live, please enter your full name and e-mail address in the form to the right, and on the big day, we'll e-mail you about the launch.
Opening page www.pocruises.com ...
Internet zone

Currency

If you go to foreign parts you'll need foreign money and one of the best names for currency is Thomas Cook. Their site features a handy currency converter and lots of helpful tips. They are at *http://www.thomascook.com.*

HANDY TIP

Get your foreign currency in plenty of time, especially if it's for a non-EC country.

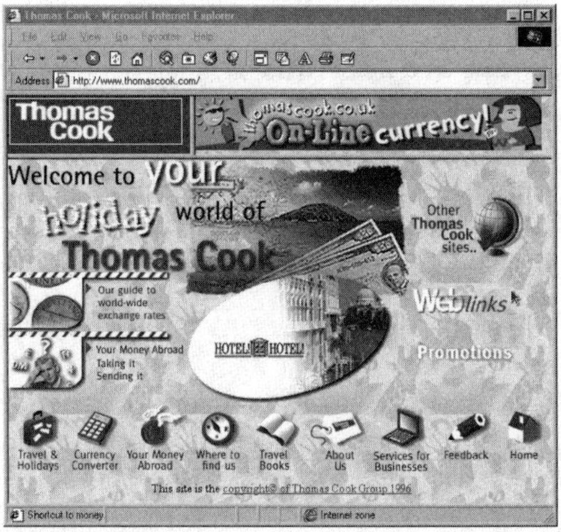
Thomas Cook - Microsoft Internet Explorer
Address http://www.thomascook.com/
Thomas Cook
On-Line currency!
Welcome to your holiday world of Thomas Cook
Other Thomas Cook sites..
Our guide to world-wide exchange rates
Your Money Abroad
Taking it
Sending it
Weblinks
Promotions
Travel & Holidays
Currency Converter
Your Money Abroad
Where to find us
Travel Books
About Us
Services for Businesses
Feedback
Home
This site is the copyright© of Thomas Cook Group 1996
Shortcut to money
Internet zone

Chapter Twelve

Leisure

All work and no play makes Jack a dull boy. Too much time in front of a computer has a similar effect. Life is too short for a non-stop round of 'work,sleep,work,sleep' with nothing pleasurable in between. If you have a leisure pursuit, chances are you'll be able to find out more about it on the web.

Covers

If you feel in need of some cultural revitalisation, try visiting a virtual museum or gallery. Whether art, theatre, cinema, museums or places of general interest, the web has it. Although second best to visiting the real place, it is sometimes useful to have a virtual visit before having an actual visit.

Try looking at *http://www.culturefinder.com.*

HANDY TIP

Many museums and art galleries have a web site. Try to visit the web before visiting the museum.

The Tate Gallery

The Tate Gallery is one of the most famous galleries in the world. If you are unable to visit the Tate in person (definitely the best idea) then you can always surf there. The site offers a great deal of information about the works on display and has an easy to find index of each artist.

There are numerous virtual museums on the net from around the world. Find out where by going to *http://nic.icom.org/vlmp.*

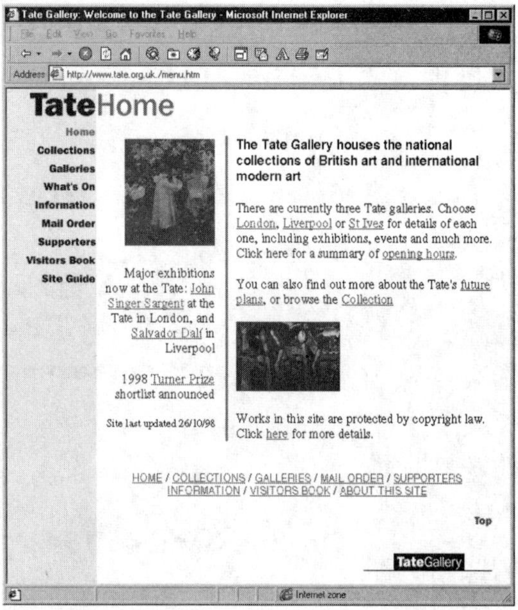
Tate Gallery: Welcome to the Tate Gallery - Microsoft Internet Explorer
Address http://www.tate.org.uk./menu.htm
TateHome
Home
Collections
Galleries
What's On
Information
Mail Order
Supporters
Visitors Book
Site Guide
The Tate Gallery houses the national collections of British art and international modern art
There are currently three Tate galleries. Choose London, Liverpool or St Ives for details of each one, including exhibitions, events and much more. Click here for a summary of opening hours.
You can also find out more about the Tate's future plans, or browse the Collection
Major exhibitions now at the Tate: John Singer Sargent at the Tate in London, and Salvador Dalí in Liverpool
1998 Turner Prize shortlist announced
Site last updated 26/10/98
Works in this site are protected by copyright law. Click here for more details.
HOME / COLLECTIONS / GALLERIES / MAIL ORDER / SUPPORTERS
INFORMATION / VISITORS BOOK / ABOUT THIS SITE
Top
TateGallery
Internet zone

Visit The Tate Gallery at *http://www.tate.org.uk.*

The Turner Prize

A cow in formaldehyde and a picture made from elephant droppings are just two of the award winners of the prestigious Turner Prize. Frankly I'm sometimes at a loss to see where the art comes in, but I'm just a simple writer.

See who's won what at *http://www.tate.org.uk./info/menui_p2.htm.*

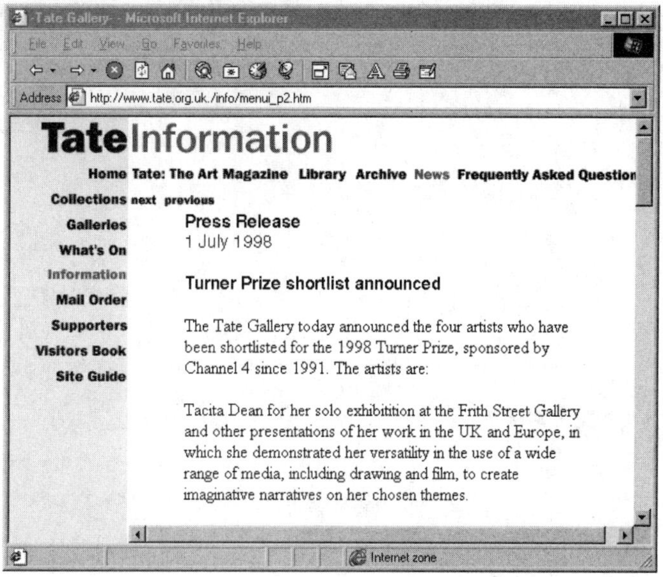
Tate Gallery - Microsoft Internet Explorer
File Edit View Go Favorites Help
Address http://www.tate.org.uk./info/menui_p2.htm
TateInformation
Home Tate: The Art Magazine Library Archive News Frequently Asked Questior
Collections next previous
Galleries
What's On
Information
Mail Order
Supporters
Visitors Book
Site Guide
Press Release
1 July 1998
Turner Prize shortlist announced
The Tate Gallery today announced the four artists who have been shortlisted for the 1998 Turner Prize, sponsored by Channel 4 since 1991. The artists are:
Tacita Dean for her solo exhibitition at the Frith Street Gallery and other presentations of her work in the UK and Europe, in which she demonstrated her versatility in the use of a wide range of media, including drawing and film, to create imaginative narratives on her chosen themes.
Internet zone

REMEMBER

This is only a small sample of related web sites.

English National Ballet – *http://www.ballet.org.uk*

Operabase – *http://www.operabase.com*

Playbill – *http://www.playbill.com*

RSC (Royal Shakespeare Company) – *http://www.rsc.org.uk*

Poetry Daily – *http://www.poems.com*

Stagebill Online – *http://www.stagebill.com*

Foundation for the Arts European – *http://www.artineurope.com*

No 10

Openness is the current philosophy and now, instead of wondering what happens behind the most famous front door in the land, you can see for yourself.

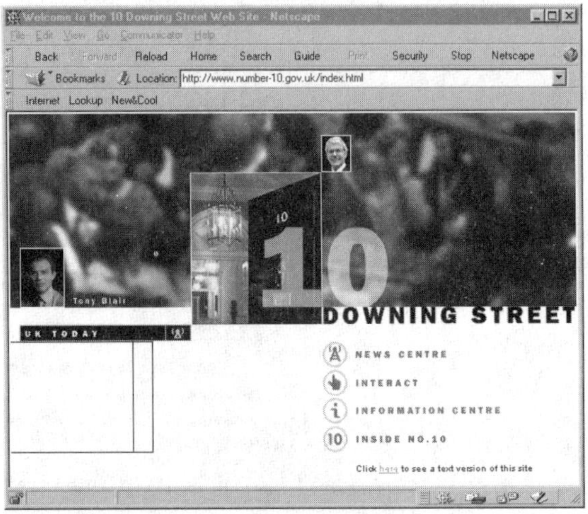

Number 10 is at *http://www.number-10.gov.uk.*

Royalty

If you don't feel you want to brave the queues outside Buckingham Palace, try finding out about the Royals from the comfort of your own armchair.

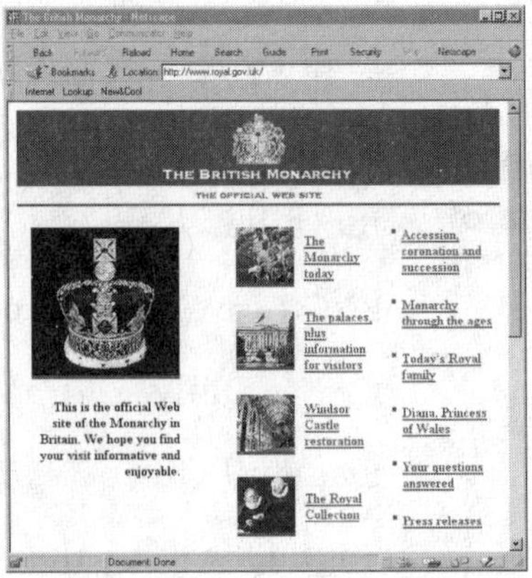

The British Monachy is at *http://www.royal.gov.uk.*

The Millennium Dome

Probably the most controversial subject at present is the Millennium Dome. Whether you agree with it or not, one thing you must concede: it's a technological marvel, even if also a technological eyesore. But the web site is one of the best around with interactive 3D graphics.

You'll need to download a sizeable module to see the 3D graphics.

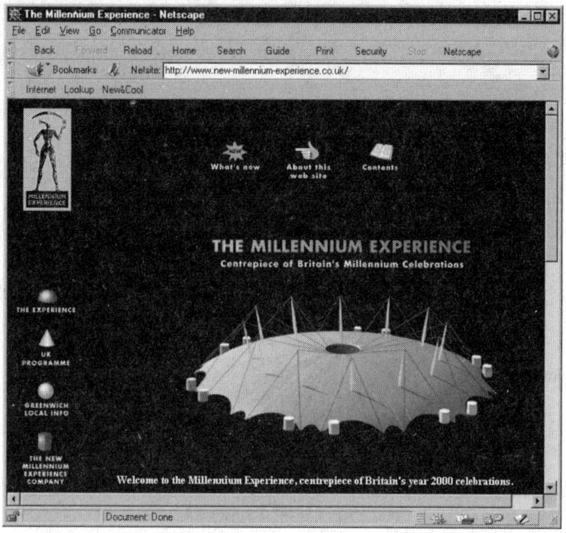

The site contains everything you could ever want to know about the Millennium Dome: from its initial concept, through its design and construction to its contents.

If you can't wait to see what the finished dome will be like, you can see it in virtual reality from this site.

Millennium Dome is at *http://www.new-millennium-experience.co.uk.*

Other interesting places to visit include:

Alexander Palace – *http://www.alexanderpalace.org/palace/index.html*

The Museum of Science and Industry – *http://www.msim.org.uk*

National Museum of Science and Industry – *http://www.nmsl.ac.uk*

Comics and Cartoons

Argon Zark!

I've always been fascinated with strip cartoons. I find them next to impossible to read, but the artwork is always superb.

Some of these screens are very large and can download slowly.

One of the best comic sites is that of Argon Zark. The graphics are as good as any comic and the stories, I'm told, are sound. Argon Zark will be found at *http://www.netaxs.com/~cparker/front/hub.html.*

Dilbert

Another excellent comic site is Dilbert which is rather like a newspaper cartoon.

HANDY TIP

Visit some of these other light-hearted sites.

Although the drawings are quite simple, the emphasis here is on the storyline. Dilbert may be found at *http://www.unitedmedia.com/comics/dilbert.*

COW (Comedy On the Web) – *http://www.comedybreak.com*

Disney – *http://www.disney.com*

Eddie Izzard Kinda Groovy Homepage – *http://www.xs4all.nl/~vonb/iz/izzard.html*

Funny – *http://www.funny.co.uk*

Wall O' Shame – *http://www.milk.com/wall-o-shame*

Films

MovieWeb

There's no shortage of information about movies on the Internet. One of the most popular is MovieWeb which lists most major films for the current year, and back to 1995.

If you don't have a very powerful modem, choose the minimum graphics setting.

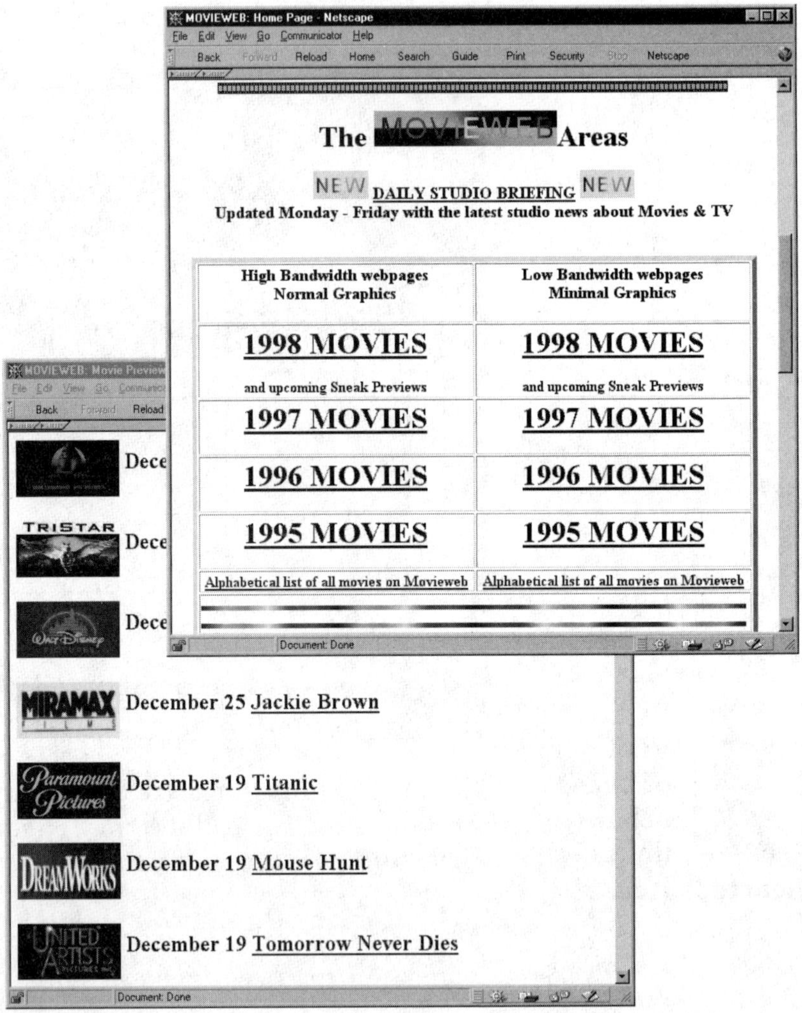

Films can be accessed by year or by film company. MovieWeb has a review of all the top movies from the major film producers. It may be found by entering *http://movieweb.com/movie/movie.html.*

Newline

This site offers a great deal of background information about films and cinema, including the facility to purchase film memorabilia on-line.

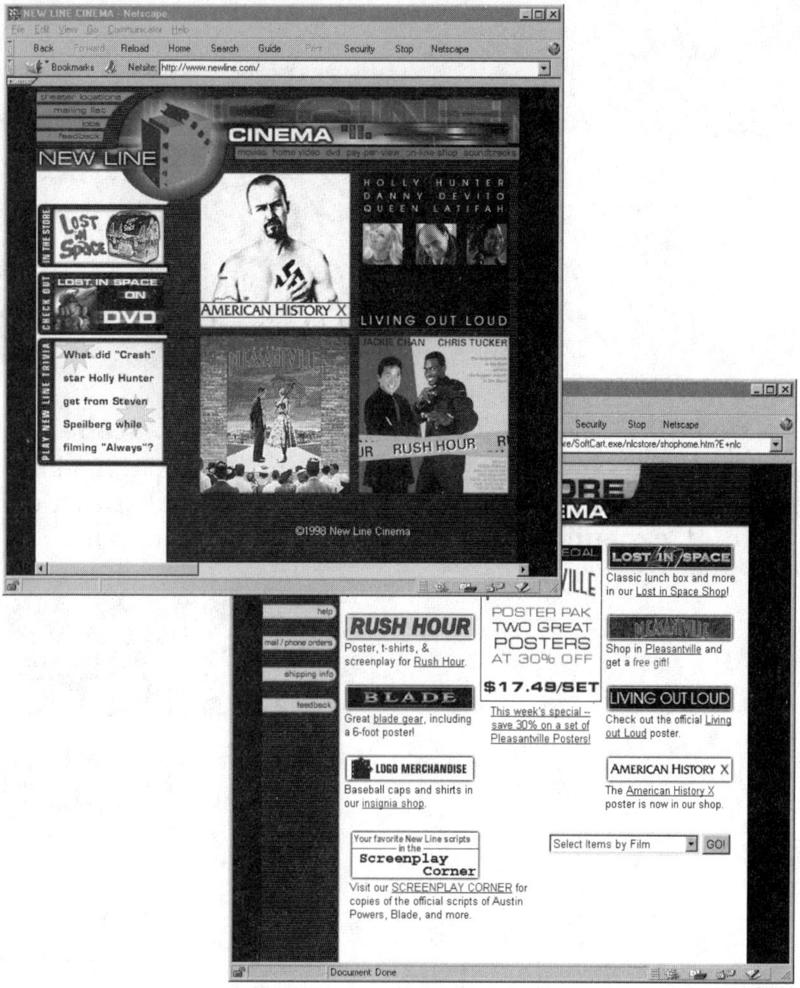

Also included is information about home cinema including DVD (Digital Versatile Disc). This is an American site so the information tends to be for that audience, but nevertheless worth a visit. Newline is at *http://www.newline.com.*

Sony Pictures Entertainment

Although shamelessly plugging their own products, this site offers a great deal to the movie buff. Information about home cinema, television and a superb studio tour make this one of the top movie sites. SPE is at *http://www.spe.sony.com.*

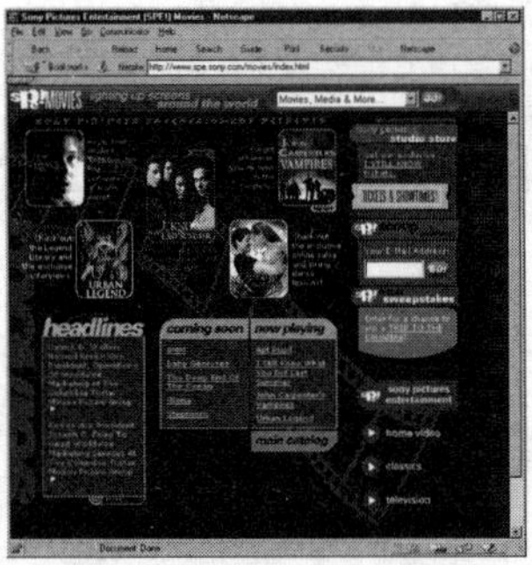

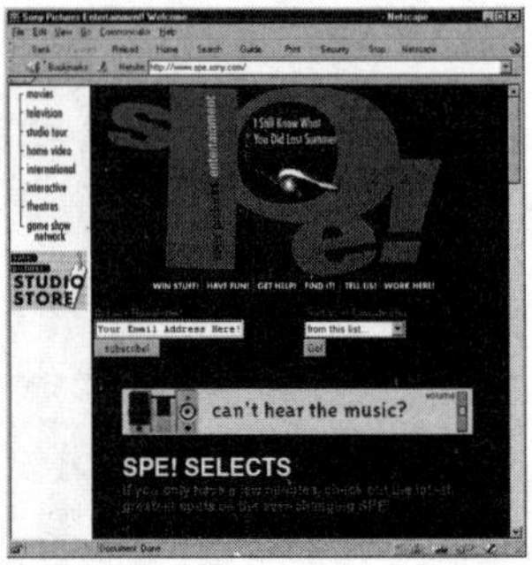

The Internet Movie Database

This is a rapidly expanding site.

This site contains information about a huge number of films. There is a powerful search facility to help you find exactly what you're looking for.

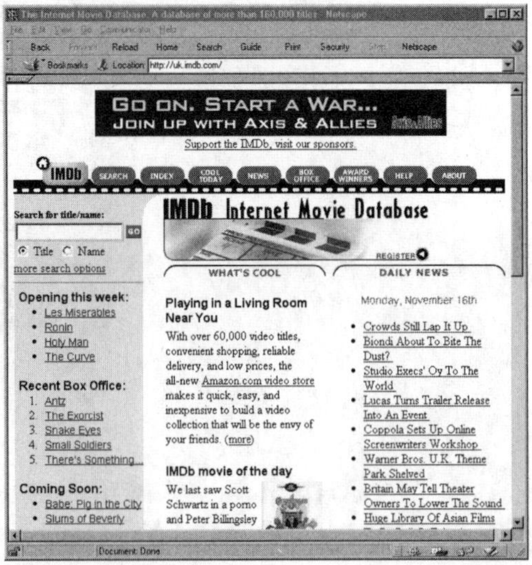

The Internet Movie Database may be found by entering *http://uk.imdb.com.*

Webring

There is also a large section of webrings on movie themes at *http://www.webring.org.*

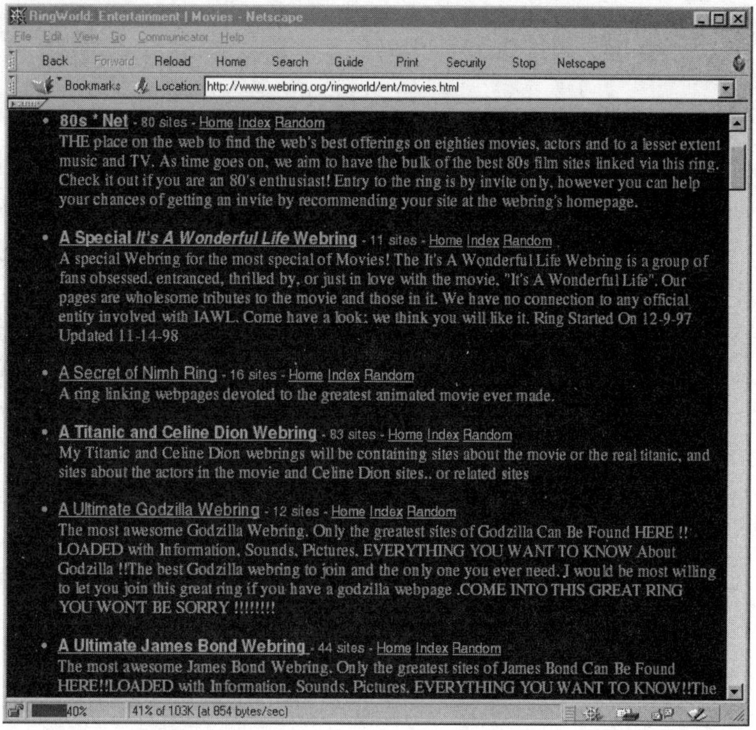
RingWorld: Entertainment | Movies - Netscape
File Edit View Go Communicator Help
Back Forward Reload Home Search Guide Print Security Stop Netscape
Bookmarks Location: http://www.webring.org/ringworld/ent/movies.html
80s * Net - 80 sites - Home Index Random
THE place on the web to find the web's best offerings on eighties movies, actors and to a lesser extent music and TV. As time goes on, we aim to have the bulk of the best 80s film sites linked via this ring. Check it out if you are an 80's enthusiast! Entry to the ring is by invite only, however you can help your chances of getting an invite by recommending your site at the webring's homepage.
A Special It's A Wonderful Life Webring - 11 sites - Home Index Random
A special Webring for the most special of Movies! The It's A Wonderful Life Webring is a group of fans obsessed, entranced, thrilled by, or just in love with the movie, "It's A Wonderful Life". Our pages are wholesome tributes to the movie and those in it. We have no connection to any official entity involved with IAWL. Come have a look; we think you will like it. Ring Started On 12-9-97 Updated 11-14-98
A Secret of Nimh Ring - 16 sites - Home Index Random
A ring linking webpages devoted to the greatest animated movie ever made.
A Titanic and Celine Dion Webring - 83 sites - Home Index Random
My Titanic and Celine Dion webrings will be containing sites about the movie or the real titanic, and sites about the actors in the movie and Celine Dion sites.. or related sites
A Ultimate Godzilla Webring - 12 sites - Home Index Random
The most awesome Godzilla Webring. Only the greatest sites of Godzilla Can Be Found HERE !! LOADED with Information, Sounds, Pictures, EVERYTHING YOU WANT TO KNOW About Godzilla !!The best Godzilla webring to join and the only one you ever need. I would be most willing to let you join this great ring if you have a godzilla webpage .COME INTO THIS GREAT RING YOU WONT BE SORRY !!!!!!!
A Ultimate James Bond Webring - 44 sites - Home Index Random
The most awesome James Bond Webring. Only the greatest sites of James Bond Can Be Found HERE!!LOADED with Information, Sounds, Pictures, EVERYTHING YOU WANT TO KNOW!!The
40%
41% of 103K (at 854 bytes/sec)

REMEMBER

For more information on web rings, see page 14.

Other Movie Sites

Aint It Cool Movie Reviews – *http://www.aint-it-cool-news.com/reviews*

Castle Rock – *http://castle-rock.com*

Cult Movies Checklist – *http://cs.bilkent.edu.tr/~tugrul/cult.html*

Film & Television Archive – *http://eng.hss.cmu.edu/filmtv*

Gods Among Directors – *http://www.godsamongdirectors.com*

Movie Cliches – *http://www.like.it/vertigo/cliches.html*

Science Fiction

Before starting on a search of the Internet for Science Fiction sites, take a look at the Science Fiction Foundation Collection at *http://www.liv.ac.uk/~asawyer/sf_info.html.* It lists most sites on the subject.

Star Trek

There are countless Star Trek sites but the official one is at *http://www.startrek.com.*

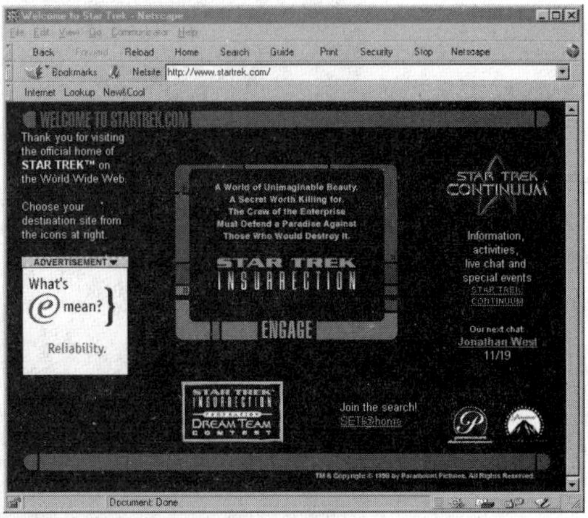

Back
Reload
Home
Search
Guide
Print
Security
Stop
Netscape
Bookmarks
Netsite
http://www.startrek.com/
Internet
Lookup
New&Cool
WELCOME TO STARTREK.COM
Thank you for visiting the official home of STAR TREK™ on the World Wide Web.
Choose your destination site from the icons at right.
ADVERTISEMENT
What's
mean?
Reliability.
A World of Unimaginable Beauty. A Secret Worth Killing for. The Crew of the Enterprise Must Defend a Paradise Against Those Who Would Destroy It.
STAR TREK
INSURRECTION
ENGAGE
STAR TREK CONTINUUM
Information, activities, live chat and special events
Our next chat
Jonathan West
11/19
DREAM TEAM
Join the search!
Document: Done

StarWars

Like Star Trek, there are countless sites dedicated to Star Wars, but there is only one official site and that is at *http://www.starwars.com.*

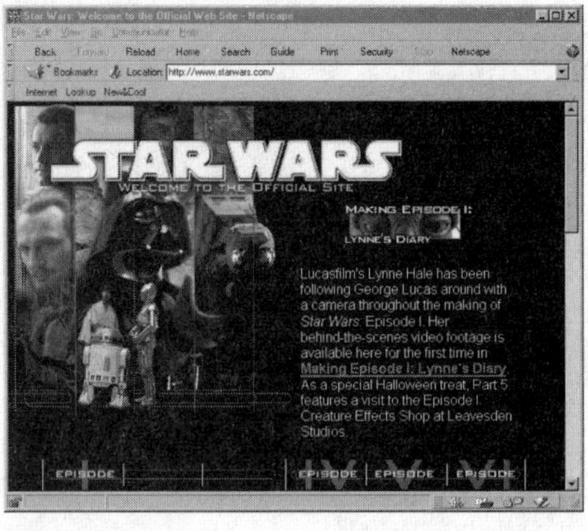

Back
Reload
Home
Search
Guide
Print
Security
Netscape
Bookmarks
Location:
http://www.starwars.com/
Internet
Lookup
New&Cool
STAR WARS
WELCOME TO THE OFFICIAL SITE
MAKING EPISODE I:
LYNNE'S DIARY
Lucasfilm's Lynne Hale has been following George Lucas around with a camera throughout the making of Star Wars: Episode I. Her behind-the-scenes video footage is available here for the first time in Making Episode I: Lynne's Diary. As a special Halloween treat, Part 5 features a visit to the Episode I Creature Effects Shop at Leavesden Studios.
EPISODE
EPISODE
EPISODE
EPISODE

The X Files

The Official X-Files web site is typical of these official Sci-Fi web sites. It contains a huge amount of background material on the series including interesting snippets about the stars.

Producers of hit shows like The X-Files waste no time in opening a web site to deal with the interest the show inevitably generates. In this site there's a full guide to each of the episodes as well as background information about the storylines.

BEWARE

Don't read this just before going to bed!

For those who are really keen, there's the chance to buy some useful items connected with the show.

The Official X-Files site is at *http://www.thex-files.com.*

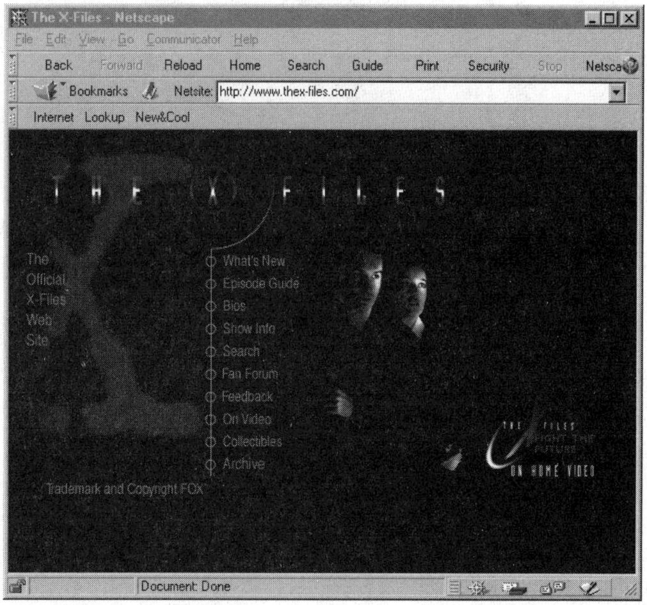

If you're really interested in buying memorabilia or collectables from a Sci-Fi film or TV series, then the Sci-Fi UK Superstore should be your first port of call at *http://www.scifi-uk.com.*

Television

Could this be the end of the Radio Times as we know it? I think not, but it is interesting that the Internet is seen as a suitable medium to expand on television and TV programmes.

All of the major TV companies have a web site in which they give programme times and additional or background information about their programmes.

Most TV companies have their own web site.

BBC TV – *http://www.bbc.co.uk*

Children's BBC – *http://www.bbc.co.uk/index/tv/childrens.html*

BBC Info – *http://www.bbc.co.uk/cdf/bbcintro.html*

This is only a small sample of related web sites.

Channel 4 – *http://www.channel4.co.uk*

Carlton – *http://www.carlton.co.uk*

Central – *http://www.centraltv.co.uk*

Sky – *http://www.sky.co.uk/channel/intro.htm*

TV Net – *http://tvnet.com*

Channel Guide – *http://www.iechannelguide.com*

Teletext

Many modern television sets are equipped to receive text which is simultaneously broadcast with the normal television signal. The 'pages' contain a variety of news and information but are limited by relatively low resolution resulting in a lack of detail both in story content and graphic display.

REMEMBER **These provide a great deal more detail than teletext on a TV.**

The internet site contains a lot more information that the TV version and is a good source of information for news, travel and television times.

Teletext – *http://www.teletext.co.uk*

T'Text (News) – *http://www.teletext.co.uk/uktoday.htm*

T'Text (TV) – *http://www1.teletext.co.uk/tv*

Television Programmes

Soaps

Many television programmes have their own website. In most cases there is a link from the site of the television company which screens the programme.

Soaps are popular on TV and also on the web as they frequently give 'the story so far'. Typical is Coronation Street which also gives information about the characters.

Not all TV websites are the official ones – some are run by fans.

Other popular soap sites are:

Eastenders – *http://www.bbc.co.uk/eastenders.home. shtml*

Brookside – *http://www.brookie.com*

Emmerdale – *http://www.sandshse.demon.co.uk/ emmerdale.html*

Fan's pages

There are many people around the world whose passion for a particular TV series knows no bounds. These loyal fans spend untold hours building sort of electronic shrines to their hobby, which is apparently collecting little-known information about obscure TV programmes.

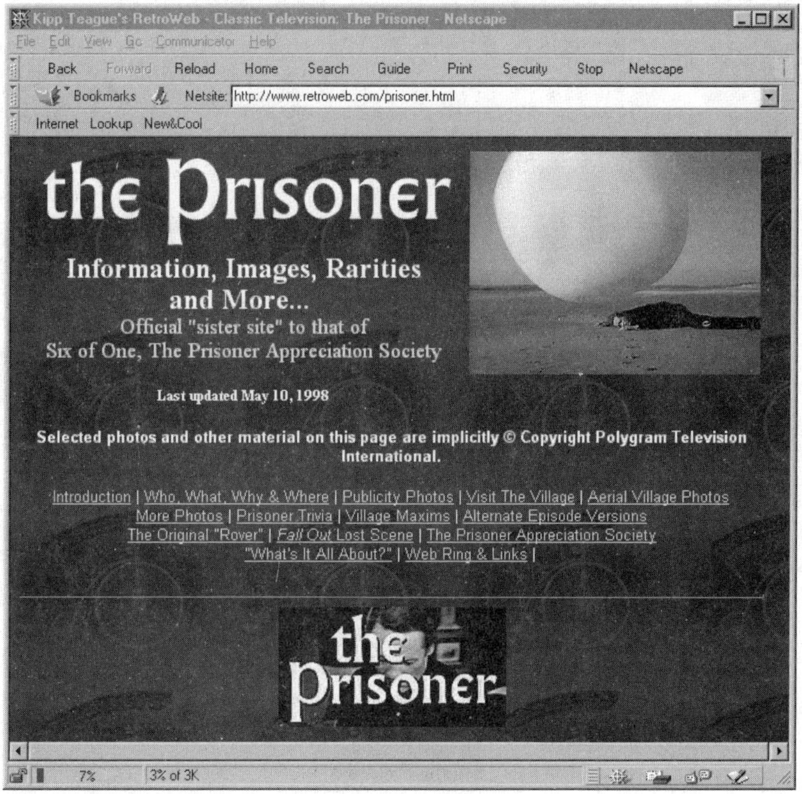

The more weird or off-beat, the more web sites appear on the subject.

Crossroads – *http://www.geocities.com/TelevisionCity/2603*

Danger Man – *http://dspace.dial.pipex.com/avalon/dman.htm*

The Saint – *http://www.saint.org*

The Prisoner – *http://www.retroweb.com/prisoner.html*

Love 'em or hate 'em, the Simpsons are currently one of the most popular TV cartoons and their web site is also one of the most popular with over 40,000 hits per month.

Sites like this can add a great deal of enjoyment to the programme by providing a considerable amount of additional information about characters and the way it is made.

On this side of the Atlantic, Nick Park's Wallace & Grommit series of stop-motion animations also have a loyal army of fans and a web site to learn more about the characters and the production.

The Simpsons – *http://www2.liglobal.com/simpsons*

Wallace & Gromit – *http://rummelplatz.uni-mannheim.de/~mfeld/wg_home.html*

There is a great deal of interest in TV programmes from the 60's, 70's and 80's. Many of the programmes from these decades are enjoying re-runs and even re-re-runs. Some stand up to time very well, others look decidedly dated.

The Sweeney is still very watchable and is enjoyed by many, although I do find it slightly embarrassing. I used to dress that way too!

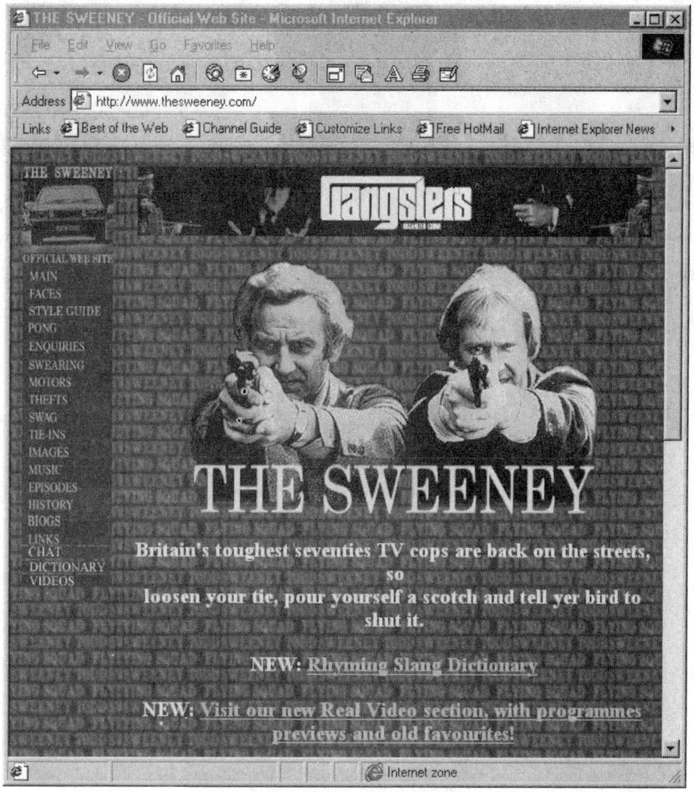

British TV is at *http://www.uktv.com*

Classic 70's and 80's UK Kids TV – *http://www.geocities.com/TelevisionCity/1011/index.html*

Soap Heaven – *http://www.geocities.com/TelevisionCity/2533*

Sport

Whatever your preference, whether a spectator or an active participant, your sport will be on the web somewhere.

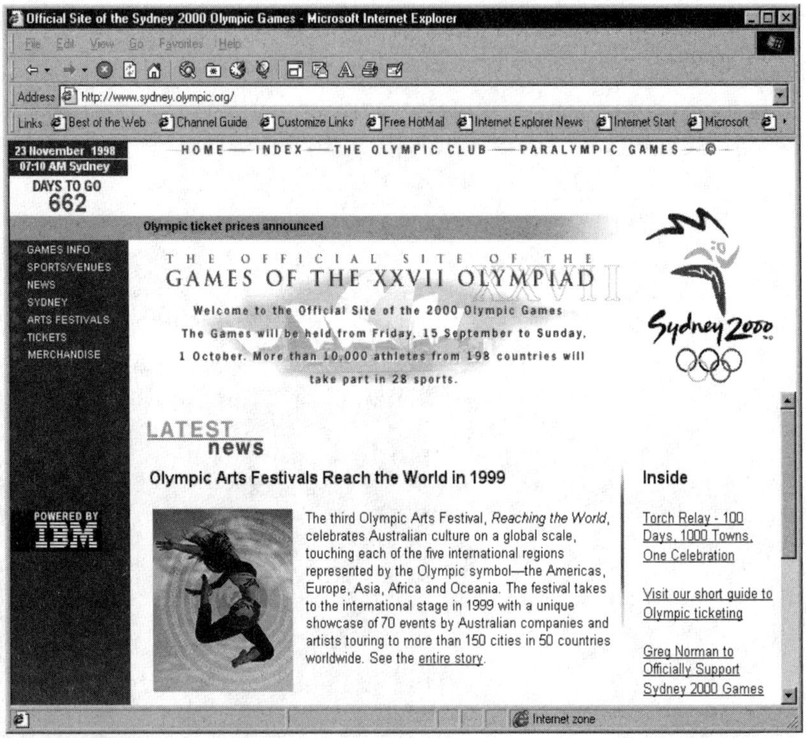

Official Site of the Sydney 2000 Olympic Games - Microsoft Internet Explorer
File Edit View Go Favorites Help
Address http://www.sydney.olympic.org/
Links Best of the Web Channel Guide Customize Links Free HotMail Internet Explorer News Internet Start Microsoft
23 November 1998
07:10 AM Sydney
DAYS TO GO
662
HOME — INDEX — THE OLYMPIC CLUB — PARALYMPIC GAMES — ©
Olympic ticket prices announced
GAMES INFO
SPORTS/VENUES
NEWS
SYDNEY
ARTS FESTIVALS
TICKETS
MERCHANDISE
THE OFFICIAL SITE OF THE
GAMES OF THE XXVII OLYMPIAD
Welcome to the Official Site of the 2000 Olympic Games
The Games will be held from Friday, 15 September to Sunday, 1 October. More than 10,000 athletes from 198 countries will take part in 28 sports.
Sydney 2000
LATEST news
Olympic Arts Festivals Reach the World in 1999
The third Olympic Arts Festival, Reaching the World, celebrates Australian culture on a global scale, touching each of the five international regions represented by the Olympic symbol—the Americas, Europe, Asia, Africa and Oceania. The festival takes to the international stage in 1999 with a unique showcase of 70 events by Australian companies and artists touring to more than 150 cities in 50 countries worldwide. See the entire story.
Inside
Torch Relay - 100 Days, 1000 Towns, One Celebration
Visit our short guide to Olympic ticketing
Greg Norman to Officially Support Sydney 2000 Games
POWERED BY IBM
Internet zone

REMEMBER This site is being prepared for the Year 2000.

Apart from sites that are almost permanent fixtures, others are published for a specific sporting event and are then removed, or at the very least forgotten forever.

Currently the sports site that is receiving a great deal of attention is the Olympics 2000 site at *http://www.sydney.olympic.org*.

At present the site is a little sparse in places but as the time of the Olympics draws nearer, it will increase in size quite dramatically.

Here you will be able to find all the latest news leading up to the big event. The site is regularly updated and is probably the leading source of information about the next Olympic Games.

Motor Sport

If, like me, you enjoy spending Sunday afternoons watching indistinguishable cars hammered by faceless drivers going round and round featureless tarmac circuits, then the web has plenty of sites to look at.

REMEMBER

This page was posted on the web within minutes of the F1 champion-ship being decided.

HANDY TIP

These are some other top motor sport sites to visit.

Formula 1 – *http://www.itv-f1.com*

NASCAR – *http://www.nascar.com*

FIA – *http://www.fia.com*

Football

Not all clubs in the football division have their own web site, but of those that do, Arsenal's must be regarded as one of the very best. Built onto a background of a piece of electronic gadgetry, presumably something to do with their sponsor, the design and layout of the site is a model of perfection.

This is how a web site should be constructed and maintained. Supporters of other clubs must be very envious.

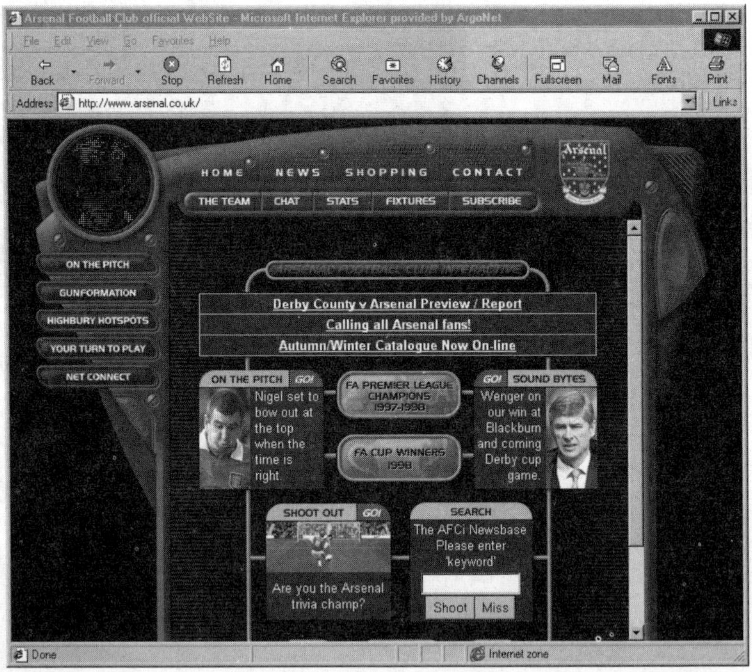

HANDY TIP

Check out this site regularly as it is frequently updated.

The site holds information about the club, their games, their victories, the players, in fact just about everything about the club.

It is regularly updated with in-depth stories about recent matches as well as previews of forthcoming matches.

Arsenal's web site is at *http://www.arsenal.co.uk* whilst FIFA's is *http://www.fifa.com.*

Other Sporting Sites

The list goes on and on, but these are some of the top sports sites.

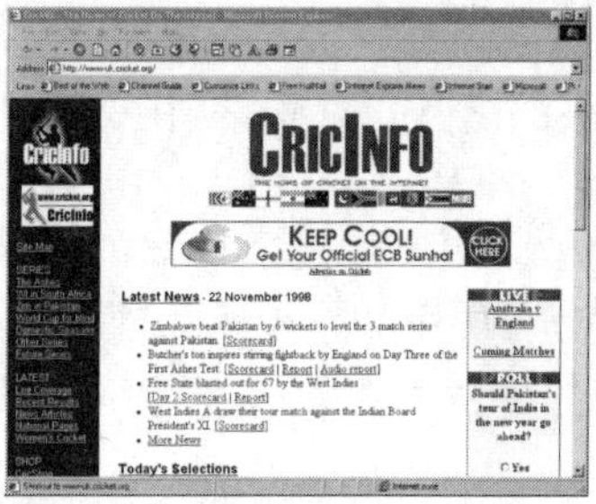

Badminton – *http://midi.external.hp.com/stanb/badminton.html*

CricInfo – *http://www-uk.cricket.org*

iGolf – *http://www.igolf.com*

Tennis – *http://www.tennis.com*

International Rugby Football – *http://www.irfb.com*

Snooker – *http://www.stud.ifi.uio.no/~hermunda/snooker*

Runners World – *http://www.runnersworld.com*

Wimbledon – *http://www.wimbledon.org*

SailNet – *http://www/sailnet.com*

Scuba.Net – *http://www.scuba.net*

Swimnews – *http://www.swimnews.com*

UK Diving – *http://www.cru.uea.ac.uk:80/ukdiving*

SkiNet – *http://www.skinet.com*

Skiing Listing – *http://ski.websmith.ca/ski*

Kids into Sport – *http://www.kidsintosport.carltontv.co.uk*

British Horse Society – *http://www.brucepub.com/bhs*

REMEMBER **This is only a small sample of web sites for sporting activities.**

Music

If music be the food of love, play on. The subjects of the music pages range from artists and composers to record companies and song listings.

The Beatles

At the last count, there were about 500 Beatles web sites – and that's not counting the foreign language ones. Selecting just one was really difficult but of them all, *http://members.aol.com/LuvBeatlez/beatles.htm* looked about the best with pages about each member, albums, films, and of course, the songs.

HANDY TIP

Use the search engines to find information about your favourite groups and artists.

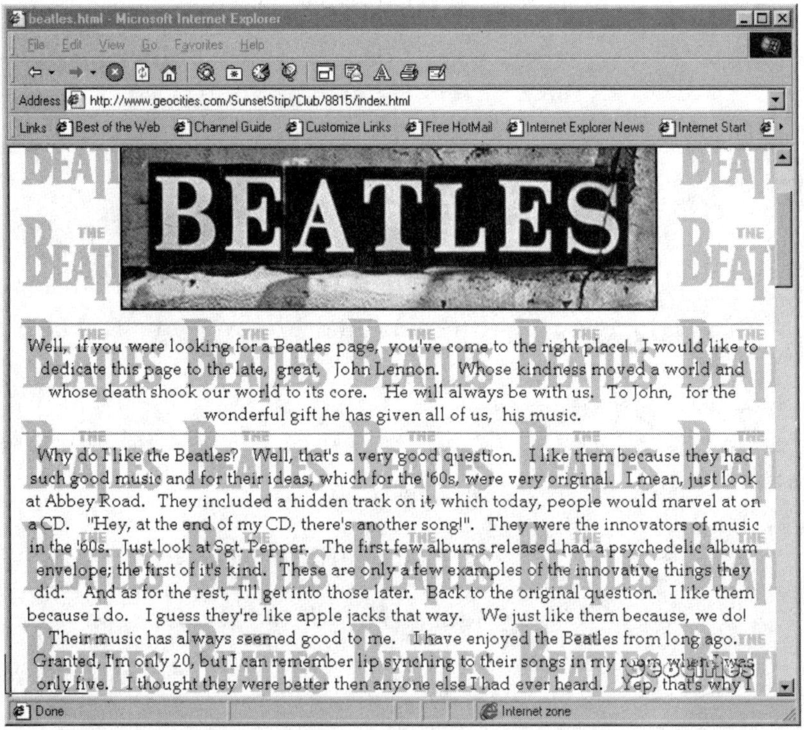
beatles.html - Microsoft Internet Explorer
File Edit View Go Favorites Help
Address http://www.geocities.com/SunsetStrip/Club/8815/index.html
Links Best of the Web Channel Guide Customize Links Free HotMail Internet Explorer News Internet Start
BEATLES
Well, if you were looking for a Beatles page, you've come to the right place! I would like to dedicate this page to the late, great, John Lennon. Whose kindness moved a world and whose death shook our world to its core. He will always be with us. To John, for the wonderful gift he has given all of us, his music.
Why do I like the Beatles? Well, that's a very good question. I like them because they had such good music and for their ideas, which for the '60s, were very original. I mean, just look at Abbey Road. They included a hidden track on it, which today, people would marvel at on a CD. "Hey, at the end of my CD, there's another song!". They were the innovators of music in the '60s. Just look at Sgt. Pepper. The first few albums released had a psychedelic album envelope; the first of it's kind. These are only a few examples of the innovative things they did. And as for the rest, I'll get into those later. Back to the original question. I like them because I do. I guess they're like apple jacks that way. We just like them because, we do! Their music has always seemed good to me. I have enjoyed the Beatles from long ago. Granted, I'm only 20, but I can remember lip synching to their songs in my room when I was only five. I thought they were better then anyone else I had ever heard. Yep, that's why I
Done
Internet zone

Most groups and solo artists of the 1950's, 60's, 70's and 80's can be located by going to *http://music.netscape. com.* Once there you'll be presented with the letters of the alphabet. Click on the initial letter of the artist's name and you'll get a list of artists beginning with that letter, from which you should find the one you're looking for.

Classical Sites

The Internet caters for all tastes – from Heavy Rock to Heavy Classical. There are countless web sites devoted to classical music. For me, the pick is Impulse Music at http://www.impulse-music.co.uk.

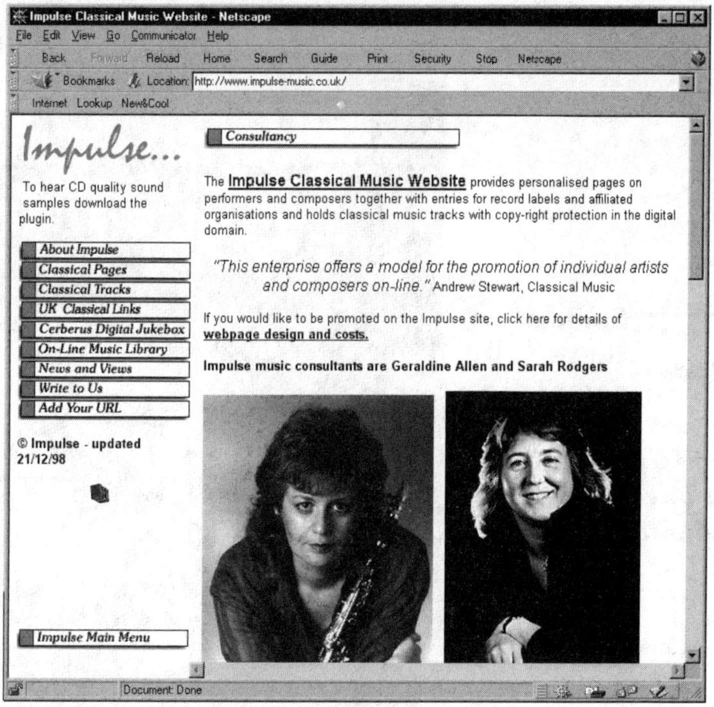
Impulse Classical Music Website - Netscape
File Edit View Go Communicator Help
Back Forward Reload Home Search Guide Print Security Stop Netscape
Bookmarks Location: http://www.impulse-music.co.uk/
Internet Lookup New&Cool
Impulse...
To hear CD quality sound samples download the plugin.
About Impulse
Classical Pages
Classical Tracks
UK Classical Links
Cerberus Digital Jukebox
On-Line Music Library
News and Views
Write to Us
Add Your URL
© Impulse - updated 21/12/98
Impulse Main Menu
Consultancy
The Impulse Classical Music Website provides personalised pages on performers and composers together with entries for record labels and affiliated organisations and holds classical music tracks with copy-right protection in the digital domain.
"This enterprise offers a model for the promotion of individual artists and composers on-line." Andrew Stewart, Classical Music
If you would like to be promoted on the Impulse site, click here for details of webpage design and costs.
Impulse music consultants are Geraldine Allen and Sarah Rodgers
Document: Done

Classical Music Web – *http://www.edu.coventry.ac.uk/music/music.htm*

Classical Choice – *http://www.cdchoice.com*

Classical Insites – *http://www.classicalinsites.com*

Classical MIDI Archives – *http://www.prs.net/midi.html*

Maestronet Home Page – *http://www.maestronet.com*

The British Music Page – *http://easyweb.easynet.co.uk/~snc/british.htm*

Virgin – *http://channels.virgin.net/channels/intro.html*

On-line Games

It is possible to play games on-line and there are several to choose from, including some from unusual sources.

REMEMBER

Some of these games can take a long time to download if you have a slow modem.

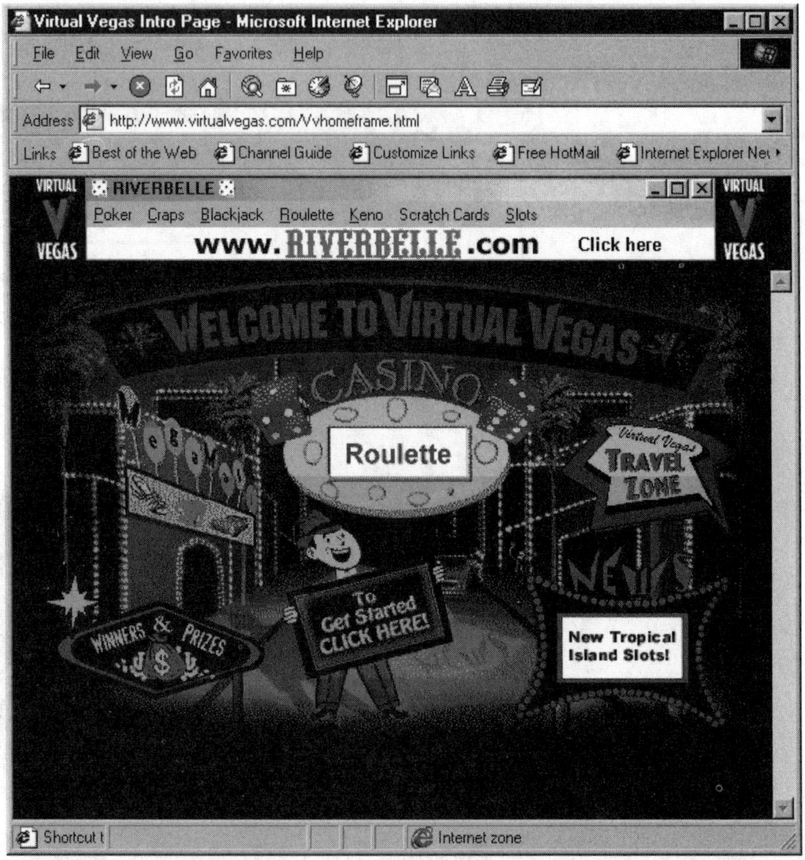

If cards, dice and roulette are your forte, Virtual Vegas at *http://www.virtualvegas.com* will provide for your every need. This site features several well known card games like Poker and Blackjack where you play the computer with virtual money.

If one-armed bandits are more to your liking, there is also an excellent game on the virtual slot machines.

Virtual Vegas also contains a link to another virtual gambling den, only this time on the Riverbelle on the Mississippi River. Riverbelle is at *http://www.riverbelle.com.*

Pacman

This is one of the very earliest computer games which has been written for the web to play on-line. You steer the hungry pacman around the maze eating up the dots. Be careful not to get eaten by one of the meanies or you'll lose a life. You can get your own back on them by eating one of the four power-pills after which the race is on to catch as many of them as you can before the power pill wears off.

Some games can be down-loaded and then played off-line.

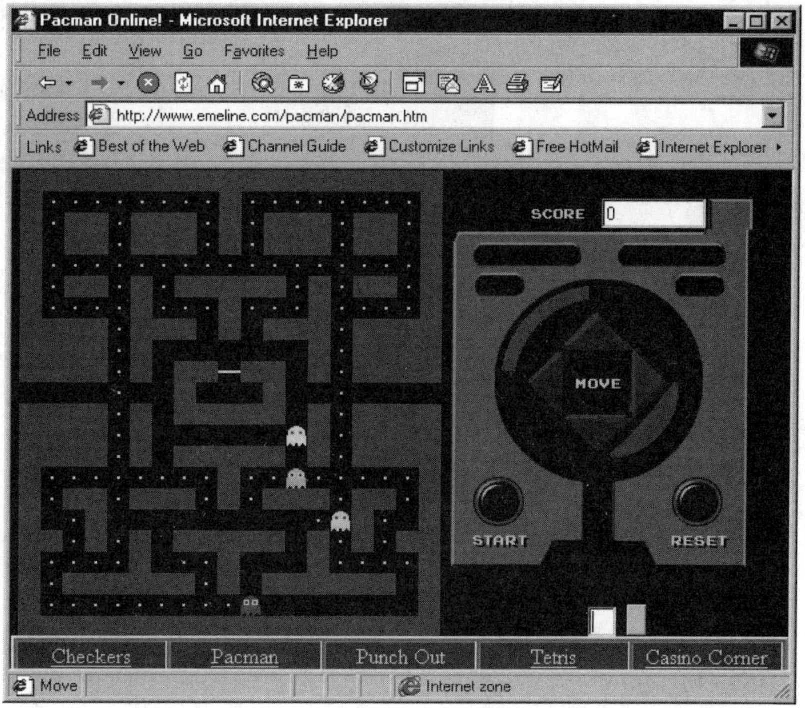

There are several versions of on-line Pacman on the web but this one is at *http://www.emeline.com/pacman/pacman.htm*

Another great game of skill and strategy is Connect 4 where you have to get four counters in a row in any direction. There are several versions of this game on the web, but one of the best can be found at *http://www.cs.monash.edu.au/cgi-bin/cgiwrap/dcron/connect_www.cgi?w=7&h=6&n=4&s=intermediate&f=human.*

Snake

You'll find games all over the Internet, and sometimes in the most unexpected places. Mobile telephone manufacturer, Nokia, incorporated a couple of games into their latest 5110 and 6110 phones. One of the games, Snake, proved so popular they put it on the web.

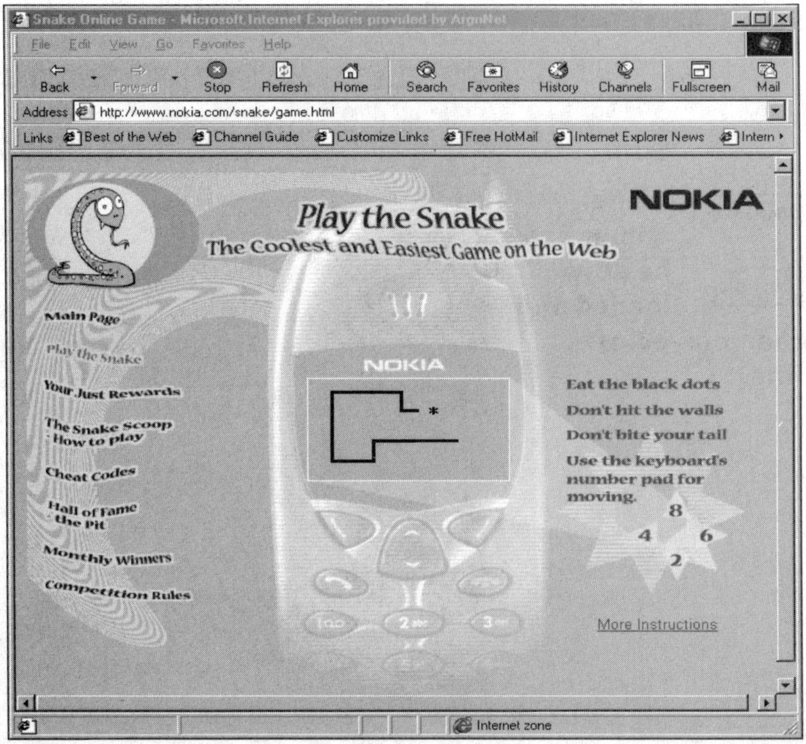

REMEMBER

On-line games pop up in all sorts of strange places.

Load up this page and you get exactly the same game played on a screen at about the same size as that of the phone. The object is to steer the snake around the screen devouring blobs that are randomly placed. Each time a blob is eaten, the snake gets a little longer. Don't hit the wall or eat your tail or the game comes to an end. If you get above 600 points it's worth entering the monthly prize competition for the highest score.

You can play Snake on *http://www.nokia.com.*

Awnings-appealshading.com Airport BAA.com

Index

energyprice: energywatch.org.uk
complain 0845 06 07 08

D

E

F